BOOK PRODUCTION
FICTION
AND THE GERMAN
READING PUBLIC
1740–1800

BOOK PRODUCTION
FICTION
AND THE GERMAN
READING PUBLIC
1740–1800

ALBERT WARD

OXFORD
AT THE CLARENDON PRESS
1974

Oxford University Press, Ely House, London W. 1

GLASGOW NEW YORK TORONTO MELBOURNE WELLINGTON
CAPE TOWN IBADAN NAIROBI DAR ES SALAAM LUSAKA ADDIS ABABA
DELHI BOMBAY CALCUTTA MADRAS KARACHI LAHORE DACCA
KUALA LUMPUR SINGAPORE HONG KONG TOKYO

ISBN 0 19 818157 4

© *Oxford University Press 1974*

*Printed in Great Britain
at the University Press, Oxford
by Vivian Ridler
Printer to the University*

PREFACE

Wir Literarhistoriker sind entweder im ganzen auf das Ästhetisch-Formale oder auf das Geistes- oder Literarisch-Entwicklungs-geschichtliche eingestellt und vergessen zu leicht, daß breiteste Wirkungen in der Geschichte der Literatur oft durch uns fernerliegende, vielleicht seltsam erscheinende Momente zustande kommen, die nicht in der Hauptsache ästhetischer oder philosophischer Natur sind . . .[1]

SINCE Herbert Schöffler wrote these words in 1922 there has fortunately been a marked change in the attitude of the literary historian, who now makes more and more use of non-literary techniques and fields of knowledge to obtain insights into literature. The scope of literary history has broadened to take in, amongst other things, social, economic, religious, and ethical considerations, and the result has been the entirely propitious one of placing literature within its context of reality and demonstrating the main stream of literary evolution. This study has been undertaken in the hope that just such a broad approach to the present subject would help to illuminate this most important period of German literature and, through its wider perspective, add to our appreciation of the general cultural background of the literary revival. The book, which is a slightly revised and enlarged version of my dissertation for the degree of M.Litt at the University of Durham, is intended in the first place for students of German literature but, in my revisions, I have also tried to bear in mind both the general interests of bibliographical scholars and also those readers interested in the sociology of literature who may have no German; for that reason translations are given not only of the quotations from German sources but also of many of the longer descriptive book-titles that are intended to illustrate points made in the text.

The narrative literature of Germany in the second half of the eighteenth century is a field where the application of purely aesthetic criteria, a worthy and most necessary exercise in itself, has nevertheless resulted in the past in an over-accentuation of individual efforts and the constant focusing of attention on more or less prominent personalities. In dealing with the novels of, say, Wieland, Goethe, and Jean Paul there is a tendency to forget that the individual author creates his work not for himself and not for future literary historians but for a collectivity or group which we call the public, and that consideration for this public determines in some measure the composition and character of his literary products; we forget, too, that other writers were also engaged, with varying degrees of success, in trying to win the favour of that same public. In short, in appreciating to the full the intrinsic and enduring worth of these individual authors we are likely to lose sight of the fact that the years from 1740 to 1800 saw the creation not only of some outstanding masterpieces, but also of modern popular fictional writing, the modern author, the modern book trade, and above all—the prerequisite for all the rest—the modern reading public. The aim of this present study is to examine some of the main factors and circumstances promoting the creation of that public and the birth of modern fiction: to consider the significant changes in the composition, organization, and attitudes of the eighteenth-century reading public and to trace the emergence of the novel as its special favourite; in doing so I hope also to indicate something of the nature of the collective life which surrounded the writers of the Classical Age.

In order to preserve continuity in the presentation of my main theme I have, no doubt, had to leave a number of questions unanswered which are also of great interest to the literary historian. The formal literary qualities of individual novels were, for example, of relevance here only in so far as they led or could lead to a widening of the appeal of narrative literature; detailed discussion of these qualities I considered to be beyond the scope of my work.[2] Similarly, the religious, philosophical, and intellectual movements of the age have been dealt with solely from the point of view of their effect on the mass of the people and on the composition of the German book market. On the other hand, what might be termed the technical and eco-

nomic aspects of bringing book and reader together have been
given full consideration—the organization of the German book
trade, the establishment of lending libraries, the rise of the profession of letters, the question of book prices, and so on—all
are, of course, of vital importance in demonstrating the development away from a book market dominated by the scholar,
particularly the theologian, towards a book market geared to
meet the demand of the new wider reading public for works of
light entertainment, particularly the novel. It is perhaps in my
closing chapter that my approach, with its change of emphasis,
most fully justifies itself; there I have attempted to reconstruct
the tastes and preferences of the various sections of the reading
public as opposed to the more usual treatment of the 'literary
public' as a united homogeneous whole.

I gratefully acknowledge the great stimulus I received from
H. Schöffler's *Protestantismus und Literatur* (Leipzig, 1922) and
from Professor Bruford's works on Germany in the eighteenth century. In my discussion of developments in the German
book trade I am deeply indebted to J. Goldfriedrich's admirable
Geschichte des deutschen Buchhandels (Leipzig, 1908–9), whilst the
work of Rudolf Jentzsch in *Der deutsch-lateinische Büchermarkt* . . .
(Leipzig, 1912) has provided me with valuable objective and
statistical information with which to reinforce the main body of
my evidence, which derives largely from the eyewitness testimony of contemporaries as recorded in memoirs, letters, in
novels themselves, and in the articles and reviews of eighteenth-
century journals and newspapers.

The study takes as its starting-point the year 1740, the date
usually chosen to mark the beginning of the German literary revival—even contemporary observers show a surprising
unanimity in seeing the years from 1740 onwards as a new era
in German literature. Whilst it is obviously necessary to select
a definite date as the starting-point of a study such as this, the
danger involved in doing so is, I think, equally obvious. One
runs the risk of creating the impression that all that had gone
before belongs to another world or another nation, having no
significance for Germany in her Golden Age—the risk in fact of

seeming to concur with the enthusiastic contemporary critic who, writing in 1784, could look back on developments on the German literary scene during the previous half-century and declare unequivocally: 'Unsere Litteratur fängt zuerst von 1740 an.'[3] I have tried to avoid this difficulty by devoting my first chapter to a summary of the situation in 1740 and a discussion of those aspects of German cultural life in the first half of the century which had played their part in contributing towards the genesis of a wide novel-reading public.

A. WARD

Newcastle upon Tyne
January 1973

CONTENTS

1

THE SITUATION IN 1740

THE German novel in the century of Baroque had been in the keeping of the aristocrat and the scholar. In these two classes of society we find both writer and public in the seventeenth century. To be a writer means to be a scholar and to take pride in the exclusive nature of one's work, whether intended for fellow graduates or for an aristocratic patron. There is no wish to address a large comprehensive public, as is evident from the type of novel offered on the German book market during these years. They are as a rule extremely long and of a learned character, demanding from would-be readers much time, often as much patience, and a comprehensive education. The novelist assumes that his public is well acquainted with the events and personalities of ancient and contemporary history, with the figures of Greek and Roman mythology, and with the works of ancient and contemporary philosophers, theologians, artists, and poets. It is taken for granted that readers will have no difficulty with the Latin, Greek, and French quotations and will understand the loan-words with which the cumbersome bombastic prose is most generously interlarded. The narrative itself is often of minor importance in such novels; rather is it considered a useful method of connecting scholarly discourses and making these more palatable. Such works, which to the modern reader are encyclopedias of knowledge rather than novels, are praised by Sigmund von Birken in these words: 'Sie sind Gärten, in welchen auf den Geschichtsstämmen die Früchte der Staats- und Tugendlehren mitten unter den Blumenbeeten angenehmer Gedichte herfürwachsen und zeitigen, ja sie sind rechte Hof- und Adelsschulen, die das Gemüth, den Verstand und die Sitten recht adelig ausformen und schöne Hofreden in den Mund legen.'[1]

It is obvious, even from such a brief summary, that the majority of these novels would appeal mainly to two classes of society—the scholar, who had the necessary education, and the aristocracy who, even if they might be lacking in the education, certainly could spare the time necessary for such an occupation as novel-reading. Many novels were especially written for the nobility. For the aristocratic reading public appeared tales of great kings, heroic princes, and beautiful princesses moving in the now fantastic, now idyllic, world of the court masquerades; such were the novels of Zesen, Ulrich von Braunschweig, Lohenstein, and later of Bohse. These novels had as their main purpose to reflect the absolutist court ideal, for in so doing they pleased and entertained their noble public. The genres especially favoured by the courts were the political novel, the *roman à clef*, the heroic novel, the pastoral romance, and of course the characteristically aristocratic forms of stage-performance like the opera, ballet, the dramas of the Silesian School, and the Jesuit drama.

A number of the writers who catered for this public were themselves of noble birth, but for the most part the actual creative work was done by university-trained court officials and high civil servants, usually of good middle-class origin like Opitz, Moscherosch, Gryphius, Lohenstein, Hofmannswaldau, and Harsdörffer; the rest were also university men in other professions, clergymen, doctors, or teachers in university or grammar school. The courts as a rule were content to set the tone and offer patronage to their particular favourites. Writer and prince go hand in hand, not because they regard each other as equals but rather because the prince is the only one who can afford to pay the writer for his work. In return, the author writes to please his master, to fit his ideals of life. Grimmelshausen had stood alone in writing out of, and for, the middle class, giving expression in realistic detail to their life and their problems, and although his lead was followed by Weise, a return was soon made in the works of Reuter to the custom of mocking the bourgeoisie or that section of it which insisted on aping the courts. The middle classes were as yet unaware that they themselves had an independent life worthy itself of portrayal. They were used to seeing themselves as the *canaille*, for in literature they were confined to comedy and the picaresque novel, neither of which was yet recognized as serious art.

Under such circumstances it is not surprising that we cannot yet speak of a broad novel-reading public; without the participation of the middle class and better-off lower classes, of the average German town-dweller, no such public for fiction could ever come into existence. What, then, was the position of the German bourgeois, his interests, and his outlook as far as literature was concerned?

If we look in vain for any general attempt during the seventeenth century to widen the appeal of literature, to enlarge the public so as to include the 'uninitiated', the middle and lower classes, so also do we fail to find any desire on the part of those classes banned from active participation in the literary life of the nation to alter this state of affairs. The merchant was quite content to leave in the hands of the professor and nobleman a literature which had no meaning to him in any case; he was both estranged from, and uninterested in, imaginative literature.

Literary historians have often explained this apathy of the German middle class of this period by pointing to the social, political, and economic conditions of the country. Thirty years of terrible warfare had devastated the towns and brought trade and industry to a standstill; this had hit the bourgeoisie more than any other class. Social pride, self-confidence, prosperity, and freedom were all lacking. The daringly enterprising and supremely self-confident bourgeois spirit present in the great towns of Germany in the Reformation period was gone. The bourgeoisie in the age of princely absolutism were humble, submissive members of society with no interest outside their own homes and families. No literature could flourish in such an atmosphere. There is no doubt that much of this is true, that the apathetic attitude of the middle class towards literature can, to a large extent, be explained by the unfavourable social conditions in Germany at the time, but another and deeper reason is also to be found; the way has been pointed by Schöffler and, more recently and with particular reference to the German novel in the Age of Enlightenment, by Gebhardt.[2] They draw attention to the interest of the same bourgeoisie in popular religious writings, which during this same time of troubles were copiously produced and widely read in almost all middle-class Protestant homes, and suggest that the fundamental explanation of their lack of interest in imaginative literature lies in the religious sphere.

We can scarcely over-estimate the importance of the part played by religion in the life of the average representative of middle-class society in Germany during the seventeenth and early eighteenth centuries. Religion was to him the highest and mightiest of all cultural and social values. In Roman Catholic areas, of course, the power of the priest was still unchallenged and, especially in country districts and the smaller towns, every aspect of the orthodox Catholic's life was overshadowed by religious considerations. And the orthodox Protestant, too, had his God before him in all his deeds and all his thoughts. Life to him was but a short transition, a short but important preparation for life eternal, and nothing was more urgent or more logical to him than to put his time on earth to good use by preparing for death and the entrance to true existence in the Kingdom of Heaven; anything which did not directly help him along the path leading to salvation was rejected out of hand as both useless and sinful. Books that might smooth this path for him were, naturally, extremely welcome.

Religious books, specially written to meet the demands and requirements of the layman, were indeed the most widespread material before the reading public during the period 1700 to 1740. Although a wide market it was not a changing one, for these religious books did not lose their appeal with time, they were never discarded as out of date, but passed on as a piece of family tradition to the next generation. Johann Arndt's *Vom wahren Christenthum*, first published in 1605, was still amongst the most widely read books in the first half of the eighteenth century. The German book market had been held by such works for about two hundred years so we may safely assume that they suited their public perfectly. They were not of a uniform type, but varied according to the section of the reading public at which they were aimed. They were written for all social classes, professions, and occupations from state official to village baker and offered guidance not only on what we would now call strictly religious matters, but also on all aspects and attitudes of life, on all practical problems with which the reader might find himself confronted—ranging from high political procedure to prenatal care.[3] Books were popular in those days because they were either edifying (*erbaulich*) or practical (*nützlich*), or both; the reader hoped to gain from his reading material both religious instruction and practical hints as to how he could shape his outer life correctly.

Interesting at this point is a list of books of 1705 entitled *Frauenzimmerbibliothekchen* containing the titles of works, a study of which is essential for 'a woman of lively intellect'. Here we see most clearly the devotional/practical dichotomy in the popular reading material of the day. Besides religious aids we find such books as *Unterwiesene Köchinn, Garten-Lust, Vade-Mecum Botanicum, Geographische Fragen, Politische Fragen, Genealogische Fragen, Haus-Vater,* and *Frauen-Zimmer-Apothekchen,*[4] but there are no suggestions for books of light entertainment for the ladies whom we now think of as having a special leaning towards such works.

The average citizen in the seventeenth and early eighteenth centuries would possess in the way of books, a copy of the Bible and of the catechism, some popular religious book (as that of Arndt), and then a calendar or almanac with perhaps a herbal or dream-book or letter-writer. This was the case even at the end of the century with Knigge's gamekeeper whose library, apart from a few devotional works from which he read a set number of pages daily, consisted solely of an old chronicle,[5] and in the nineteenth century we still read in Keller's *Drei gerechte Kammacher* (1856) of Jungfer Züs Bünzlin, who besides the Bible had '. . . a small book . . . entitled: *Golden Rules of Life for the Woman as Fiancée, Wife, and Mother* and a dream-book, a letter-writer . . .'.

Important for the future development of the reading public is the fact that this religious literature was widely read not only in the towns, but also in the country districts. The situation would, in most cases, be the same as that described in *Sebaldus Nothanker* (1773–6) where we learn that such devotional and instructive books were popular, and even bought by payment in kind, in the peaceful principality where the hero led his at first so quiet life.[6] Such books first gave reading a place in almost every man's life and cleared the printed word of that mistrust which the mass of the nation must have felt for so long against the near magic of these incomprehensible 'symbols'. Through them also the intellectual *niveau* of the reading public was raised considerably and the last result of this line of development was that the coming middle-class fictional literature found an extensive and receptive public prepared for it.

For the present, however, this same public which showed such an interest in popular religious writing had no time for anything entertaining. Reading was to the middle class not a pastime but a serious business, a useful occupation where something profitable was to be learned which would help the reader, directly or indirectly, to gain salvation.

Here lies the deeper reason for the general lack of interest of the bourgeois in imaginative literature. For the orthodox Protestant the norm for all action, whether it be at work or in leisure hours, was the Bible, and in his Lutheran translation the German middle-class townsman would read and obey: 'Der ungeistlichen aber und altvettelischen Fabeln entschlage dich; übe dich selbst aber an der Gottseligkeit.'[7] There are two important elements here. The first is the *ungeistlich*, the unholy or profane; this cannot possibly help the Christian to win salvation, more it awakens in him the desires of his unsound fleshly nature. The form of profane works is also repulsive, for it flows like honey and might arouse displeasure at the cold religious dogma which is more necessary to man, so even if the material of a work is religious and the form irreligious, i.e. too cultivated, too polished, the whole work must be repulsive to the good Christian. Bodmer's translation (1732) of Milton's *Paradise Lost* was, for example, forbidden by the Zürich censors, 'da es eine allzu romantische Schrift in einem so heiligen Themata sei'.[8] Klopstock had to withstand the same reproaches against his *Messias* (1748-73), and that many still saw the laudable side of such works in their instructive content is shown by Goethe's description of Rat Schneider's attitude to Klopstock's epic poem.[9] The same protests against worldly literature were still being put forward as had been advanced two centuries earlier by Tschudi (1505-72), who would 'wol leiden, daß man alle Romans, auch den besten nicht ausgenommen, auf einen Hauffen würfe und mit Feuer ansteckte',[10] for people preferred to read them rather than the Bible and other devotional works. Such protests, it is true, also show that fiction was, however, read but the important point is that for the man who took his religion seriously novels were for long a 'forbidden fruit'.

The next moment of repulsion is to be found in the word *Fabeln*, fables. All fiction was considered idle, useless, and vain by a religion of truth, by a faith with such a concrete conception of the doctrine of salvation. Thus we find the German Grandison of the parody by Musäus asking later in the century if the material of Richardson's novels was based on the truth, for if not they were no better than fairy-tales and not worth reading.[11] It is of interest here too to hear Scott on the subject of novels and novel-reading:

> Excluding from consideration those infamous works, which address themselves directly to awakening the grosser passions of our nature, we are inclined to think, the worst evil to be apprehended from the perusal of novels is, that the habit is apt to generate an indisposition to real history and useful literature; and that the best which can be hoped is, that they sometimes instruct the youthful mind by real pictures of life, and sometimes awaken their better feelings and sympathies by strains of generous sentiment, and tales of fictitious woe.[12]

The middle-class person of the mid eighteenth century in Germany is in complete accord with these sentiments; when he reads he wishes to draw useful conclusions from his reading in the form of either shining examples or terrible warnings.

This fanaticism for truth explains many of the characteristics of the rising middle-class novel. Biographies of pious people were, and still are, a favourite reading material of the serious Christian, for they provide a model on which to base one's own religious and moral life. Thus, after the new secular spirit of the eighteenth century had freed the novel from attacks from a purely religious angle, we see a marked preference for biographies; many of the first family novels show biographical elements in their composition and for the rest of the century all novelists give detailed descriptions of the life of the main characters and often the subsidiary ones, too. We shall see this branch of taste reflected in the Leipzig book-catalogues in the many novels whose titles are just proper names. The biased attitude towards works of fiction also explains the time and trouble taken by writers in prefaces to assure their public that their story is perfectly true and is merely copied from genuine documents or consists solely of extracts from family papers left behind for posterity.[13] It helps to explain, too, the popularity and extensive use of the letter form in fiction, for the directness of the letter helps the illusion that all is true; in this case the novelist very often remains anonymous and insists that he has only fulfilled the duties of an editor.

The novel, then, was attacked because of its profane character, and because it was fictional writing. Finally, the material of novels also led to violent protests from conscientious citizens. Their worldly content glorified earthly well-being and often amounted to nothing but a series of exciting and meaningless adventures. In all cases they were found immoral, especially in the realm of eroticism, leading to ever-changing and ever more piquant representations. Criticism of the genre because of this pernicious effect on the nation's morals had been lively throughout the whole of the seventeenth century; typical is the following extract, aimed also, it will be noted, at the old chap-books which were still a favourite reading material in the eighteenth century and about which more will be said later:[14]

Was haben die verdärbliche Schriften nicht für Unglück und Nachteil angerichtet als der *Amadis, Splandian, Florisant, Tristant, Tirant,* und dgl. Narrenteidigungen, als *der Kärker der Liebe, Ritter Pontus, Peter mit den Silbren Slüsseln, Lancilot, Melusina, Goffroy mit dem Zane* und dgl. Fatsepossen mehr.[15]

These attacks had culminated in G. Heidegger's *Mythoscopia Romantica, oder Discours von den so benannten Romans, d. i. erdichteten Liebes- Helden- und Hirtengeschichten, von deren Ursprung, Einrisse, Verschiedenheit, Nütz- und Schädlichkeit, samt Beantwortung, Einwürfen und andern Remarquen* (Zürich, 1698), and continued throughout the eighteenth century, too (though later critics differentiated between good and bad novels, not condemning the whole genre out of hand).

In 1742, for example, the Swiss publisher Lindinner was forbidden to print advertisements for 'schlechte und liederliche Bücher und Romans' in his *Wochen-Blättlin*.[16] Novelists, too, quite often joined in the fight against 'the soul-destroying fiction' on the market, drawing particular attention to the danger in allowing young girls access to such reading material; in 1776 we find Hermes writing: '. . . gute Romanen mag man den jungen Mädchen immerhin geben; aber leider! wo sind die guten? Ich habe . . . keinen gesehen . . .'.[17] The strength of the tradition behind such utterances is most clearly shown when we find even the violent opponent of Protestant asceticism, the arch-enlightener C. F. Bahrdt, writing in 1789: 'Am meisten hütet euch vor jener Menge kindischer Mährchen, Komödien und Romanen, welche euch nicht weiser und tugendhafter machen und dagegen eure Phantasie anfüllen . . .'.[18] Even as late as 1826 we find a faithful protector of public morals advising parents to avoid the use of the word *Roman* in front of children and servants so that the desire to read them will not be awakened,[19] and when the literature of this time tells of a 'fallen maiden' we often read that the way was prepared for the villain by the girl's mania for novel-reading (e.g. in Richardson's novels, in *Fräulein von Sternheim*, *Sebaldus Nothanker*, *Kabale und Liebe*, and numerous others).

Such were the objections which faced the novel in the eighteenth century, and although attacks became less frequent as the century proceeded, during its first few decades no true Christian dared openly declare himself a novel-reader. Clearly, before the middle and upper-lower classes of German society could come into consideration as possible members of a novel-reading public two things had to happen: firstly, society and culture in general would have to undergo a process of secularization, freeing the life of the German *Bürger* from the grip of religion and the dictatorship of parish priest and parish minister, and secondly, writers would have to meet this development half-way by producing works of secular literature which were both acceptable to the conscience and relevant to the life of the serious-minded citizen. It is in the achievement of these two things that the importance of the years 1700 to 1740 in the history of the German novel lies.

Secularization is in fact the theme that unites that group of often conflicting forces which were active in Germany during the first half of the eighteenth century—Pietism and the German version of the English and French Enlightenment, which together brought about a total intellectual reappraisement and introduced a whole new system of social, ethical, religious, philosophic, and aesthetic values.

The German Pietist was essentially an individualist in revolt against the idea of collective belief, against communal Christianity with its collective rules and regulations. The Church and her ministers with their eternal polemics and cold impersonal dogma he saw as a barrier between himself and his God, and in their place he put the 'invisible church' to be found in the feeling of each individual and in the realm of personal religious experience. The once solid community of believers was divided into individual souls, each of which bore the responsibility of seeing to its own salvation, to gain which each man must first be convicted of sin so that God's grace might come upon him in the hour of conversion, the climax of his life on this earth. The foundations of this new movement amongst German Protestants had been laid generations earlier by such men as Sebastian Franck (1499–1542), Valentin Weigel (1533–88), Jakob Böhme (1575–1624), and Johann Arndt (1555–1621), but it was only under the leadership of Philipp Jakob Spener (1635–1705) that Pietism became firmly established, finding supporters in all parts of Protestant Germany and amongst men and women of every age and all social ranks.

The 'invisible church' of the Pietists had, as already stated, no need of pastor and no place for dogma, and it is this rejection of dogmatics and clerical omnipotence that removed one of the greatest barriers to the freeing of society from the iron grip of the Church. This in itself is an important development when considering the genesis of a novel-reading public, but there are also other aspects of Pietism which had a far-reaching influence on the history of the German novel.

Perhaps the most important of these is the stress laid on feeling. Formerly individual feeling had to be suppressed, anything which might distinguish one from the main body of Christians had been avoided but now the inner life of man as an individual was a subject of general interest. The rule of the heart had commenced. It had won its recognition in the religious field, but with no church discipline, with no objective system of faith to check excesses, the Pietists' unsound worship of feeling was soon to result in the secular field in boundless enthusiasm, over-sensitivity, and sentimentalism.

With every soul looking to its own salvation it is not surprising that we find each believer probing into his own inner life to see if he could make any improvement anywhere. From being a necessity of religion it gradually became merely fashionable to write one's findings down in the form of confessional autobiographies; diaries were kept by everyone who took his religion seriously and letter-writing, so important in the political, gallant world for the furthering of useful friendships, was now used to exchange feelings and to keep friends informed of each other's progress and spiritual welfare. Correspondence was started even with strangers whose fame as letter-writers had spread throughout the land. It is in such writing with its self-observation that we find the roots of the new science of psychology—then known characteristically as *Seelenkunde*[20]—and of such soul-analysing works as *Anton Reiser* and Jung-Stilling's *Lebensgeschichte*. Here too, we find a further explanation for the immense popularity in later years of the novels in biographical, letter, and diary forms.

The influence of Pietism in the social sphere is also of vital importance to the literary historian. Originating in the middle class, it had spread to all classes of society during the first half of the eighteenth century. There were adherents found even amongst the aristocracy, the most notable names in this respect being Seckendorff, Uffenbach, Canitz, and Zinzendorf. This represented the first storming of the social barriers in Germany, and this development in social and intellectual life was balanced by a corresponding development in literature. As long as each social class had its own definite range of feeling, its own particular conflicts, interests, and problems, then any literary work, irrespective of any intrinsic artistic value, could enjoy influence only in that social sphere in whose world of feeling and ideas it moved—as, for example, in the novel of the seventeenth century. But when the barriers between the classes started to disappear, and when a common interest on the basis of Pietism and the new philosophy of Rationalism was formed, then the time was favourable for the establishment of an art the rudiments of which were known to all and had a meaning to all, consequently an art whose influence was not of necessity limited to one social community. Conditions were therefore favourable for that exceptional general interest in literature and the world of books which now typifies the second half of the eighteenth century.

Finally, the Pietist movement did much to restore the former self-confidence of the middle and better-off lower classes of German society; these were the classes which had suffered most from the general political instability in the land and more especially from the ravages of the Thirty Years War. Pietism became the source of a new life where sentiment, too, had an important part to play, and this new life was adopted almost unanimously by those classes exiled from art by the aristocratic world. The 'small man' now began to play a part in the intellectual life of the nation and began to long for education and instruction so that he might fit himself for his new and important role in life. Just how eager a public the writings of the Pietist leaders found may be gathered from an article by the staunch orthodox Protestant, Valentin Löscher (1673–1749), in his journal *Unschuldige Nachrichten* (founded 1701). He demands that the censorship and suppression of pietistic literature should be introduced, and continues: 'Dies bedauern wir am meisten, daß dergleichen giftige Dinge nicht allein am allermeisten gekauft und gelesen werden, sondern auch viel eher Verleger finden, als was zu Gottes Ehre und Beförderung des Guten gemeint ist.'[21]

The publishers would know what was a good commercial risk; they would know that there was a new intellectual spirit abroad and that it was the many ordinary citizens of Germany and not merely the few scholars who would buy such works. A genuine thirst for knowledge was now to be found in the once intellectually apathetic middle-class society. There would be many in Germany who could say of the Pietist movement the same as James Lackington had said in England of the Methodists: 'It was by their preaching that I was taught to call upon God for his grace to enable me to turn from my vicious course of life, and through which I became a real Christian. It was by their means also that I was excited to improve a little my intellectual faculties . . . and it is well known that many, very many, instances of the same kind might be adduced.'[22]

It was in this longing for improvement of the intellect that the second great force of this period, that of Enlightenment, came to the aid of the ordinary man. That is one of the most important aspects of the new philosophy of Rationalism from the literary point of view; it freed literature and culture in general from the grip of the scholar, especially the theologian, and by its movement for the popularization of knowledge prepared a middle- and upper-lower-class public for the coming great age of German literature.

To the great thinkers of the period, *Aufklärung* might mean primarily a closer connection between the various branches of natural science; they might rack their brains about the whys and wherefores of existence, but to the average middle-class

German of this time it was a case of a totally new intellectual
atmosphere taking over. Typical is the change in the attitude
to the world and to earthly things. Protestant orthodoxy demanded that every expression of life be in service of God and so
long as the Church could keep this idea a living force she was in
command and need give no account of herself to her followers.
The orthodox Christian simply believes, without examining
critically, the doctrine of his Church; his father had done the
same and had gained salvation. His faith is not the result of the
triumph of his reason but rather his inherited privilege. In
contrast to him comes the new eighteenth-century *Bürger*, the
modern man and dweller on this earth, now feeling much more
economically secure and gaining in respect enjoyed. Self-
confidence, a sceptical attitude, and individualism of will and
feeling, give him his stamp. He is educated and wishes to add
constantly to his fund of knowledge and it is this feeling of
intellectual superiority which now compels him to call the
Church to account for her doctrines in order to satisfy his
reason. He can no longer believe blindly, but must first examine
and convince his rational mind; he regards those who stick
unshaken and unquestioning to their belief as inferiors, as
'dependants', as 'limited'. When he does believe, then it is the
result of his own conviction and not of tradition or authority.
The followers of the new philosophy are filled with a great hope
of clearing up all life's mysteries and problems and of showing
the real worth and supremacy of man. To be human no longer
means to be a sinner, for with reason as the criterion the doctrine
of original sin cannot retain validity, or at least requires a much
less radical interpretation than the orthodox Protestant Church
allowed. And how could man be ever mindful of eternity when
life in this, the best of all possible worlds, was so manifestly
propitious? God, to the eighteenth-century bourgeois, is lovable
and understanding, the human being is good, life is good, and
the evil in the world is a negative element, a lacking of perfection, but certainly nothing positive and not a punishable crime
of humanity in general.

Yet Orthodox and Rationalist managed to work together at
first. As long as the tendency of the new philosophy towards
atheism remained latent, friction was negligible, and one thing
at least they both had in common—the complete rejection of

sentiment, by the Orthodox as *Heterodoxie* and *Enthusiasmus* and
by the Rationalists as 'animalische Trübungen der Vernunft'
('animal disruptions of man's reason'); and then, in the early
stages, reason was actually used to serve God and the Faith. The
work of Gottfried Wilhelm Leibniz (1646–1716) is characteristic in this respect. He attempted to give the Christian faith
a rational foundation, to characterize revealed religion as something above, but not contradictory to, man's reason. But of
more significance from our point of view are the writings of
Christian von Wolff (1679–1754). The influence of Leibniz on
him is conspicuous. In fact, Wolff really said what Leibniz had
said before him, but there is one important difference between
the two philosophers: Leibniz had preached the new doctrine
only to the learned, writing for the most part in French and
Latin, whereas Wolff turned his attention to the nation as
a whole; he was, as Hegel well called him, 'der Lehrer der
Deutschen', the first German scholar to set any store by a large
public. Middle-class society has at no other time and in no other
nation been so systematically schooled as was the German
bourgeoisie by Wolff. That he should write in German was
the natural result of his policy of regarding every German as
a potential convert. The effect of this alone on the development
of a reading public and also on the development of German as
a literary language[23] can scarcely be over-estimated; Gottsched
wrote later:

> Kaum hub man an, auf deutsch zu lehren,
> Zum Trotze der Lateiner-Zunft:
> Gleich stieg der Wahrheit Glanz zu Ehren,
> Der Pöbel selbst bekam Vernunft.[24]

The importance of Wolff as a philosopher does not belong
here; important to us is the effect which he had on his contemporaries. He taught his public to think philosophically, that is,
independently of theology. Philosophy had, up to then, been
shackled with the chains of theology, but now it was freed
and was able to become the main study and almost the common property of the eighteenth century. This was linked with a
general demand for more opportunities for the ordinary man to
educate himself. We find John Stuart Mill writing of the same
movement in England: 'So complete was my father's reliance
on the influence of reason over the mind of mankind, whenever it

is allowed to reach them, that he felt as if all would be gained if
the whole population were taught to read, if all sorts of opinions
were allowed to be addressed to them by word and in writing . . .'.[25]

Like Leibniz, Wolff did not use the reason of man to attack
the doctrinal foundations of the Church but sought rather to
reconcile reason with the articles of faith; he had nothing in
common with what he termed 'the tasteless free-thinking of the
English'. This conciliatory attitude found complete favour with
the German bourgeoisie, which was proud to think rationally
but still wished to retain its faith. In clear and simple language,
his own language, the ordinary man could now read of, and
understand, the fundaments of the Christian religion—in yet
another sphere the minister of the Church had become dis-
pensable.

It is also of importance to our present theme to note that
Wolff also turned his attention to rationalizing the practical side
of everyday life, dealing with problems which had a definite
topicality to the German middle class and which had for so
long been neglected by the religious-minded orthodox writers.
His two works—*Vernünftige Gedanken von der Menschen Thun und
Lassen zur Beförderung ihrer Glückseligkeit* (1720) and *Vernünftige
Gedanken von dem gesellschaftlichen Leben der Menschen und insonder-
heit dem ganzen Wesen zur Beförderung der menschlichen Glückseligkeit*
(1721)—each enjoyed five editions in a short time, quite an
achievement for any work in those days. This type of useful
reading material was clearly more congenial to the aspiring
middle class than such gloomy tracts as the orthodox *Kunst aller
Künste, vermittelst deren man vergnügt leben und sterben könne.*[26] The
great importance of the last-named of Wolff's works, however,
lies in the fact that it brought the bourgeois ethical code into
credit and condemned the loose morals of the so-called gallant
world. This accent on man's ethics would also find an eager
public in middle- and upper-lower-class society, for, since dog-
matic religion had now lost its influence on large sections of the
community, a new support for religion was required; it was
found in the realm of ethics, and Christianity was henceforth
to be preached with the accent on ethics—a development which
was to have a great effect on the coming middle-class novel.

It was perhaps natural that the most bitter opposition to

Wolff's ideas, once they had reached the bulk of the bourgeoisie, was offered by the Pietists whose whole devotional life was founded on the doctrine of original sin, and it was indeed their leaders, Lange, Breithaupt, and Francke who succeeded in having Wolff banned from Halle and all Prussian territories in 1723. On his triumphant return in 1740, however, his textbooks were to be found in every school and his theories prevailed in almost all the German universities and had given rise to a critical school of theology in Halle itself. Besides the broad mass of the German middle class, many of whom had received their Wolffian philosophy in the more vernacular formulation of Gottsched, his followers included princes and state ministers, Protestant clergy and Jesuits; a sure sign of the widespread interest in Wolff's teachings is the appearance in the thirties of lexicons to help the ordinary man to understand his works, and if Wolff himself is to be believed, even peasants read his *Logik*.

We may say, then, that the first prerequisite to the growth of a wider reading public had been achieved by about the year 1740. Pietism and Rationalism had together broken the hold which the Church had previously enjoyed over society and culture. Feeling had, at least amongst certain sections of the community, at last gained recognition; the Bible and dogma had been replaced by reason and ethics as life's criteria and, most important of all, the new spirit was evident not just in a small group of learned scholars but in the whole bourgeoisie; they now constituted, in Schücking's famous expression, 'der neue Geschmacksträgertypus'.[27] The atmosphere was now favourable for the development of a popular secular literature. Even in Spener and Thomasius we can see promise of a change in the attitude to profane literature. The only harm which Spener could see in novel-reading was the 'waste of precious time', whilst Thomasius in the January volume of his journal *Monatsgespräche* (1688) defends the reading of novels as a pastime and praises Abraham a St. Clara if only because he is amusing; a sense of humour is something good in itself; the prudes read their editions of Petronius and other 'fleshly works' in secret and excuse themselves by their interest in the language, why then cannot the ordinary man have a little light entertainment in his leisure hours? The new secular spirit was already beginning to take effect. If writers could now produce works of fiction which were acceptable to the respectable citizen then a public for these works would be found.

For much of the period 1700 to 1740, however, the heroic gallant novel was still predominant, with writers of the so-called 'Lohensteinische Schule' still turning out the endless stories, after the manner of *Die römische Octavia* (1677), in which almost without exception the setting is exotic and women play the main parts; the most successful of these seventeenth-century novels, most notably Ziegler's *Asiatische Banise*, were still being reprinted. Just what was expected of a novel in these years is shown most clearly by a definition to be found in Amaranthes's *Frauen-zimmerlexikon* (Leipzig, 1715): 'Romain seynd allerhand ver-liebte Geschichten und Erzählungen derer Götter, Helden, hohen Standes — auch anderer Personen, mit allerhand heim-lichen und wundernswürdigen Liebes-Intrigen angefüllet.'[28] Such was the legacy of the previous century; the term 'novel' had become synonymous with 'love-story', and although 'other persons' could figure in the narrative we are left with the distinct impression that heroes of high social standing are most welcome. August Bohse, called Talander (1661–1730), one of the most characteristic writers in this branch of fiction, gives us an indication of the aims of novelists in writing such stories and also of the type of public at which they are directed; in the Foreword to *Verliebte Verwirrung der Sicilianischen Höfe* (1725) he writes: 'Ein rechter Mann wird einem zeigen, wie man die Höflichkeit praktiziert, tapfere Taten üben, sich gegen honette Frauenzimmer bescheiden aufführen, mit Standespersonen der Gebühr nach umgehen und als ein kluger Mann in aller Kon-versation sich erweisen solle.'[29] Besides entertaining his public he also instructs them in the art of being a success at court. Readers, aristocratic and otherwise, who looked simply for an amorous tale, exciting adventures, and a foreign setting would be well served here, but this was hardly the type of fiction to appeal to German middle-class society.

Even where writers followed in the steps of Weise and Reu-ter, giving their stories a realistic, contemporary setting, they still clung to the inevitable love-story and usually with such an over-accentuation of sexual relationships that their products swiftly joined the ranks of that branch of fiction known as the *Skandalroman*. The most popular writers in this group were

Christian Friedrich Hunold (1680–1721) who wrote under the name of Menantes, and Christian Friedrich Henrici (Picander) (1700–64).

Courtly romance and *Skandalroman* could never win over the German bourgeoisie to the novel-reading public and so the way was left open for a foreign work. The immense popularity of Defoe's novel *The Life and Strange Surprising Adventures of Robinson Crusoe of York* (1719) in Germany bears witness to the growing desire of the middle class to participate in the literary life of the nation. Defoe (1661–1731) was, of course, writing for an English public; he says himself that his readers were 'of the middle state, or what might be called the upper station of lower life',[30] but so similar were the spiritual and intellectual atmospheres of the two nations, especially in middle-class society, that the novel found a reception in Germany which must scarcely have been equalled since. Its impact on the German literary scene is well known, but it is as well to be reminded of it briefly here in our present context. Within a year of its publication there appeared three translations, the most important being *Das Leben und die gantz ungemeine Begebenheiten des Robinson Crusoe* (Frankfurt and Leipzig, 1720); the same year saw five editions of this translation and further editions followed in 1721, 1731, 1745, 1765–6, and 1773. A veritable flood of imitations soon appeared. For the next sixty years the German book market was all but swamped by the so-called 'Robinsonades'.[31] A catalogue of the year 1746 lists for the period 1721 to 1745 alone Brandenburg, Dutch, French, Italian, Nordic, Persian, Polish-Prussian, Saxon, Silesian, Swabian, Swedish, Spanish, 'Teutsch', Thuringian, medical, clerical, and ethical Robinsons; there was further a 'book-dealing Robinson' and even a 'Jungfernrobinson'.[32]

Robinson Crusoe must have come as a revelation to people accustomed to the Frenchified atmosphere of the courtly heroic, historical, and gallant novels. Here was a story which had not only a meaning but also a certain topicality to the average German citizen. When the English seaman, cut off from all other thoughts on his lonely desert island, turns to a still contemplation of his God, and when after his considerations he arrives at a firm conviction of the goodness of Providence, the German reader could recognize in this tale the story of his own religious experiences. Had not he too, starting out from the

Rationalist idea of the best of all possible worlds, arrived at the
very same conclusion as Robinson? It is this firm belief and
trust in the goodness of Providence that finds itself so perfectly
portrayed in Defoe's story, thus explaining much of its success
in Germany. On the other hand, the adventurous content of the
English novel had quite a good deal in common with the already
established branches of fiction with their love of exciting incident
in far-off places. Its title alone would attract the attention of
the followers of these tales; strange and surprising adventures
were promised, and Robinson Crusoe was as outlandish and,
it follows, as interesting a name as was, say, Happel's *Kaiser
Xunkius*. They would not be disappointed on reading the novel
either. Exciting sea-voyages, pirates, slave-traders, the strange
lands of Algeria and Brazil, a shipwreck on a desert island, and
cannibals were the fare they were used to and enjoyed in their
reading material. To these already popular elements Defoe the
business man, the man who wished to live by his pen, added a new
ingredient, a religious message especially aimed at middle-class
society. For the first time we find a novel which appealed to
both of these once rigidly divided reading publics; future
writers did not fail to notice Defoe's technique here, and with
the coming together of these two groups we can naturally
expect a larger public for each work. That Defoe's novel, however, was most appreciated as the presentation of an exceptional
inner experience, as the story of a soul, or in other words, that
it found most of its readers amongst the bourgeoisie, is proved by
the fact that none of the many imitations, all of which sought to
emulate the Englishman's success by following the adventurous
framework and making it into the main content, was as well
received by the public as was the original. Defoe, by making his
story acceptable to the virtuous, had introduced the German
middle class to fiction; his novel was, in fact, the first of the
'sugared pills' which were to be showered on the reading public
in the second half of the century.

The best and most popular of the German 'Robinsonades'
was Johann Gottfried Schnabel's (1692–?) *Wunderliche Fata einiger Seefahrer, absonderlich Alberti Julii, eines gebohrnen Sachsens und
seiner auf der Insel Felsenburg errichteten Colonien* (1731–43, in four
volumes). For the framework of his story Schnabel borrows the
form of *Robinson Crusoe*, the idea of a shipwreck on a deserted

island, but he develops Defoe's ideas further by shipwrecking not one, but four travellers (three men and one woman) who must now seek to live in harmony as a group. This picture of the ideal social community is then contrasted most strongly with the society of Germany as known to his contemporary public; all the ideas current amongst the German middle class, the call for social reforms, the fight of right against wrong, rational against irrational, the new sense of social responsibility known to the age as 'Tugend', the new secular role allotted by many to human sentiment—all find their expression in *Insel Felsenburg* but it is noteworthy that the author finds his ideal so improbable that he places the action in a far-away unknown land, his Utopia, so that it may appear credible to his readers; the new spirit, with its stress on piety, loyalty, honesty, and sincerity was not yet strong enough to venture into the open and suggest the immediate application of its ideas in German society itself. Schnabel had, however, given the ideas a concrete formulation and his novel became something very like a social manifesto setting forth the hopes and aspirations of wide sections of the German community.

It is significant that forty years later the book-dealer and author Friedrich Nicolai (1733–1811) could tell us that the most well-read books in the country districts of Germany were first, religious and devotional literature and then, Schnabel's *Felsenburg*.[33] The novel, in fact, took on a role similar to that of Bunyan's *Pilgrim's Progress* in England; it was found next to the Bible in all pious middle-class homes. Nicolai's evidence is proof not only of the book's long-lived popularity[34] and wide public but also of the respect in which it was held by that wide public, and respect was something which not even the most optimistic critic could have prophesied for the novel at the beginning of the century. Prejudice against the novel was so strong at this time that this aspect alone of Schnabel's book cannot be stressed too much. Written not by a scholar but by an ordinary barber-surgeon of Stolberg-Wernigerode for a middle-class public, and of such a character that it could be read quite openly and indeed to some profit by self-respecting, God-fearing citizens, *Insel Felsenburg* did much to prepare the way for the coming period of bourgeois culture with its secular literature and wide reading public.

When considering the position of the German novel about the year 1740 it might seem that the obvious procedure is to turn to the theorists of the period and that means, in this instance, to the Leipzig school of Gottsched and to the Swiss critics Bodmer and Breitinger, but we look in vain in their main critical works for any treatment of the novel as a separate and worthy genre. Nor could it be otherwise. The novel as we now know it was only gradually coming into existence during these years and was not yet recognized as a serious form of art; it was, in fact, being evolved because of the sudden appearance of a large reading public whose tastes and preferences had no place in the technical talk of literary men; readers simply wanted something to read which was related to their everyday lives and expressed in language they could understand—it was a question of 'demand' rather than 'theory'. Thus we find, as the modern critic John Wain has pointed out, that the originators of the modern novel 'were mostly men who had no literary theories at all, but simply wrote to fill a gap; if they did start with a theory, then it was a theory of parody, of ironic deflation'.[35] Wain is referring here particularly to Defoe, Richardson, and Fielding but the same holds good for Germany if we add to the 'theory' of parody that of imitation; men like Gellert, Hermes, Knigge, J. G. Müller, and Nicolai all improvised their novels in response to a demand, wrote 'to fill a gap' and not to satisfy any abstract theories of art.

More informative than the theorists on the subject of the German novel and its future is that branch of writing which, prior to 1740, was stopping the same gap referred to above, meeting the growing demand from the middle class for its own reading material—the field of journalistic literature; this was where the future novel-reading public served its apprenticeship, made the transition from devotional to secular literature and acquired many of the tastes that were later to be catered for by novelists.

With the opening decades of the eighteenth century there began what might be called the era of journalism. By the year 1715 the situation in Germany was such that a contemporary commentator could declare, 'daß viele Buchläden nicht mehr Buchläden, sondern Journal-Läden heißen möchten, auch die Buchhändler mehr Journal-Memoriale als Bücher-Memoriale zu expediren und zu verschicken hätten . . .'.[36] In 1718, for example, there appeared no less than 101 magazines (63 in German, 21 in Latin, and 17 in French), in 1720, 88 magazines (50 in German, 21 in Latin, and 17 in French), in 1724, 96 magazines (65 in German, 18 in Latin, and 13 in French). This magazine literature was most varied in content. Of the 48 journals in German appearing in 1716 we find 22 of general scholarly and literary content, 2 historical and political, 5 combining the above types, 10 theological, 2 moral weeklies, 2 'Swedish Tales' (*Schwedische Famen*), 1 philological, 1 pedagogic, 1 on books and disputations, 1 of miscellaneous content, and 1 *Journal der Journale*.[37]

It will be seen that most of these journals would appeal only to a scholarly public; only two groups can come into consideration as reading material for a larger public and therefore of importance in the matter of future taste in the reading of fiction. The first of these groups is the historical journal, not of course the type which specialized in imperial declarations, decrees, treaties, etc., and whose public would clearly be limited. There were other much more popular journals aimed at the average newspaper reader, bringing the latest news, rumours, and 'secrets' of court-life, the life-stories of princes and their followers, the adventures of court-mistresses and favourites and the like—all regarded as 'history' in those days; such a magazine was the very popular *Europäische Fama, Welche den gegenwärtigen Zustand der vornehmsten Höfe entdecket* (1702–56). Then for the reader merely seeking entertainment were those magazines which presented contemporary history in a satirical vein, anecdotes, strange fates of great men, horrible stories of tyrants and aristocratic scoundrels, vivid descriptions of bloody battles, great fires, floods, sieges, etc.; the favourite of this group was the *Gespräche in dem Reiche derer Todten, Nebst dem Kern der Neuesten Merkwürdigkeiten und sehr wichtig darüber gemachten Reflexionen* (1718–44). The public which bought such reading material would also find much to their taste in the heroic gallant novels when they could afford them, and they would also have most definite demands to make of the fiction-writers of later years.

The second group of journals which looked beyond the circle of university-trained specialists for its public was that directed particularly at the sober practical-minded bourgeoisie—the moral weeklies, after the fashion of the English *Tatler* (founded 1709), *Spectator* (founded 1711), and *Guardian* (founded 1713). In these weeklies the German Enlighteners, the representatives of the progressive attitude of the bourgeoisie, found a mouthpiece through which they could address and instruct the whole nation—a distinct sign of the awakening of the old self-confidence of the middle class after years of servile submission to the aristocracy. They now wanted to lead their lives according to rules made by themselves or their equals.

As it was an essentially middle-class literature it was natural that the first imitations of the publications of Addison and Steele appeared in places where the bourgeois spirit of old had remained most intact; the first appeared in Hamburg which, because of its lively trade connections, stood most under English influence. Here were published *Der Vernünftler* (1713), *Lustige Fama* (1718), and *Der Patriot* (1724). Zürich and Berne were quick to follow this lead, Bodmer setting the pace in his Zürich *Discourse der Mahlern* (1721–3). During the period 1723 to 1728 there appeared eight such weeklies in Leipzig, nine more were added by Hamburg, and one each from Frankfurt, Wahrburg, Dresden, Eisleben, Bautzen, and two giving no place of publication. In the state of Hanover, whose Elector was now King of England, even the smaller towns, Hanover itself, Göttingen, and Celle, for example, had their own moral weeklies and as the century proceeded their number increased remarkably. Before 1740 there were on the average ten such weeklies founded each five years; twenty-eight were founded from 1741 to 1745; twenty-seven from 1746 to 1750; forty-four from 1751 to 1755; and twenty-nine from 1756 to 1760.[38] Naturally they did not suddenly just disappear from the German book market, but after 1760 their day was over and their numbers steadily declined. Their task and their public had been taken over by the middle-class novel much of whose character is surely foreshadowed in the content, style, and aim of these weeklies.

There is no place in them for the latest rumours revolving round court society, foreign royalty, and great potentates. Here the subject is simply the German bourgeoisie, the human being, his life, his joy, and his sorrows on this earth. 'Unser Gegenstand ist der Mensch mit allem, was zu dem Menschen gehört' ('Our subject is man, and everything pertaining to man') we find in the first number of *Maler der Sitten* (1746). From the world of exciting incident attention was now turned to the inner life of man, to his everyday surroundings, and to the most intimate community of human society, the family, especially to the woman and her domestic problems. Amongst the favourite themes of these weeklies we find education by far the most recurrent, with the main accent again on the woman, for it was through her in her capacity as mother that the coming generation could most effectively be brought up in an enlightened manner. Religion, too, was a favourite topic, and always discussed from the point of view of the layman. Other subjects frequently dealt with include nursing, marriage, fashions, superstition, intolerance, gambling, thrift, loan-words, etc.

The aim of the moral weeklies is first and foremost to instruct, but in as pleasant and entertaining a manner as possible. The various editors realized that the way to win readers was not by writing dry eulogies on the virtues of man but by introducing concrete examples of the correct way to live, in the form of an entertaining narrative. Thus they would find both more readers and more success in their crusade against vice. Moral instruction takes the form of story, satire, dialogue, or, for the more personal approach, letter. It is obvious from the titles of the moral weeklies that real paragons of virtue are to be led before the public for their praise, admiration, and imitation, e.g. *Der Patriot*; *Der Biedermann*; *Der Menschenfreund*; *Die Matrone*; *Die mühsame Bemerkerin*; *Die vernünftigen Tadlerinnen*; *Die vor sich und ihre Kinder sorgfältigen Mütter*.

The German middle class was, as we have seen, by no means without reading material before the advent of this magazine literature, but formerly its leisure hours had been spent exclusively in the reading and study of popular religious literature, though often with a stong practical bias. Not the least important aspect of such journals as the moral weeklies is the fact that they introduced the broad mass of the bourgeoisie to a secular reading material which, because of its serious and Christian nature could, and did, gain their respect. The reading habit grew. Brockes's *Hamburger Patriot* (1724–6) could boast of 5,000 subscribers as early as 1724. Gottsched's *Biedermann* could write as early as 1727: 'Ihr seid es etliche Jahre her gewohnt, liebe Landes-Leute, daß ihr wöchentlich ein paar moralische Blätter durchleset . . .',[39] or again: 'Von den französischen Grenzen bis nach Moskau sind ohngefähr 300 deutsche Meilen; soweit wird *der Patriot* hochgeschätzt.'[39] Even allowing for the perhaps pardonable enthusiasm of an editor we may be sure that these weeklies really did have a wide public and enjoy great popularity.

Polite literature had won the trust of the middle-class public. The moral weeklies and such 'transitional' novels as Defoe's *Robinson Crusoe*, Schnabel's *Insel Felsenburg*, and later the novels of Richardson and his German imitators had given this public a reading material which was in accord with the more secular spirit of the century and yet not so revolutionary as to give rise to suspicions in the mind of the good Christian as to whether it was right or wrong to read it. Just as in their former reading matter they were being sermonized, given a text which was both 'edifying' and 'practical', and if it was now also 'entertaining' then that could only mean that the 'sermon' would be followed much more eagerly. What possible objection could there be to a work with a title like *Pamela, oder die belohnte Tugend (Pamela, or Virtue Rewarded)*. And so the generation of the forties and fifties went on to read what perhaps their fathers, and most certainly their grandfathers, would have condemned as worldly, soul-destroying fiction.

One final indication of the literary climate in Germany in 1740 may be obtained from a glance at the position and circumstances of writers about that time. For much of the first half of the century the social standing of men engaged in producing works of imaginative literature was the most humble imaginable. Even the court poets with their relatively secure, paid appointments at one of the larger courts enjoyed but little respect in society in general. Weise writes in his . . . *curieuse Gedanken von deutschen Versen* (1691): 'Heute bezeichnet der Name Poet als kaiserlicher Titel eine Art gelehrten Adels, steht aber sonst in großer Verachtung.'[40] To be called a novelist (*Romaniste*) was an insult.[41] Both for social and financial reasons a writer had to have some other means of support besides his pen. In earlier days Fischart and Grimmelshausen had ended their lives as state officials, Opitz became a historiographer, Fleming travelled as Oldenburg ambassador to Russia and Persia, Simon Dach lived from his professorship, Harsdörffer,

Hofmannswaldau, and Brockes were town councillors; whoever tried to live from his pen alone, like Zesen and Günther, ended in poverty and contempt.

The writer depended on his main occupation or profession for any social respect he hoped to enjoy and if possible kept his literary activity secret. Weise says later in the afore-mentioned work: 'Die Dichtkunst wird erst ästimirt, wenn der Mann etwas anders daneben hat, davon er sich bei Mitteln und Respect erhalten könne. . . . Opitz' unsicheres Leben wird gewiß kein Vater seinem Sohn wünschen.'[42] The professions where we find most of the middle-class writers of the first decades of the eighteenth century are those of teacher or headmaster at grammar schools, university professor, clergyman, or finally merchant or independent citizen.

There was as yet no profession of letters. This was the period of which Goethe could write: 'Die Produktion von poetischen Schriften wurde als etwas Heiliges angesehen und man hielt es beinahe für Simonie, ein Honorar zu nehmen oder zu steigern.'[43] The contemporary attitude was that it was enough if the author was saved the risk of financing the publication of his works himself: 'Der Autor, er mag etwas oder nichts vor seine Arbeit bekommen haben, verliehret doch nichts dabei und kan sich gar wol zu Frieden stellen, wenn er siehet, daß seine Schrift mit begierigen Augen gelesen wird.'[44] It was not an uncommon practice even later in the century for publishers to pay authors in books. Practically the only literary men to earn money from their writing were the occasional poets; turning out poems to celebrate festive occasions at court, and later in bourgeois circles too, was amongst students quite a common method of financing one's studies—Geßner, for example, kept himself alive at the University of Jena from 1710 to 1712 by writing birthday, wedding, and funeral poems in German and Latin. Gottsched himself was not above earning money this way, whilst the court poet Johann von Besser assures us that writing had contributed most not only to his happiness, but also to his purse.[45] Still it was quite usual even for court poets to have some secondary occupation and source of income; von Canitz was, for instance, in addition to poet, diplomat and *Hofrat* too.

If Goethe referred to the production of poetical works as 'something sacred', then the respect and social esteem enjoyed by writers was by no means in proportion to their 'high calling'. All authors had to defend themselves against the reproach that it was unseemly to have any connection with the creative side of poetry, aristocratic poets because of their social rank, and those of the middle class because of the waste of valuable time involved in writing. The court poets defend themselves by saying that composing verse is, of course, not their main occupation; this would be a sure way of ruining oneself socially. Baron von Canstein in his Preface to the 1700 edition of Canitz's *Nebenstunden* considers it both unnecessary and undesirable to pass on to posterity the author's name and memory, for appearance in print would surely debase both. Noble and bourgeois poets alike sought, therefore, to hide their identity by the use of pseudonyms (e.g. Weise = Catharinus; Mencke = Philander von der Linde; Hunold = Menantes; Gressel = Celander; Henrici = Picander; Schnabel = Gisander or 'der Ungenannte'; Hagedorn, Haller, and Liscow wrote anonymously.[46] Von Ziegler was rather braver than his noble colleagues and declared openly, 'that a quill-feather in the hand becomes the nobility just as well as a plume-feather on the hat'.[47]

Bourgeois poets, in their defence, never tire of assuring us in their prefaces that they have not wasted any time in writing since they have used only their leisure hours for this purpose, and so are still good citizens really. A glance at the book-catalogues of this period reveals a host of such *poetische Nebenstunden*, even the respectable merchants of Hamburg not being averse to publishing the 'products of their free time'.[48] But the impression that one was engaged professionally in writing imaginative literature must be avoided at all costs.

With the third and fourth decades of the century, however, come definite signs of an improvement in the position of writers, an improvement based firstly on the new character and function of polite literature, and secondly on the subsequent widening of its appeal which have already been noted. When literature added to its aim of entertaining the reader that of instructing and edifying him also, then both literature and men of letters gained in respect; and gradually the literary activity of people who already held a socially respected position helped the profession as a whole to gain further esteem as when Gellert, for example, a man of taste, learning, and high reputation, published his novel *Leben der schwedischen Gräfin von G.* in 1747.

Of vital importance to writers, especially writers of prose fiction, was the second point—the widening of the appeal of literature, since this obviously meant more sales and, ultimately, the chance of winning financial security. The writer's whole conception of his public changes.[49] The age of the Maecenas, the court poet, and courtly occasional poet was over, the predominance of the essentially aristocratic forms of prose fiction was ending; poets no longer saw their public as the small and extremely select circle gathered round their patron, and novelists needed no longer to aim their stories at a restricted section of German society. Writers now see before them an unlimited public. Weise was in this respect a precursor of the new spirit; he writes as early as 1672: 'Über Fürsten und Herren haben andere genug geklaget und geschrieben: hier finden die Leute ihren Text, die nicht viel vornehmer sind als ich.'[50] Schnabel wrote his *Kavalier* (1738) especially for the German youth 'whether they be noblemen or commoners', and on the subject of reading he writes seven years later:

> Also bleibt es dabey, das [*sic*] lesen, schreiben und conversiren allen Ständen nützlich seye, die Mächtigen finden in denen Schriften einen klaren Spiegel, die Staats-Männer einen magnetischen Com-pass, wie sie ihre Ruder lenken und wo die Ancker einzusenken sind, die Mittel- und Bürgerlichen Standes sehen, daß eine Tugendhaffte Lebens-Art nützlich- und rühmlicher als eine Lasterhaffte sey, und . . . so hat auch der Bauern-Stand bey dem erzehlen-hören seine Aufmunterung. . . . Allen Ständen ist etwas kluges zu lesen, zu schreiben und zu conversiren sehr nützlich, und der Mittel-Stand kan sich mit der Zeit dadurch dem höheren fast gleiche schwingen, wenn das Glücke dabey favorisirt, und der vergallte Neid nichts dazwischen machet. Auch der geringste Stand kan auss denen Historien einen Trost, und Muth schöpfen.[51]

The potential public for imaginative literature, formerly the select few of court and academic circles, was now the whole of German society. The age of the patron was ended, that of the publisher about to commence.

2

THE EVIDENCE OF THE LEIPZIG
BOOK-FAIR CATALOGUES

A CONTEMPORARY observer writing in 1690 on the *Nützliche und Fürtreffliche Buch-Handlung* points out the difference existing then between the book-dealer and the cloth-dealer; the cloth-dealer, like most merchants, has both producers and consumers, he gets his wares straight from the looms and sells them again to princes and lords, ladies and cavaliers, and also to artisans and peasants, 'whereas the common herd hardly ever contaminates the bookshop'. For the book-dealer, producer and consumer are one and the same—the scholars: 'Seine Wahren sind von- und vor niemand als Gelehrten; keufft iemand von and'n Professionen zu Zeit'n ein Teutsch- oder bey andern Nationen in seiner Mutter-Sprach gestelltes Büchlein so geschiehets zufälliger Weise und selten daß daruff keine Rechnung oder Staat zu machen.'[1] The modern reader can scarcely conceive the gap between the scholarly literature dealt with by all the best bookshops and the, to all intents and purposes, literatureless 'other professions' who now and then, but only by chance, buy 'ein teutsch Büchlein'.

This was the situation at the beginning of the eighteenth century. The book market was dominated by the scholar, particularly, as we shall see, by the theologian. During the next fifty or sixty years, however, the new secular and enlightening spirit was to bring about great changes in the composition of the German book market. The learned works for the scholar, written for the most part in Latin, were displaced by German works, written with an aim to popularize knowledge amongst all classes of society; the theological and popular devotional literature gave way to a secular literature of entertainment, predominantly narrative in character. These changes are mirrored most clearly in the book-catalogues of the Leipzig fair during these years.

We are most fortunate in having in these catalogues the most unbiased and objective source imaginable. They alone can give a true picture of the German book market in far-off days, listing as they do the books considered worthy of being brought to the fair; here we see the interests of the reading public and through them the actual composition of that public. Since the autumn of 1564 half-yearly catalogues of the new printed works appeared, first as a private undertaking, and then as the official organ of the book trade. They gave the titles of books to be brought to the Easter and Michaelmas fairs of both Frankfurt am Main and Leipzig. From 1564 to 1594 there exists only a Frankfurt catalogue, from 1594 to 1749 both Frankfurt and Leipzig catalogues appeared, after which publication of the former stopped. In mid nineteenth century the Leipzig catalogue, too, ceased to appear; the publication since 1797 of the *Hinrichssche Verzeichnisse* had made its appearance superfluous.[2] The evidence of these catalogues gives a most concrete picture and most conclusive proof of the momentous changes and developments in the composition of the book market during the eighteenth century.

The Easter fair catalogue of 1650 shows the following composition:[3] theology alone takes up 41·4 per cent of the total book production, history 20 per cent, philosophy, science, philology, etc., together 16·9 per cent, law 7 per cent, medicine 5·8 per cent, against which imaginative literature is represented by 5·1 per cent of production. In this same catalogue no less than 71 per cent of the books offered are for a Latin-reading public; 16 per cent of the total are theological works in German, and so together scholarly Latin works and German theological writings take up 87 per cent of the total book production, leaving only 13 per cent for a public not reading Latin and not interested in theology.

In the 1701 catalogue we see that Latin has already lost considerable ground. Here we find that 55 per cent of the books offered are written in Latin, and that theological works in German account for a further 24 per cent; thus 21 per cent of the items are for the not so learned public. Then by 1740 the number of Latin works sinks to 27 per cent, German theological writings still cling to a high 31 per cent, leaving for the non-theological German-reading public 42 per cent of the books offered.

The development over ninety years then was as follows:

	1650	1701	1740
	%	%	%
Latin works and German theological works together	87	79	58
Rest	13	21	42

The use of Latin, the language of the learned and symbol of the scholarly book market, was slowly passing away. Taking into account the total annual production, as opposed to the items offered in one half-yearly catalogue, we find that German works predominated over those in Latin from the year 1692 onwards. Interesting in this respect is the big difference between university towns and others; of the books appearing in Hamburg during the period 1700 to 1709 only 27 per cent were in Latin, for Jena the figure is 58 per cent, and, showing the picture in south Germany, 40 per cent of the books published in Augsburg during the same period were in Latin, as against Tübingen with 81 per cent.[4] By the year 1740 the use of Latin even in theological works had diminished most markedly; the Easter catalogue of that year lists 251 Lutheran, 8 Roman Catholic, and 23 Calvinist works, of which only 36, 2, and 2 respectively are written in Latin. German, which had long been strongly represented in imaginative literature and Protestant theology, was next adopted by historians, then by medical men and philosophers, and finally by that faculty whose language even today is all but incomprehensible to the layman—law. By the end of the century the rule of Latin on the German book market had well and truly ended; the Easter fair catalogue for 1770 had still shown 14 per cent of its items written in Latin, but that for 1800 aims less than 4 per cent of its contents at the Latin-reading public in Germany.

The fact that 55 per cent of the books announced in the 1701 catalogue were written in Latin might at first seem a big limitation to the possibility of sales, but this is not really so. These books were written for the scholar, and if they had been written in German, sales would not have increased at all, rather would the sale abroad of these German learned works have suffered a marked set-back. And, when finally a fall in the number of Latin books did set in, it was not a case of saying in German

what was formerly said in Latin but rather was it an attempt
to appeal to a much wider public than that offered by scholarly
circles. Instead of the huge systematic encyclopedias so beloved
of seventeenth-century collectors, and proudly displayed in ela-
borate bindings, we find simple lexicons for the layman, bound
in boards; history was popularized by biographies of famous
people, geography by popular travel descriptions, and, most
important from our point of view, the popular religious and
devotional works were displaced by a secular literature of entertainment. This latter development is evident from the catalogues
of the second half of the century by which time the secularizing
influences of the new intellectual spirit were taking effect.

We have already seen that during the first half of the century the most popular and widespread reading material was the
religious and edifying literature written especially for the layman. It was at the cost of this branch of literature that the
interest in—and, it follows, the production of—works of polite
or imaginative literature of entertainment grew. The catalogues
of 1740, 1770, and 1800 show the following relationships
between theology and imaginative literature.[5]

1740

Theology		Imaginative Literature	
	%		%
ALTOGETHER	38·54	ALTOGETHER	5·83
Including:		Including:	
Works for the expert	18·41	Narrative Literature	2·65
Works for the layman	19·08	Drama	0·26
		Poetry	1·32

More than one-third of the total production consists of theology; this is possible only in a religiously minded culture, and
that these writings were not meant in the first place for university-trained theologians, clergymen, etc., is shown by the fact
that a little more than half of the religious works are in the form
of simple instruction, sermons, etc., for the average Christian.
In the face of this no importance can be given to imaginative
literature with its 5·83 per cent, even less to narrative literature
with its 2·65 per cent of the total production. The picture
changes very considerably by 1770.

1770

Theology	%		Imaginative Literature	%
ALTOGETHER	24·47		ALTOGETHER	16·43
Including:			Including:	
Works for the expert	12·67		Narrative literature	4·02
Works for the layman	10·84		Drama	3·67
			Poetry	3·23

Theological writings have decreased considerably in percentage and inside this group, too, the situation has changed; most of the religious works are now intended for the scholarly theologian. The demand of the laity for instructive religious works has lessened a good deal. Imaginative literature, on the other hand, has increased remarkably. The 1800 catalogue shows the end of the development, the almost complete secularization of popular reading material.

1800

Theology	%		Imaginative Literature	%
ALTOGETHER	13·55		ALTOGETHER	21·45
Including:			Including:	
Works for the expert	6·03		Novels	11·68
Works for the layman	5·80		Drama	2·49
			Poetry	1·32

Imaginative literature has now overtaken theology, and inside the former group over one-half of the production is made up of novels. We see the development clearly from the following table comparing the production of popular devotional works with that of imaginative literature:

	1740	1770	1800
	%	%	%
Religious literature for the layman	19·08	10·84	5·80
Imaginative literature	5·83	16·43	21·45

We are forced to the conclusion arrived at by Jentzsch, 'that the ground lost by devotional literature and collections of sermons had been gained by imaginative literature and the fine arts'[6]—in other words, that the part of the public that had made up the main contingent in the market for religious literature of instruction had now turned to secular literature, especially to the novel, for its new reading material.

Up to 1740 there was comparatively little to show at the Leipzig fair in the way of imaginative literature as a whole, let alone fictional prose. The 1710 catalogue[7] lists 149 general works in German (i.e. not including theology, law, and medicine), of which thirty-nine dealt with history and politics, twenty with geography, mostly travel descriptions, and only fifteen are concerned with belles-lettres. The latter include the poems of Philander von der Linde, two anthologies of poems, three of Christian Weise's works, a collection of Lohenstein's works, three courtly novels, Philander von Sittenwald's *Jocoseria*, Celander's *100 Historien*, and *Schauplatz der Bösheiten aller bösen Weiber*. The Easter fair of 1720 saw only eight articles offered under the section for imaginative literature and these were all poetical works except Johann von Besser's collected works and one courtly love-story. The situation is much the same in 1730 when amongst ten articles we find seven poetical works (Brockes and Günther are both represented), two courtly love-stories and one 'Robinsonade'.

How different, however, is the picture in 1740! From the Leipzig Easter catalogue for this year it is obvious that we are standing on the threshold of a new period in German fictional writing, though the position of polite literature as a whole is still relatively weak. The section headed *Schöne Künste und Wissenschaften* (i.e. imaginative literature, fine art, and music) contains forty-four titles, or 5·83 per cent of the total book production; the demand in this sphere, then, played no greater part in the German book market than that in philosophy (also 5·83 per cent) and came a long way behind the demand in theology (38·54 per cent), law (12·85 per cent), and history and geography (11·38 per cent). Of the forty-four titles offered, music accounts for seven items; the fine arts have no representative at all in this catalogue. The poetical works are still very much in the shadow of the deep-seated learned tradition; of a total of ten, two deal with neo-Latin poetry, four are short didactic poems and fables, and three are anthologies; courtly occasional poetry, also, it will be remembered, strongly imbued with learned tendencies, finds a very typical representative in the last work of this group: *Die in eine Parforce-Jägerin verkleidete Poesie, bey hohen Königl. Lust-Jagen am Fest-Tage St. Hubertus in einem Gedichte . . .*—in representative folio. The five works dealing with the theory of the arts also place the accent on scholarly poetry and are obviously intended for the expert; the most important items here are Gottsched's journal *Beyträge zur critischen Historie der deutschen Sprache, Poesie und Beredtsamkeit*, Bodmer's *Critische Abhandlung . . .* and Breitinger's *Critische Dichtkunst*. The dramatic field shows only two products, and one of these is a translation from the French (Voltaire's *Marianne*), the other dealing with ancient learned material: *Die Begebenheiten des Telemachs . . . .*

Only in the realm of narrative literature do we find anything like a strong production. This branch of literature is represented by twenty works, 45·45 per cent of the imaginative literature section. While the poems and literary theoretical works were written with an eye to a scholarly public, here we see the lighter reading material intended for a larger public; at the same time, two types of novel offered in this catalogue also illustrate the way in which fiction was broadening its appeal so as to attract the serious-minded, but by no means learned, reader. Firstly, there is the type which indicates in its title the earnest ethical content of the story, making the book acceptable to the pious citizen who was used to the edifying and instructive literature of the theologians; such titles as the following must put even a work of fiction beyond reproach: *Abbildung eines klugen und tugendhafften Frauenzimmers . . . oder . . . der Marquise . . . (Portrait of an Intelligent and Virtuous Woman . . . or . . .)*, or, *Leben . . . oder die durch ihre tugendhaffte Aufführung glücklich gewordene Bäuerin (Life . . . or the Peasant-Woman whose Virtuous Conduct brought her Happiness)*. Secondly, in answer to the demand for truth in all reading material, there are the novels which adopt the outward form of biography thus helping considerably the illusion that the story is based on fact; the strength of this taste for 'truth in fiction' is manifest in the many *Leben und Begebenheiten . . . (Life and Adventures . . .)* now to be found on the market. Amongst others, we find in the 1740 catalogue: *Leben und Begebenheiten des Obristen Jaques . . . (Defoe); Leben und gantz ungemeine Begebenheiten der Mylady . . . vermählten Baronessin . . .; Leben der Marianne oder angenehme Begebenheiten einer vornehmen Gräfin*; *Rethima oder der schönen Geogianerin . . . Geschichte.*

For the rest, the narrative literature announced here still mirrors the tastes of a reading public which finds pleasure in long-winded titles, which likes its share and more of the adventurous, extraordinary, and colourful elements of fictional writing, a public which, though showing an apparent interest in the individual, has a marked preference not so much for the human being in general as for persons of high rank and if possible from a foreign country, too. The average German *Bürger* might be turning more and more to novels for his reading material, but he and his life were not yet figuring prominently in the content of those novels. No fewer than eleven of the twenty works in this section contain in their title some appellation of social dignity such as *Graf, Gräfin*; *Marquis, Marquisin*; *Mylady*; *Baroness*, etc.—characters whose lives had been one mass of adventure, remarkable events, and dangerous moments. The popularity of such novels is clear when we meet such a comparatively large number of these related types: *Curiose und seltsame Lebens-Geschichte des beruffenen Signor Fioraventi welcher bishero unter dem Nahmen als Marquis Danies bekannt ist (Curious and Strange Life Story of the Infamous Signor Fioraventi, hitherto known as . . .)*; or *Der Englische Welt-Weise oder Historie des Herrn Cleveland, eines natürlichen Sohnes des Cromwells (The English Philosopher or History of Mr. Cleveland, a Natural Son of Cromwell)*; or *Merkwürdige und wahrhafftige Historie des Grafen Bellestor und des Fräulein von Cespedes (Remarkable and True History of . . .)*.

A taste for the adventurous and also for things foreign is likewise revealed in another branch of narrative literature, that of the now well-established and popular 'Robinsonades', two representatives of which are found here: Pellander's *Thüringischer Robinson*, and *Der Philosophische Seefahrer oder die Begebenheiten des . . . auf einer neu entdeckten Insul . . . (The Philosophical Seaman or Adventures of . . . on a Newly Discovered Island)*. We may also ascribe the following work to the same taste: *Wundersame Unterredungen aus dem Reiche derer Todten als Telemaque des Ulyssis Sohn und der berühmte Engländer Robinson Crusoe einander dasselbst angetroffen . . . (Strange Conversations from the Realm of the Dead when Telemachus, son of Ulysses, and Robinson Crusoe, the Famous Englishman, met each other there . . .)*.

The all-but-dead gallant novel with its courtly milieu and adventurous love-story finds its last representatives in this catalogue in Menantes's *Europäischer Höfe Liebes- und Helden-geschichte 3. Th. (Stories of Love and Heroes from the Courts of Europe)* (1st edn., 1704) and in *Der mühsame aber doch unermüdete Liebes-Aventurieur, wie solcher den Berg der Liebe nach vielen Beschwerlich-keiten endlich übersteiget und die Anmuths-vollen Gegenden mehr als irrdischer Ergötzlichkeiten glücklich erlanget (The Adventures of the Tired yet Tireless Gallant, relating how after numerous Difficulties he at last negotiates the Mountain of Love and happily attains the Pleasant Regions of more than Earthly Delights).*

A collection of short stories, so-called *nouvelles historiques*, whose material is taken from the Middle Ages, but whose characters speak, think, and act like eighteenth-century citizens appears under the title of *Hundert Neue Neuigkeiten oder auserlesene Historien, 7, 8, 9, 10 und letzter Theil* by Frau von Gometz. And finally, also serving purely for entertainment, are two more works bringing stories and other pieces: *Kurtzweiliger Historien-Schreiber, in welchen auserlesene, lustige und possirliche theils schertz-theils ernsthaffte Historien und Geschichten erzehlet werden,* and Lehm's *Angenehmer Zeitvertreib bey langen Nächten und sonst müßigen Stunden.*

The names of the characters in the works of fiction offered in the 1740 catalogue betray a strong preference for a foreign atmosphere and indeed, of the twenty books listed in this section, no less than ten are translations, eight from French and two from English. Here, too, we are proved to be at the beginning of a new period of German fiction; for the next fifty years or more translations were to contribute a fair proportion of the fictional works available to the German reading public.[8] We see, then, in this catalogue three important developments: (1) The number of titles under imaginative literature rises steeply to forty-four. (2) A change of taste is visible in the turning away from the heroic gallant novel to a type of fiction more general in its appeal, quasi-biographies with the accent, however, still on persons of high social rank. (3) We see, too, the beginning of the period of industrious translating activity in an attempt to satisfy the growing demand amongst the reading public for works of fiction.

As far as organization in the book trade is concerned, all was ready by mid century for Germany's great literary revival, and it was only the extensive use made of this organization during the next few years which necessitated the reforms of the late eighteenth and early nineteenth centuries. Three things characterize the German book trade at the beginning of our period: business was conducted on an 'exchange basis' as opposed to 'cash trade', the professions of bookseller and publisher were invariably combined, and their personal attendance at at least one of the book fairs was essential if the system was to be at all workable. These trade fairs were held three times a year at both Frankfurt am Main and Leipzig, but by the beginning of the eighteenth century the Leipzig fair was by far the more important—certainly in the book trade and, in fact, in most other branches of commerce.[9] Of the three trade fairs held annually at Leipzig the Michaelmas and Easter meetings were the most important to the book trade; that at Easter saw the most business transacted.[10] The publisher-dealer would visit that city at the time of the fair, bringing with him his recent publications, and there he would 'set up shop', displaying advertisements and title-pages in the street outside his lodgings. The first week was quite often devoted to social calls, after which he would visit the most famous publishing houses, show his title-pages, haggle for a while about price and value, and then each party would decide how many copies of each other's books they were prepared to accept. The last few days of the fair would then be spent sitting in his rooms with his own bills and books, hoping and waiting for callers bringing more business. Only very rarely did money ever pass between dealers; if the reckonings did not happen to balance each other at one fair, the difference was generally left to stand over till the next, and thus many houses remained permanently in barter with each other. After the fair the dealers returned home, each with a varied stock of books to sell to his customers.

As pointed out by the contemporary critic Johann Stephan Pütter, Germany possessed in this respect an advantage over every other European nation.[11] In Holland, England, France, and Italy bookshops had trade as a rule only with their own publishing firm; there were no book fairs, and publishers usually dealt only in cash or at most with mutual accounts and ultimate cash settlement; potential customers had first to find out the publisher of the work wanted, which was difficult enough in itself, and then buy it from him for cash, or else they could find a book-dealer who had an account with the publisher concerned and ask him to order it for them—all without seeing the work and with no possibility of returning it if they were dissatisfied. Whereas in Germany, any work which appeared at the fair was within a matter of weeks circulated through all Germany, listed in numerous printed catalogues, and announced in many journals, newspapers, learned and political magazines, and the like. The customer did not first need to seek the publisher, but simply walked into a bookshop where books were always on show no matter where or by whom they were published; any book-dealer would undertake to obtain any work whatever, and regular customers at least could always return unsatisfactory purchases. Pütter can say in all truth: 'Diese ganze Einrichtung des Teutschen Buchhandels ist für das Publikum so bequem, als es nur möglich ist, und als kein ander Land in Europa sich rühmen kann.'[12]

By mid eighteenth century, moreover, book-dealers were becoming more conscientious in their work and we begin to hear many complaints about dealers who were giving the trade a bad name because of their scanty education. Admittedly, there were as yet very few booksellers who shared the idealistic conception of the duties of the profession that shines, for example, through Perthes's *Memoirs*, but neither were there many who would agree with the Emperor Joseph when he declared that the selling of books required no more education than the selling of cheese.[13] It was by now agreed that to be a successful and worthy book-dealer, at least a knowledge of Latin was necessary and a smattering of other languages desirable; a long apprenticeship, rounded off by a trip abroad, were now looked on as essential before a man entered the trade proper as a master. The fight was now started against the 'Auch- und Nicht-Buchhändler'—those who had gate-crashed the trade and sold books merely as a side-line to their real job. The main offenders in this respect had been students who had failed their examinations, preachers who quite often preceded their sermons with a summary of the stock of books they had for sale, and teachers and professors who even undertook to fulfil orders from the public.

In the purely quantitative aspect of book production too the

fourth and fifth decades of the eighteenth century clearly con-
stitute a milestone in the history of the German book trade,
marking at long last the complete recovery of that trade from
the set-backs suffered in the Thirty Years War. Production had
just reached its peak in 1619 with 1,668 printed works appearing, whereas for the period 1654 to 1694 the average yearly
production was only 826, and even in the following fifty years
it was possible to maintain an average of only 1,127 works.
More than one hundred years were required to reach something
like the former level of production, until during the years 1746
to 1756 there were on average 1,347 new publications appearing
annually on the German book market.[14] The book trade, the
essential 'middleman' between writer and public, was ready to
play its part in meeting the demand of the German reading
public for more and still more books.

An analysis of the contents of the Lepizig book-catalogue for
the Easter fair of 1770 demonstrates the increased importance of
imaginative literature on the German book market one generation later and shows us some of the tastes and preferences
prevalent in the reading public which had seen, if perhaps not
always noted, the appearance of German translations of
Richardson's novels (1742 onwards), the publication of Gellert's
Schwedische Gräfin (1747–8), Lessing's *Miss Sara Sampson* (1755)
and *Minna von Barnhelm* (1767), Wieland's *Don Sylvio von Rosalva*
(1764) and *Agathon* (1766–70), and the first three volumes of
Klopstock's *Messias* (1751–69). What did the bookshops stock
for the German novel-reader four years before the appearance
of Goethe's *Werther* ?
   In 1740 imaginative literature had accounted, with forty-four
titles, for 5·83 per cent of the total book production; the 1770
catalogue, on the other hand, lists under the heading of *Schöne
Künste und Wissenschaften* no fewer than 188 works (181 in German, seven in Latin), and imaginative literature, taking up
16·43 per cent of the total book production, thus becomes the
second strongest group of publications on the market. Theology
still leads with 24·47 per cent but, as we have seen, most of the
religious writings are now intended for the expert. Devotional
works for the layman (123 items) no longer outnumber the works
of imaginative literature, and this swing towards a secular,

entertaining reading material becomes even more pronounced if one takes into account the popular periodicals now on the market (thirty-four items, including nineteen moral weeklies). For comparison it may be noted that history and geography together account for 9·61 per cent, medicine 7·95 per cent, mathematics and natural sciences 6·206 per cent, and law 5·33 per cent of the titles offered in this catalogue.

Thirty years previously narrative literature had been the only branch of imaginative literature which had shown signs of a large and almost mass production. By 1770 both poetry and drama also might be said to show this characteristic. While in 1740 the production of narrative literature was much higher than that of poetry and drama, in 1770 we find the three of them at approximately the same level: narrative literature 4·02 per cent (forty-six works), drama 3·67 per cent (forty-two works), and poetry 3·23 per cent (thirty-seven works) of the total book production.

The 1770 catalogue lists fourteen theoretical works on the arts in general (one of which is Nicolai's famous journal *Biblio-thek der schönen Wissenschaften und freyen Künste*), thirteen on fine art, and eight on music. There are twenty-eight publications of collected works and works on individual writers offered, and of these no fewer than twenty-two relate to Gellert who had died one year previously. Six of these are actual works by Gellert (including the fifth edition of *Die schwedische Gräfin*); the other sixteen works are on Gellert himself, three of these actually dealing—as early as 1770—with the books occasioned by his death. The new atmosphere abroad in Germany, the increased intensity of interest in literary affairs, could scarcely be better demonstrated than by this massive and immediate reaction to the death of a man of letters and one whose work had done so much to gain recognition for the novel as a worthy genre, for writing as an honourable occupation, and for novel-reading as a respectable pastime.[15] It was, in this respect, from Goethe that Gellert's perhaps most fitting epitaph came—itself a commentary on the history of the German novel-reading public: 'An Gellert, die Tugend und die Religion zu glauben, ist unserm Publicum beinahe eins.'[16]

In 1740 poetry had accounted for 1·32 per cent of the total pro-duction and all the ten works listed had been of an exclusively scholarly nature; the 1770 catalogue offers thirty-seven poetical works (3·23 per cent) and of these only six show either courtly or scholarly elements (three of them are in Latin)—the rest announce themselves simply as *Gedichte*. There are fifteen collections of poems. Of the poetical works only four can be proved to be translations and all four are from the English.

Dramatic literature, too, occupies a different position from that which it had in 1740. The 1740 catalogue had only two works (0·26 per cent) to show in this field but in 1770 this branch of literature is represented by forty-two works (3·67 per cent). With the increased production in the dramatic field appears the controversy about the effect which the theatre could have on the nation's morals; typical of such writings is: *Sendschreiben an einen Freund . . . ob man aus einer Komödie mehr lernen könne, als aus einer erbaulichen Predigt* (*Epistle to a Friend . . . Reflecting on whether one can learn more from a Comedy than from an Edifying Sermon*) by T. Sinceri (the pseudonym used, with not a little comic irony, by a writer named Schwindel). The 1770 catalogue lists seven collections of plays, seven single plays or dramas (*Schauspiele*), five tragedies, and eleven comedies, including a new edition of Lessing's *Lustspiele* and the second edition of his *Minna von Barnhelm*. Nineteen of the forty-two dramatic works are known to be translations (eight from English, eight from French, and three from Italian).

Compared with 1740, narrative literature also has made advances in production, though not so strikingly as in drama and poetry—after all, there had already been something like a process of mass production in the narrative field in 1740. As against the twenty works (2·65 per cent) offered in 1740, the 1770 catalogue lists forty-six works of narrative literature (4·02 per cent). It is the light-entertainment novel intended for the greater public which dominates the field. The fictional works are in many ways similar to those of 1740; the *Leben und Begebenheiten . . .* are still very well represented though one development is that the title is now often shortened merely to *Begebenheiten . . .*; this is in all probability just a case of abbreviation (the *Leben* being understood), but it suggests also that it was no longer quite so necessary for writers to stress the sincere biographical content of their stories. Double titles are frequently encountered, with the sub-titles drawing attention to the remarkable, wonderful, adventurous, or ethical content of the book—titles in fact seem to play a role not unlike that of film trailers today in the cinema trade, that of whetting the prospective customer's appetite.

The main accent is once more on adventure and remarkable events, on characters who distinguish themselves by high social rank and thrill-packed lives. Of the forty-six works in the narrative field, seventeen can with safety be placed in the category of *Leben und Begebenheiten . . . (Life and Adventures . . .)*; *Begebenheiten Ferdinands Grafen von . . .*; *Der englische Weltweise oder Historie des Herrn Clevelands . . .* (in 1740 catalogue too); *Die Ausländer in der Schweiz oder Begebenheiten des Herrn von . . . (The Foreigners in Switzerland, or Adventures . . .)*; *Bewundernswürdige Begebenheiten eines Uhrmachers, wie auch dessen Reisen . . . (The Remarkable Adventures of a Clock-Maker, also containing his Journeys . . .)*; *Merkwürdige Lebensumstände Elias Beudels, eines Fischers Sohnes . . . (The Strange Life-History of Elias Beudel, a Fisherman's Son . . .)*. Non-aristocratic heroes, it will be noted, are beginning to make their appearance even in this branch of fiction. Fifty years after the publication of *Robinson Crusoe* we still find stories obviously inspired by the English novel: *Der Schiffbruch und Begebenheiten des Herrn Pet. Viaud, eines Schiffcapitain . . . (The Shipwreck and Remarkable Adventures of . . .)*; *Der neue französische Robinson oder Begebenheiten . . . (The New French Robinson, or . . .)*. Eleven of these novels in the 'life and adventures' category have males as their main characters, and the other six, mostly with long-winded subsidiary titles, have a heroine as the focal point: *Die glückliche Lotteriespielerin oder Geschichte des Fräulein Tolet, welche . . . (The Lucky Gambler, or History of Miss Tolet . . .)*; *Wunderbare Fata und merkwürdige Lebensgeschichte einer gebohrnen Wienerin . . . (The Wondrous Fate and Remarkable History of a Viennese Lady . . .)*; *Die schöne Sängerinn oder Begebenheiten der Marquisinn . . . (The Beautiful Singer, or . . .)*.

A branch of fiction not present in 1740 is the novel which simply announces itself as a *Geschichte* and lays no stress on the adventurous or extraordinary elements in the story but merely on the history of the personality concerned. The term *Geschichte* would seem in fact to have been a sort of title of honour used by novelists to distinguish their 'true histories' from the fictional, and therefore, to many, still suspect *Romane*.[17] If a double title is used here then the second element is intended to appeal to the reader's sentiments, asking at once for understanding and sympathy: *Die gezwungene Ehe, oder Geschichte Sir Georg . . . (Marriage under Constraint, or . . .)*; *Die Sprache des Herzens oder Geschichte . . . (The Language of the Heart, or . . .)*. Most of these novels, however, are quite content with *Geschichte der . . .*, followed by the heroine's name: . . . *der Miss Beville*; . . . *der Miss Sidney Bidulph*; . . . *der Lady Henriette Hanbury*; . . . *der Gräfin von Zurlock*. So far is this simplification of titles carried that Wieland's short story could appear as *Combabus, eine Erzählung*.

As will already have been noted we still find very many main characters of high social standing and foreign extraction; the titles most frequently used are 'Miss', 'Lady', 'Marquisin', 'Graf', 'Gräfin', and 'Sir'. One group of novels, however, gives only the Christian name of the hero or heroine, adding no information on their social standing, so that we can say that the person concerned was introduced to the reader simply as a fellow human being and one whom he can meet as an equal; but even here sub-titles often betray a preference for a foreign setting. Other additions to the title point again, in the manner stated above, to the emotional, compassionate element in the story: *Betsi, oder der Eigensinn des Schicksals, Eine englische Geschichte (Betsy, or The Wilfulness of Fate, an English Story)*; *Charlotte, oder der großmüthige Freund, eine englische . . . (Charlotte, or The Noble-Minded Friend, an English . . .)*; *Amalie oder einige Züge der wahren Großmuth, eine deutsche . . . (Amalia, or Some Features of True Nobleness of Mind, a German . . .)*; *Isabelle oder die Stiefmutter, eine spanische . . . (Isabella or the Stepmother, a Spanish . . .)*. Readers who preferred a more exotic setting were not forgotten: *Chmki, eine cochinchinesische Geschichte . . .*; *Zingha, Königinn von Angolo (sic), Eine afrikanische . . .*; *Zemin . . . eine morgenländische Erzählung (Zemin . . . an Oriental Tale)*.

Three novels draw particular attention to the fact that they are written in letter form: *Sylvie und Moleshoff von Donat nach Art der Heldenbriefe*; *Geschichte Agathe von St. Bohaire . . . in Briefen verfasset*; *Briefe zwischen Herrn von St. Evremond und Herrn Waller . . .* This branch of fiction had been enjoying great popularity in Germany ever since the appearance of Richardson's novels, where the letter form had been used primarily to create a sense of participation in the mind of the reader and to lend an air of verisimilitude to the story; they had been an instant success and this success in itself, of course, goes a long way towards explaining the large number of epistolary novels on the German book market in the second half of the century—the public liked Richardson and demanded that other writers should copy his efforts and produce similar family novels in similar form. But by the 1770s a further factor was coming into play, related to the first and likewise ensuring the success of novels in letter form. Richardson's novels had heralded the age of Sentimentalism, the following generation lived through the climax of that movement, and what better way was there of giving expression to the subjective world of human emotions than through that most personal of forms—the letter. It was by now the fashion in sentimental circles to write revealing letters to one's friends about the state of one's heart or that of a mutual acquaintance. Letters on this subject, received from others, were a favourite reading material of whole circles of 'kindred spirits'. Goethe was impressed by this same thing amongst the friends of Sophie von Laroche:

... es war überhaupt eine so allgemeine Offenherzigkeit unter den Menschen, daß man mit keinem Einzelnen sprechen oder an ihn schreiben konnte, ohne es zugleich als an mehrere gerichtet zu betrachten. Man spähte sein eigen Herz aus und das der anderen und bei der Gleichgültigkeit der Regierungen gegen eine solche Mittheilung . . . griff dieser sittliche und literarische Verkehr bald weiter um sich. Solche Correspondenzen, besonders mit bedeutenden Personen, wurden sorgfältig gesammelt und alsdann bei freundschaftlichen Zusammenkünften auszugsweise vorgelesen. . . .[18]

Small wonder that the epistolary form long remained the special favourite of wide sections of the German reading public and was soon to produce in *Werther* the best seller of the century.

Two travel novels, both of which are still remembered today, are listed in the 1770 catalogue: Sterne's *Yoricks empfindsame Reise* (New Edition); and Hermes's *Sophiens Reise von Memel nach Sachsen* (vols. i and ii). The third volume of Hermes's novel appeared in 1771, volumes iv and v followed in 1772. Although *Sophiens Reise* did not occasion unlimited enthusiasm or become the general favourite of the day as did, say, Sophie von Laroche's

Fräulein von Sternheim (1771) or Nicolai's *Sebaldus Nothanker* (1773–6), it did become a kind of 'house book' (*Hausbuch*), a family reference book that no middle-class home of the eighteenth century could afford to be without. Hermes's novel is, in fact, found even today in the libraries of many old families where one looks in vain for the more famous literary products of the same period. All in all, *Sophiens Reise* would seem to be the novel which was read as eagerly and as universally during the last thirty years of the eighteenth century as was Freytag's *Soll und Haben* (1855) during the latter half of the nineteenth century; both novels must have been experienced by the greater contemporary public as the truest and most characteristic picture of their own life and times.[19]

Finally, there are three novels in the 1770 catalogue which cannot be included with safety in any of the above categories: *Vornehmer Thor*; *Zeitvertreib eines Soldaten vom Regiment*; and Marmontel's *Belisar*.

In addition to single novels, however, there are a number of collections of novels and short stories, from which single novels were frequently advertised and sold separately: *Romane und Feyenmährchen in 5 Theilen*; *Versuch in rührenden Erzählungen* . . .; *Landbibliothek zu einem angenehmen und lehrreichen Zeitvertreibe*; *Unterricht und Zeitvertreib für das schöne Geschlecht* . . .; *Abendstunden oder Sammlung von* . . .; and *Neue Abendstunden* . . . . Even here, it will be noted, stress is laid on the instructive ('lehrreich', 'Unterricht') besides the entertainment ('angenehm', 'Zeitvertreib') value of the works.

Translations are not always named as such in the Leipzig catalogue but of the forty-six works in the field of narrative literature no fewer than sixteen are known to be translations (eight from French, five from English, one Italian, and two collections from various languages).[20] Nor does the catalogue always name the author of the books offered, but Jentzsch, working from other sources, tells us that a certain Christian Heinrich Korn sent no fewer than seven works to this fair alone. Clearly, the day of the 'quill-driver' had dawned, and Lichtenberg could ask, 'Ob es nicht zuträglich wäre, zur Bequemlichkeit der Setzer gewisse Namen ganz gießen zu lassen'.[21]

The most important development evident in the 1770 catalogue, however, is—to draw attention to it once more—that imaginative literature is now predominant over the religious literature for the layman; the situation of 1740 has now been reversed. There is now a larger market for entertaining works of dramatic, poetic, and narrative literature than for devotional works of instruction.

The catalogue for the Leipzig book fair of Easter 1800 completes our picture, illustrating as it does so clearly and so concretely the great change in the interests catered for by the German book trade in the eighteenth century. By 1800 theology (including popular devotional works) claims only 13·55 per cent (348 items), imaginative literature, on the other hand, accounts for 21·45 per cent (551 items) of the total book production and now constitutes the largest single group of publications on the market. The following table, in which percentages have been taken to the nearest whole number, shows the broader developments over sixty years:

	Percentage of total production		
Easter Fair	1740	1770	1800
	%	%	%
Imaginative literature, popular periodicals, popular philosophical works, Taschenbücher, biographies, and travel descriptions	10	23	30
Theology, including popular devotional works	38	24	14
Primarily for the scholar. Law, medicine, political science, maths., natural sciences, history and geography (less biographies and travel descriptions). General scholarly works	49	43	41
Practical affairs. Agriculture, industry, engineering, commerce, pedagogy, 'house books', etc.	3	8	14

From the detailed figures for individual subjects, given in Appendix I of this study, it can be seen that only three of them decrease in relative importance during this period, namely theology, law, and works of a general scholarly nature; four groups of publications claim a comparatively constant proportion of the market: philosophy, philology, history and geography, and popular periodicals; all others show a both absolute and relative increase in production over the years. Broadly speaking, we can say that the development was away from theology and general scholarly works towards works of light entertainment, on the one hand, and books dealing with the practical side of life, on the other.

The increased interest in works concerned with *Die schönen Künste und Wissenschaften*, however, is no longer equally distributed amongst the various branches of this type of reading material, as had been the case in 1770. The 1800 catalogue offers only nine works on the general theory of belles-lettres, and fine art accounts for a fairly modest thirty items (one in Latin); music, on the other hand, has risen from 0·7 per cent to 3·43 per cent of the total book production and with eighty-eight items is now almost equal to poetry and drama combined—of these eighty-eight publications, however, nineteen are in French and six in Italian. Poetical works had accounted for 3·23 per cent of the total production in 1770, but now only 1·3 per cent of the market (thirty-four items) goes to poetry; one reason for this relative decrease may be found in the fact that journals, almanacs, and *Taschenbücher* were by this time devoting considerable space to poems, thus lessening the demand for separate volumes. Half of the poetical works are anthologies, the stress being on contemporary rather than the older German poets (Schlegel, Schiller, and Ramler are represented). Dramatic literature, too, loses the equality with narrative literature which it had enjoyed in 1770; in 1800 it accounts for 2·49 per cent (sixty-four items) as against 3·67 per cent of the total production in 1770; amongst the sixty-four items in the dramatic field we find eleven general theoretical works, seven theatrical periodicals, nineteen plays (*Schauspiele*), ten tragedies, and thirteen comedies.

This catalogue, then, shows a notable decrease in the demand for poetry and drama as a reading material. In 1800 the process of literary mass production is most evident in the novel; the supremacy of narrative literature as a popular reading material was now established. The increase in production in this branch of writing since 1740 is nothing short of remarkable. In 1740 narrative literature had constituted only 2·65 per cent of the total book production, in 1770 the increase had been only slight, to 4·02 per cent, but in 1800 we find it represented by no fewer than 300 items, 11·68 per cent of the total production. The development in the three genres may be tabulated thus:

Easter Fair	1740	1770	1800
	%	%	%
Narrative literature	2·65 (20 items)	4·02 (46 items)	11·68 (300 items)
Poetry	1·32 (10 items)	3·23 (37 items)	1·32 (34 items)
Drama	0·26 (2 items)	3·67 (42 items)	2·49 (64 items)

Production in the field of narrative literature in 1800 is greater than that in law, or medicine, or history and geography together, and is very nearly as great as that in theology (13·55 per cent)—a convincing testimony to the change which in sixty years had taken place in the reading public and its interests as served by the book trade; we now have a wider reading public which looks mostly for entertainment, mainly in the form of the novel.[22] This is evident from the large number of this genre brought to the Leipzig fair and is also substantiated by the fact that from the Easter fair of 1797 novels (and plays too) were listed separately from other literature under their own rubric *Romane*, suggesting that novels were now so popular (and so numerous) that a quick survey of the new publications in this field was felt desirable.

Any division of the 300 novels listed in the 1800 catalogue must needs be into large, obvious groups; Jentzsch has drawn attention to a valuable guide in this task in the *Allgemeines Repertorium der Litteratur für die Jahre 1785–1800*.[23] It is sufficient here simply to indicate these broad divisions without detailed characterization; the last chapter of the present study contains a discussion of the different sections of the German reading public to which these various types of novel might appeal.

The great majority of the novels offered in 1800 are to be found in the *Allgemeines Repertorium* under the heading, 'mit Voraussetzung der wirklichen Welt; ohne historische Grundlage' ('set in the world of reality; without historical basis'); 106 of the 300 novels are in this class. We have noted earlier that in 1770 as against 1740 the interest in the everyday world of realities had gained ground against the interest in the strange and fantastic adventures of high-ranking persons; this trend in taste has continued to 1800. This is evident from the number of novels whose titles consist simply of the Christian name of the hero or heroine, possibly with a sub-title setting the correct mood and pointing to the character development, or to the compassionate element in the story; nothing is said either of high rank or remarkable adventures: *Die schöne Caviere oder der Sieg der Unschuld* (. . . *or the Triumph of Innocence*); *Rosalinde oder die gerettete Unschuld* (. . . *or Innocence Preserved*); *Sidonie, das Opfer einer unnatürlichen Mutter* (. . . *the Victim of an Unnatural Mother*); *Amanda oder der Weg zum Heiligthum. Aus den Papieren eines Einsiedlers* (. . . *or the Path to the Sanctum. From the Papers of a Hermit*); *Heliodora oder die Lautenspielerin aus Griechenland* (. . . *or the Lute-Player from Greece*), etc. But we find too that, throughout the catalogue, alongside the novels with a clearly foreign setting is an increasing number of stories with German heroes or heroines; with more and more readers demanding that fiction be related to their own sphere of experience, writers begin to make much greater use of book-titles and everyday German proper names which establish their characters as individuals set in the context of real contemporary life in Germany: *Karoline Stahlhelm oder die Folgen des Leichtsinns* (. . . *or the Consequences of Frivolity*); *Sophie von Woldow oder die leidende Tugend* (. . . *or the Pangs of Virtue*); *Clärchens Geständnisse. Seitenstück zu Röschens Geheimnissen* (*Clärchen's Confessions. Counterpart to Röschen's Secrets*); *Marianens Schäferstunden* (*Marianne's Hours of Love*); *Reinhard oder Natur und Gottesverehrung* (. . . *or Nature and the Worship of God*); *Franz Damm oder der Glückliche durch sich selbst* (. . . *or the Man who won his own Happiness*); *Werner oder die Hütte des Seemanns* (. . . *or the Seaman's Cottage*), etc. Other novels do not even name the leading character: *Karakterprobleme*; *Gemälde des menschlichen Herzens* (*Portrait of the Human Heart*); *Kabalen des Schicksals* (*The Intrigues of Fate*), etc.

Stories with a strong biographical element are represented by Jung-Stilling's *Heimweh* and Mirabeau's *Erstes Abentheuer*, but much more numerous are the novels which simply tell the story of two lovers: *Sophie und Oskar*; *Fernando und Bianka*; *Lenardo und Blandine*, etc. Some titles rely purely on the treatment of love to attract readers: *Liebe und Untreue* (*Love and Infidelity*); *Das Glück und das Grab der Liebe* (*Love's Joy and Love's Doom*); *Leben und Liebe* (*Life and Love*), etc.; others, hoping to appeal also to readers of thrillers, add a suitable secondary title: *Die stille Ecke am Rohr-teiche oder Anton und Edda* (*The Secluded Spot by the Reed-Pond, or ...*), etc.

A branch of fiction strongly characteristic of the new interest in purely human, bourgeois, and domestic material is the family novel, which had found no representatives in the 1770 catalogue and yet was a favourite reading material at the end of the century; by 1800 it had in fact already become the *Trivialroman* of the official histories of German literature: *Eduard. Der Zögling der Natur. Ein Familiengemälde* (*Edward. Nature's Pupil. A Family Portrait*); *Familiengeschichte*; *Onkel Warm und sein schönes Mümchen, eine Familiengeschichte*; *Geschichte der Familie des Herrn Macarius Bohn, oder die Launen des Glücks* (*... or the Whims of Fortune*), etc. The wide interpretation put on the term *Familiengeschichte* and also its 'customer-appeal' is well illustrated in this catalogue by the writer who offers his public ... *eine Familiengeschichte, worin verschiedene Entführungen und Seeräubergefechte vorkommen* (*... a Family Novel, containing Various Seductions and Sea-Fights with Pirates*).

The French Revolution and events connected with and arising from it provide many novelists with their material and motifs—the fate of the *émigrés*, the separation of lovers owing to political circumstances and other similar themes as treated for instance by Goethe in *Hermann und Dorothea*; *Die Ausgewanderten* (*The Émigrés*); *Dourbeil und Celiane oder Geschichte zweier Liebenden während der Tyrannei des Robespierre* (*... or History of Two Lovers during the Tyranny of Robespierre*); *Julio, Graf von Albino ... Eine Familiengeschichte italienischer Emigranten* (*...a Family History of Italian Émigrés*); *Marki von Gebrian, oder Ränke und Schwänke eines französischen Emigranten* (*... or Tricks and Pranks of a French Émigré*); *Die Heldin der Vendee ... Romantische Geschichte des jetzigen Krieges* (*The Heroine of Vendée ... Romantic Story of the Present War*), etc.

Yet we still find amongst such competition the old 'Robinsonades' holding their own as favourites of the public; their number cannot be established with certainty but the following novels certainly did owe their inspiration to Defoe's novel: *Der einsame Inselbewohner, oder Robert Surrais Schicksale in zween Welttheilen* (*The Lonely Islander, or Robert Surrai's Fateful Adventures in Two Continents*); *Robinsons wunderbare und merkwürdige Schicksale zu Wasser und zu*

Lande; mit Bildern für den Bürger und Landmann (Robinson's Strange and Remarkable Adventures on Land and Sea; with Illustrations for Townsfolk and Countrymen); *Graf Robert und sein Freund St. Michael, oder die Fürsten von Orimbul und Bambuk, neu entdeckte Inseln an der Küste von Afrika (. . . or the Princes of Orimbul and Bambuk, newly discovered Islands off the Coast of Africa)*, and similar travel stories like *Reisen in unbekannte Länder und merkwürdige Begebenheiten auf denselben (Journeys to Unknown Countries and Strange Adventures experienced there)*.

The increased interest in the education of youth and in the perfecting of man in general is manifest in narrative literature, too, in the greater number (twenty-two) of novels which show some moral or pedagogic aim. Just such a novel had indeed been one of the 'best sellers' of the 1790s—Karoline von Wobeser's *Elisa, oder das Weib wie es seyn sollte (Elisa or Woman as she ought to be)* (1795) which will be discussed fully at a later stage.[24] In the 1800 catalogue alone we find eleven imitations and variations on Wobeser's theme: *Henriette, oder das Weib wie es seyn kann (Henriette, or Woman as she can be)*; *Das Weib wie es ist (Woman as she is)*; *Robert, der Mann wie er seyn sollte (Robert, Man as he ought to be)*; *Moritz und Auguste, oder die Kleinen, wie sie seyn sollten (Moritz and Augusta or the Youngsters as they ought to be)*; *Fritz, der Mann wie er nicht seyn sollte (Fritz, Man as he ought not to be)*, etc. In addition to these we find other novels written with some didactic purpose in mind: *Wilhelm Ehrenpreiss und Caroline Sebastiani, oder der Spiegel für Ehegatten und die es werden wollen (. . . or a Guide for Married People and Those who would become such)*; *Geschichte der Familie Frebeni, oder die Hölle auf Erden (History of the Frebeni Family, or Hell on Earth)*; *Gehorsam und Treue, oder Franz und Louise. Eine Erziehungsgeschichte (Obedience and Loyalty, or . . .)*, etc.

Also requiring mention is the large number (thirty-one) of satirical and humorous novels, a branch of the genre which found but few representatives at the 1770 fair. Amongst this group of novels we meet, of course, with specimens of various grades, ranging from those whose sole aim was comic effect and entertainment to the more serious literary and period satires of Jean Paul, two of whose works are offered here: *Der Titan,* and *Clavis Fichtiana seu Leibgebesiana.* Most of this fiction is now forgotten: *Meppen Bocksbarths Abenteuer und Weiber (Meppen Bocksbarth's Adventures and Wives)*; *Biographien der Hahnreye oder*

Ehestandskroniken für geplagte Ehemänner (*Biographies of Cuckolds or Marriage-chronicles for Tormented Husbands*); *Bocksprünge und Narrenstreiche der menschlichen Vernunft* (*Capers and Caprioles of Human Reason*); *Fragmente in Sternes Manier* (*Fragments in the Manner of Sterne*), etc.

Finally, there is the large group of novels, not present in 1770, then termed *historische Romane* which included all the various branches of this type of fiction, the *Ritter-, Geister-, Zauberer-, und Räuberromane*; the catalogue for Easter 1800 offers seventy-seven works of this nature. On the one hand, these pseudo-historical novels are little more than the above stories of contemporary lovers, heroes, and families simply laid in the past; on the other hand, however, their very setting betrays a strong and genuine interest in historical material, even if the picture of past days as presented by the popular novelists is often quite false. Some stories find their setting in ancient history (Scipio was a very popular character), but the majority deal with German history, especially in the 'dark Middle Ages', where the world of monks, knights, castles, secret passages, and dungeons provided writers with far more possibilities for intrigues, and vivid, terrible, and moving scenes than did the dry present. The taste for such reading material had been nurtured in wide sections of the reading public by the popular historical journals referred to earlier and also, as we hall see, by the old chap-books by reprints of some of the more spectacular specimens of and seventeenth-century fiction; novelists knew of this taste and now set out to make the most of it in what was in many respects 'the poor man's *Sturm und Drang*'.

It is in this branch of fiction-writing that the process of literary mass production is most evident, the pace being set by the most successful works like, for example, Veit Weber's *Sagen der Vorzeit* (*Legends of Prehistory*) (1787–98). The 1800 catalogue offers in this line: *Sagen der Ungarischen Vorzeit*; *Sagen der Österreichischen Vorzeit*, and many others with sub-titles like *Geschichte der Vorzeit* or *Sagen der Vorwelt*, etc. Many novels name some historical personality as the focal point of their story: *Rudolph von Werdenberg, eine Rittergeschichte*; *Saladin, Aegyptens Beherrscher am Ende des 12. Jahrhunderts*; *Bernhardt, Herzog zu Sachsen*; *Moritz, Churfürst zu Sachsen*, etc. The vast majority of this group, however, emphasize the supernatural, terrifying elements in the story; this would seem to be the bait most likely to catch a customer: *Wippo von König-stein oder die Todtenhöhle am Fichtelberge, Eine Geistergeschichte* (. . . *or the Cave of the Dead on Mount Fichtel, a Ghost Story*); *Mathilde von Rappenschwyl oder das unversöhnliche Rachgespenst* (. . . *or the Irrecon-cilable Avenging Spirit*); *Die Todtengruft im Geisterschlosse oder . . . (The Funeral Vault in the Castle of Ghosts or . . .)*; *Die Mitternachts-glocke . . . (The Midnight Knell . . .)*; *Das Bildnis mit den Blutflecken. Eine Geistergeschichte . . . (The Blood-spattered Portrait . . .)*, etc. The Easter Fair of 1800 also brought its quota of tales of ghost-seers and exorcists, whose literary stock had since Schiller's *Geisterseher* (1789) risen considerably: *Der Geisterbanner, eine Geschichte aus den Papieren eines Dänen . . . (The Exorcist, a History contained in the Papers of a Dane . . .)*; *Die Geisterseherin oder die Zerstörung von . . . (The Ghost-seer or the Destruction of . . .)*; *Graf Moritz von Portokav, oder zwei Jahre aus dem Leben eines Geistersehers* (. . . *or Two Years in the Life of a Ghost-seer*), etc. Three 'robber' novels by Vulpius, the most popular writer of this type of story, are offered: *Rinaldo Rinaldini* (3rd, 4th, and last parts), *Rinaldo Rinaldini* (3rd, new, and cheaper edition of the whole work), and *Glorioso, der große Teufel.*

Related to the taste for tales of prehistory is the interest in old folk-tales and legends, which now appeared in considerable numbers either in collections or as separate works: *Volks-Sagen*; *Oesterreichische Volksmährchen*; *Wintermährchen*, etc. Then we find, too, oriental tales and fairy stories in greater number than was the case in 1770; this taste was catered for by a collection of works called *Die blaue Bibliothek aller Nationen*, and by individual works such as *Dya-Na-Sore* (2nd edn., in 5 vols.); *Prinz Ama-ranth . . .*; *Das Lamm unter den Wölfen*; *Geschichte des Prinzen Kamarupa und der schönen Komalata . . .*; *Korane, ein morgenländisches Mährchen*, etc.

There are, finally, sixteen novels which, owing to lack of information on them, cannot with certainty be assigned to any of the groups mentioned above. But besides individual novels, mention must also be made of collections of fictional works such as *Bibliothek für Romanleser*; *Der Romanfreund*; *Romane der Aus-länder*, etc.; there were also smaller collections by single, often anonymous, authors: *Geschichten und kleine Romane*; *Gemälde aus dem häuslichen Leben*; *Gemälde und Erzählungen aus dem gesellschaft-lichen Leben*; *Verirrungen des menschlichen Herzens*, etc.

Symptomatic of the highly commercial, competitive atmosphere of the German book market at this time is, in addition to the many imitations of one-time best sellers like *Elisa*, the frequency with which one meets the sub-title *Ein Gegenstück/ Seitenstück zu* . . . (*Counterpart to* . . .), followed, of course, by the title of some 'box-office success'; we also find quite often—and certainly much more frequently than was the case in 1770— that writers name their other successes on the title-page in an attempt to boost sales: . . . *vom Verfasser des Jägermädchens* (*By the author of the Huntress*), etc., or else they assure us that they have followed the example set by an established favourite: *eine Geschichte in Webers Manier*. There are, however, only six examples of new editions in the novels announced here.

Of the 300 items of narrative literature offered in this catalogue fifty-two are known to be translations. There are twenty-seven works translated from the French, eighteen from English, four from Spanish, and one each from Dutch, Danish, and Russian; it is interesting to note, however, that in the realm of chivalrous, robber, and ghost novels England leads the field with eight contributions and France is in second place with four. The English novel-reader shared with his German contemporary a marked taste for gripping tales of brave knights and daring robbers, though his over-all appetite for works of fiction was by all accounts nowhere like so large; Professor Ian Watt, working from a number of sources, estimates ('with the greatest possible reserve') that from 1770 to 1800 an average of forty novels appeared annually in England—a total of about 1,200 over three decades, whereas the German reading public were 'fed' a similar total during five or six years of the nineties alone.[25]

It goes without saying that the vast majority of the novels offered on the German book market through the Leipzig book-fair catalogues served only to satisfy the demands of the day as contemporary reading material and were then forgotten; unfortunately, their inferior literary quality has also condemned them to oblivion in the official histories of German literature and German culture in general, with the result that the Classical Age of German literature frequently appears to us to be surrounded by a dazzling blaze of idealism which can so easily lure us into false interpretations of the prevailing mood and tastes. These now forgotten works are in fact much more representative of the age and its general atmosphere than are the works of the great writers, and clearly our picture of eighteenth-century Germany is incomplete without them, as incomplete as any picture of our own times which ignored the tastes reflected in the mass of popular 'paperbacks', the 'Ian Flemings', 'Dennis Wheatleys', and 'Agatha Christies', ignored too the present-day cinema trade and television productions which have to a great extent taken over many of the functions of popular fiction. The above survey of the items announced in the 1800 catalogue discloses to us not the interests of small, exclusive, intellectual circles, but the preferences and tastes of the greater reading public, the prevailing if not the enduring spirit of the age; it also reveals much of the essential atmosphere of the German literary scene: the immense mountain of reading material devoured by the German public, the strong preference of that public for works of fiction, the intense pressure upon writers to meet that public's uncritical demand for light entertainment, and the extent to which writers succumbed to that pressure, yielded to popular tastes, and indeed exploited them, turning out countless variations and imitations of proven popular themes with a rapidity and lack of refinement never before seen in the German book trade.

Contemporary critics, too, were well aware of the poor literary quality of these novels; their remarks leave no doubt on that score, nor on the fact that these works enjoyed a very wide public. Critics were, for example, not a little disturbed at the effect which such novels had on the education and taste of their many readers; one reviewer declares, referring particularly to the *Leben und Begebenheiten . . . (Life and Adventures . . .)* type of story,

daß diese Art von Romanen nicht einmal beim Krämer einen Nutzen haben könnten, weil sie, ehe sie dahin kämen, schon durch so viele Hände gegangen sind, daß sie bereits abgenutzt sind; sie dienen zum Beweis, wie der gute Geschmack in unseren geschmackvollen Zeiten noch gar nicht anfangen will, allgemein zu werden, und das Publikum im ganzen betrachtet sich lieber an solchem Pompernickel begnügen, als mit besser zugerichteter Speise sättigen läßt.[26]

The harm which these novels are doing to the genre as a whole is also noted: 'Aber selten wenden gute Köpfe ihre Zeit darauf

Romanen zu schreiben. Diese Produkte des Witzes sind durch die vielen Sudler beynahe ebenso herabgesetzt wie die Gelegenheitsgedichte.'[27]

Yet it would be wrong to regard this fictional literature as the exact eighteenth-century equivalent of the *Kitsch*, the cheap sensational novels and love-stories, the 'shilling shockers' and 'penny dreadfuls' of later days. The novels listed in the 1800 catalogue showed themselves openly on the market, were available in every lending library, and found readers, as we shall see, even amongst the better-educated members of the public, including those who were soon to lead German literature into the Age of Romanticism.[28] In the most esteemed literary newspapers and journals—the *Jenaer Literatur-Zeitung*, the *Leipziger Jahrbuch, Allgemeiner Literarischer Anzeiger, Neue Allgemeine Deutsche Bibliothek*, etc.—they received attention and were reviewed seriously even if, in the majority of cases, unfavourably, which is by no means the case with the sensational novels of our own times. Detailed comment on the present controversy about what, precisely, constitutes *Kitsch*[29] lies beyond the scope of this present study, but for the reasons given above and for those set forth and fully documented in her own work I would support the contention of Marion Beaujean[30] that these eighteenth-century novels were considerably more than what we in the twentieth century understand by the term *Kitsch*. Nor, indeed, is the expression *Trivialroman* a completely felicitous choice in this present context as it is in itself, of course, a value judgement and one so pejorative in tone that the literary historian who wished his work to be taken seriously was for long dissuaded, by this very 'label', from any treatment of any branch of 'sub-literature'. A number of critics, Marion Beaujean and Hans Foltin[31] amongst them, have provided what could be the answer to this confusion in terminology by suggesting that we distinguish between *Trivialliteratur* and *Hochliteratur*, but recognize also that there is between these two poles a further category—*Unterhaltungsliteratur*; it is, I feel, in this last group that the novels mentioned above should be placed—as *Unterhaltungsromane*. At the same time, one cannot but admit that Schiller does seem to anticipate many of the present-day *Kitschanalytiker* and, incidentally, provide them with a model of clarity and lucidity, in his comments on some of the sickly-sentimental works on offer on the German book market: 'Sie bewirken bloß Ausleerungen des Thränensacks und eine wollüstige Erleichterung der Gefäße; aber der Geist geht leer aus, und die edlere Kraft im Menschen wird ganz und gar nicht dadurch gestärkt.'[32] However, whether Schiller, in referring to the authors of these works as *Schundskribenten*, had precisely the same type of writer in mind as have modern critics when referring to *Kitschautoren*, has to my mind not yet been fully established.[33]

By the end of the eighteenth century, then, the German book market presented a very different picture from that which we saw in 1740. From a total production of 755 items offered at Easter 1740, to a total of 2,569 items at Easter 1800, from 28 per cent in Latin to under 4 per cent, from a market dominated by the theologian to a market granting pre-eminence to imaginative literature, and—most spectacular of all—from twenty works of narrative literature announced at Easter 1740 to 300 at Easter 1800. Clearly, the driving moment behind book production was now the reading public's pronounced taste and gargantuan appetite for light entertaining works of fiction. The novel had gained that prominent place over other literature which it has maintained to this day.

3

THE GROWTH OF THE
NOVEL-READING HABIT

Johann Georg Sulzer (1720–79), while staying in Berlin
in 1747, wrote as follows to Bodmer: 'Das gemeine Publikum
liest wenig. . . . Es ist kaum zu glauben, wie wenig Menschen in
diesem Lande lesen. Was von weitem oder von nahe zum Hofe
gehört, liest fleißig, um sich den Ekel des Müßigganges zu
vertreiben. . . . Von den anderen ist kaum hie und da einer der
zum Lesen Zeit hätte.'[1] Even fourteen years later in 1761 Sulzer
must admit that if there is another public besides that compris-
ing the learned members of society, then he has not met with it
up to now; he continues: 'So lange die Bücher blos in den
Händen der Professoren, Studenten und Journalschreiber sind,
dünkt es mich kaum der Mühe werth, für das gegenwärthige
Geschlecht zu schreiben.'[2]

How different are the opinions given by critics later in the
century. Reading, once a rare pastime indulged in only by the
few of the privileged social classes, was by the end of the century
regarded as one of life's necessities by all classes of German
society. As early as 1779 the situation had changed so much that
Wieland could write: 'Nie ist mehr geschrieben und mehr
gelesen worden.'[3] Kant writes in 1798: 'Die Leserey ist zum
beinahe unentbehrlichen und allgemeinen Bedürfniß geworden.'[4] The years from 1740 onwards were seen even by
contemporaries as a new era in German literature, one critic,
as already mentioned, going so far as to declare: 'Unsere
Litteratur fängt zuerst von 1740 an.'[5] They were well aware
that it was an entirely new type of literature that was now to be
had on the book market; books were no longer written merely
for the scholar and the aristocrat but for the whole of German
society. We read in 1795: 'Man lieset selbst da, wo man vor
zwanzig Jahren noch an kein Buch dachte; nicht allein der
Gelehrte, nein auch der Bürger und Handwerker beschäftigt

sich mit Gegenständen des Nachdenkens.'[6] Schiller, too, speaks of 'das immer allgemeiner werdende Bedürfnis zu lesen, auch bei denjenigen Volksklassen zu deren Geistesbildung von Seiten des Staats so wenig zu geschehen pflegt.'[7]

Almost every journal of the latter half of the century writes at some length on the *Lesewut* ('craze for reading'), *Lesesucht* ('mania for reading'), or *Leseseuche* ('reading plague') and tells how the pastime of reading is becoming daily more widespread; reading is now a common pastime even in the lower classes and not only amongst men but amongst women, too. In 1780 we read, for example, in the *Deutsches Museum*: 'Heutiges Tages ist nicht leicht ein Frauenzimmer von einiger Erziehung, das nicht läse; der lesende Theil findet sich jetzt unter allen Ständen, in Städten und auf dem Lande, sogar die Musketiere in großen Städten lassen sich aus der Leihbibliothek Bücher auf die Hauptwache holen.'[8]

Möser speaks of the 'unersättliche Leselust aller Stände' ('insatiable appetite for reading material in all the social classes'), and Meiners tells us of an ordinary peasant who had read the works of Frederick the Great; we hear, too, of a tailor of Hanau who had a library of 3,600 volumes.[9]

There was naturally no shortage of prophets who foresaw in this development the end of all domestic bliss and honest conscientious workmanship. Möser, in his *Patriotische Phantasien* (1774–86), longs for the return of the days when girls spent their time spinning and weaving instead of reading novels; wives should have better things to do than seeking entertainment from novels.[10] The mayor of a 'small imperial town' writes in 1776 to the *Deutsches Museum*: 'Sollten diese unsre armen Mädchen die Kühe melken, so saßen die über einem Buch das sie nicht verstanden.'[11] A Silesian newspaper complains in 1806 that the daughter of a middle-class family, who should be working in the kitchen, is more often to be found reading her Goethe and Schiller, while the spoiled country lass exchanges her spinning-wheel for a Kotzebue drama.[12] The fashionable craze for reading is criticized on a somewhat higher level by Lichtenberg; he claims 'daß die Buchdruckerei Gelehrsamkeit zwar mehr ausgebreitet, aber im Gehalt vermindert hat. Das viele Lesen ist dem Denken schädlich.'[13]

A great period of prosperity was experienced by the German

book trade, which found itself compelled to make some reforms in its organization so as to be able to deal with the increased demand for books.[14] So great were the profits to be made in the trade that contemporaries now for the first time saw the book trade as a money-making business just like any other branch of commerce, along much the same lines as Defoe had noted in England in 1725: 'Writing . . . is become a very considerable Branch of the English Commerce. The Booksellers are the Master Manufacturers or Employers. The several Writers, Authors, Copyers, Sub-Writers and all other operators with Pen and Ink are the workmen employed by the said Master-Manufacturers.'[15] Fichte, writing in 1805 put it thus: 'An die Stelle anderer, aus der Mode gekommener Zeitvertreibe trat in der letzten Hälfte des vorigen Jahrhunderts das Lesen . . . . Das neue Bedürfniß erzeugte ein neues Gewerbe, durch Lieferung der Waare sich zu nähren und zu bereichern strebend: den Buchhandel.'[16]

The production of books was increasing every year in Germany, until a Swiss newspaper could report in 1799: 'Alle Jahre werden zwischen 6 bis 7 tausend neue Bücher gedruckt; nebst dem schreiben über 20 tausend Menschen ums Brot. So etwas hat keine Nation noch gesehen.'[17] From the year 1721 to 1763 the fair catalogues show an increase in production of 265 items; during the next forty-two years, 1763–1805, the increase was by 2,821 items. This increase made the deepest impression on contemporaries and in not a few cases filled them with a fear for the future of German literature; from 1785 onwards we can find scarcely one journal which does not call attention to the dangers of this *Vielschreiberei* ('ceaseless pen-pushing'). A contributor to the *Deutsches Museum*, for example, writes: 'Ich verstehe nicht die Kunst derjenigen dreytausend deutschen Büchermacher, welche in drey Jahren viertausend siebenhundert und neun Bücher verfertigen konnten.'[18] Lichtenberg summed up the situation as follows: 'Wenn England eine vorzügliche Stärke in Rennpferden hat, so haben wir die unsrige in Rennfedern.'[19]

The catalogues of the Leipzig book fairs are, as we saw earlier, a good guide when considering the increase in book production, but they by no means list all the books printed. The catalogues for 1780, for example, list 2,095 German works;

Nicolai, however, estimates for the same year, working from his business correspondence, the total of German books and treatises as 5,000 originals and translations. Reckoning editions of 1,000 copies, these two estimates give us a total of between 2,000,000 and 5,000,000 copies of new books circulated yearly amongst a population of about 20,000,000.[20] For comparison it may be noted that eighteenth-century England, where Johnson felt he could speak of a 'nation of readers', saw a fourfold increase in the annual book production (excluding pamphlets) during the century; the annual output from 1666 to 1756 averaged less than 100, and that from 1792 to 1802 was 372, in a population of about 6,000,000.[21] On the subject of bookselling, as opposed to book production, however, it is worth recording that James Lackington, bookseller in Finsbury Square, London, writes: 'According to the best estimation I have been able to make, I suppose that more than four times the number of books are sold now [1791] than were sold twenty years since.'[22]

But besides a quantitative, there was also a qualitative change on the German book market. The days of the thick collections of sermons, the medical works in folio, the heavy reference works, and the huge 'opera omnia' were over; scholars were no longer the only customers of the German book-dealers and writers were out to please their new master, the wider reading public. The following advice is given to writers of the eighties by Magister Reiche: polemic treatises have but little appeal for the reader of today, at any rate no profit worth speaking of can be made from them; sermons, devotional literature, and exegetical works depend too much for their success on the writer's reputation; pedagogy is now a hackneyed theme and, besides this, there is too much competition in this field from Campe and Weiße; works requiring a mature and speculative mind are now out of fashion.[23] The age of the octavo and duodecimo had arrived.

The public was now turning to what contemporaries termed *die unterhaltende Lektüre* ('entertaining reading material'). The *Deutsches Museum* (August 1780) tells us that theological, medical, philosophical, and philological works are now enjoying but poor sales; more popular is *die angenehme Lektüre* ('pleasant reading material'). And at the auction described in the farcical

comedy, *Die Gelehrten-Versteigerung* (1781), theologians were
hard to get rid of, whilst poets and novelists were in very great
demand. The bookseller Wilhelm Fleischer of Frankfurt am
Main informs us in 1792 that the favourite reading material of
the day is novels, poems, and comedies.[24] Another contemporary
observer writes in 1783: 'Unser Zeitalter verträgt tüchtige und
gründliche Schriften nicht, es achtet sie nicht. Nur Überset-
zungen aus dem Englischen und Französischen, nur Romane,
nur witzige Tändeleyen, das sind seine Schooshündgen, das
sind seine Puppen.'[25] In similar vein we find a reviewer in 1784
despairing of Germany's future 'so lange *Romanen-Krämer in
Leipzig* sich durch den Verlag von *Werthers Leiden, von Siegwarts
Klostergeschichte* und *solchen Lumpenschriften* ganze Landgüter
erwerben werden, da hingegen die besten moralischen Bücher
oft zu nichts anderem, als Käse und Butter-Krämern zum
Gebrauch dienen.'[26] Lessing, too, was well aware of this situation
when writing about Wieland's *Agathon*; he wonders whether he
can, in fact, call it a novel and continues: 'Roman? Wir wollen
ihm diesen Titel nur geben, vielleicht, daß er einige Leser mehr
dadurch bekömmt.'[27]

The publisher planning his annual visit to the Leipzig fair,
then, realized that he would find very few of his colleagues
interested in serious scholarly works with their small and exclusive public, and so he made sure that works of light entertainment were well represented amongst the titles he had to offer.
Recent research by Marion Beaujean and Jochen Schulte-
Sasse,[28] based on sources other than the Leipzig catalogues, has
confirmed that the tables reproduced in Chapter 2[29] do give a
true picture of the broad development over these years; the more
detailed figures that they produce, however, show that the
'battle' between novel and drama to win the public's favour was
a much closer thing than the Leipzig catalogues of 1740, 1770,
and 1800 alone would suggest. At the same time, the results that
they obtain do highlight one of the fundamental difficulties of
accurate bibliographical research in this period. Working from
Kayser's *Vollständiges Bücher-Lexikon . . .* (Leipzig, 1836) Beaujean
has listed decade by decade the total production of new novels,
and Schulte-Sasse places her figures alongside those of his own
count (from the same source) of new plays, excluding translations, giving the following picture:

	Plays	Novels
1750–60	125	73
1761–70	304	189
1771–80	1,069	413
1781–90	1,135	907
1791–1800	1,002	1,623
1801–10	1,029	1,700

The predominance of plays in the early part of this period is, to say the least, surprising but the picture then changes considerably when we see the results of Marianne Spiegel's extremely well-researched and documented study, which unfortunately stops short at the late 1760s;[30] drawing on a wider selection of bibliographical sources, and including both new editions and translations she lists for the period 1750–60 a total of 315 novels (against Beaujean's 73); 258 titles are listed for the years 1761–9. My own count from Heinsius's *Verzeichnis . . .* (Leipzig, 1813) produced the following figures, in which are included all novels and collections of short stories published in German, whether original works or translations; both new and repeated editions were counted, in so far as the latter were listed at all in the catalogue; multi-volumed novels were counted as one item and dated by the appearance of the first volume (see also Appendix II):

	Over 5 years	Per decade		Over 5 years	Per decade
1740–4	53	157	1780–4	449	972
1745–9	104		1785–9	523	
1750–4	130	209	1790–4	820	1,746
1755–9	79		1795–9	926	
1760–4	65	200	1800–4	1,429	2,207
1765–9	135		1805–9	778	
1770–4	183	443	Period 1700–39	108	
1774–9	260		No date of publication	395	
			1700–1809 : TOTAL	6,437	

The Swiss bookseller Johann Georg Heinzmann, estimated the number of novels, originals and translations, which had appeared in Germany between 1773 and 1794, 'to be safe', at no fewer than 5,850; the same man tells us that during the 1790s novels were appearing at the rate of 300 a year.[31]

Much clearly depends on the differing techniques and starting-points of the various research workers—whether, for example, translations and new editions should be included in such counts; but over and above this, such discrepancies as in the above are regrettably unavoidable in view of the lack of any *one* exact and complete bibliographical source. What can be said with certainty, however, is that by the 1790s the novel had clearly won, and was to keep, pride of place in the belles-lettres section of the German book market. When, in 1797, we find the Leipzig catalogue introducing for the first time the separate rubric *Romane*, it is evidence not only of the greatly increased production in this field but also of the need that was felt to provide prospective customers with a convenient and detailed form of reference to the latest works of fiction.

Clearly the most important factor helping in the growth of the novel-reading habit is to be sought in the novel itself, in the type of fiction produced by writers from mid century onwards. We have already seen how works like *Robinson Crusoe, Insel Felsenburg*, and the popular moral weeklies with their dual nature, combining a secular entertaining form with a high ethical content, had won the respect of the bourgeoisie for imaginative literature. Richardson's novels had continued this trend; a biographical excerpt is told in a pleasant and entertaining manner—mostly in letter form—but the story is not an end in itself, entertainment is not the novelist's main aim, and so every action, every mood is examined and analysed down to the last minute motivation. The English novelist is just as concerned about the spiritual well-being of his readers as were the theologians who produced religious works for the layman, but he transforms the positive religious element into pure moral instruction and relates the doctrines of his Church to real life. If he appears more secular, then it is, as he himself says, because he purposely compressed the religious passages so that they would be more palatable to those readers who were most in need of them and who might otherwise be tempted to omit these passages in their reading.[32] How dear these passages were to him, however, is shown by his publication in 1755 of *A Collection of the Moral and Instructive Sentiments, Maxims, Cautions and*

Reflexions, Contained in the Histories of Pamela, Clarissa and Sir Charles Grandison. By giving the material of the older edifying literature a new dress, an entertaining cloak, he makes a concession to the changing taste of the serious yet more secular-minded reader of his day and at the same time hopes to win 'converts' from amongst the ranks of the already confirmed novel-readers who looked primarily for entertainment in their reading matter. In the Epilogue to *Clarissa*, for instance, Richardson says that it has been his aim to 'investigate the great doctrines of Christianity under the fashionable guise of an amusement'. Richardson was, in short, a combination of novelist, preacher, and something akin to missionary, and it was this that won him so many readers in Germany and such a large following of admirers and imitators amongst German men of letters.

In Gellert's eyes, for example, literature was primarily concerned with furthering moral ends, and so it is not surprising when, in recommending books to his students, he can add Richardson's novels to his list of religious and edifying works and moral weeklies, although he is fully conscious of the novelty of his action in praising novels from the University Professor's chair. He writes in the tenth lecture of his *Moralische Vorlesungen* (published posthumously in 1770):

> Zu dieser Classe [der moralischen Gedichte] zähle ich ferner die guten prosaischen Gedichte, besonders die Clarissa und den Grandison. Aber wie? Romane von dem philosophischen Katheder anzupreisen? Ja, wenn es Werke eines Richardsons sind, so halte ich ihre Empfehlung für Pflicht . . . . Ich habe ehedem über den siebenten Theil von Clarissa und den fünften des Grandisons, mit einer Art von süßer Wehmut einige der merkwürdigsten Stunden für mein Herz verweint; dafür danke ich dir noch jetzt, Richardson.[33]

When a respected and religiously minded man like Gellert starts to praise novels in public, and even honours the genre with a product of his own, the last suspicions against the worldliness of the novel must, even in Christian circles, be discarded. The novel could now be read quite openly by true Christians once Gellert and other religious men had shown their approval. And the newly won public were not betrayed in their trust; the German novels of the Age of Enlightenment outshone their English models in the worship of virtue, in magnanimity, moral tendency, and pulpit style'. Books now began to find their way into households where once nothing, or at most the Bible, was read; a contemporary critic, Thomas Abbt (1738–66), sums up Gellert's work in this respect as follows:

> Für ganz Deutschland ist es ohne Widerrede Gellert, dessen Fabeln dem Geschmack der ganzen Nation eine neue Richtung gegeben haben. Sie haben sich nach und nach in Häuser, wo sonst nie gelesen wird, eingeschlichen. Fragt die erste beste Landpredigerstochter nach Gellerts Fabeln? Die kennt sie! nach den Werken andrer Dichter? kein Wort! — Dadurch ist das Gute in Exempeln, und nicht in Regeln, bekannt, und das Schlechte verächtlich gemacht worden.[34]

The way was prepared, then, by the instructive type of imaginative literature like the fable, and hymns, too, but soon these were followed by the novel, which in the hands of the Enlighteners was just another means of bringing instruction to the people. No genre was more suited to the purpose of instructing by 'examples and not by rules' and if the taste of broad sections of the reading public now demanded that their edifying literature be entertaining, too, then the novel could also fulfil this requirement most admirably.

The German 'novel of the present' (*Gegenwartsroman*) in the Age of Enlightenment is characterized in its various aspects by the names Gellert, Joh. Timotheus Hermes, 1738–1821 (*Geschichte der Miss Fanny Wilkes* (1766), *Sophiens Reise von Memel nach Sachsen* (1770–2), *Für Töchter edler Herkunft* (1787), *Für Eltern und Ehelustige* (1789), etc.), Moritz Aug. von Thümmel, 1738–1817 (*Wilhelmine* (1764), *Reise in die mittäglichen Provinzen von Frankreich im Jahre 1785–86* (1791–1805), etc.), Joh. Karl Aug. Musäus, 1735–87 (*Grandison der Zweite* (1760–2), rewritten as *Der deutsche Grandison. Auch eine Familiengeschichte* (1781), etc.), Adolf Franz Friedr. Freiherr von Knigge, 1752–96 (*Der Roman meines Lebens* (1781–3), *Geschichte Peter Clausens* (1783–5), *Über den Umgang mit Menschen* (1788), *Die Reise nach Braunschweig* (1792), etc.), Joh. Gottwert Müller, 1743–1828 (*Siegfried von Lindenberg* (1779), *Komische Romane* (1784–91), *Die Herren von Waldheim* (1786), etc.), Joh. Gottlieb Schummel, 1748–1813 (*Empfindsame Reisen durch Deutschland* (1770–2), *Fritzchens Reise nach Dessau* (1776), *Spitzbart, eine komi-tragische Geschichte für unser pädagogisches Jahrhundert* (1779), etc.), Joh. Jak. Engel, 1741–1802 (*Der dankbare*

Sohn (1771), *Titus* (1779), *Herr Lorenz Stark, ein Charaktergemälde* (1801), etc.), Friedr. Nicolai, 1733–1811 (*Leben und Meinungen des Herrn Magisters Sebaldus Nothanker* (1773–6), *Freuden des jungen Werthers* (1775), *Geschichte eines dicken Mannes* (1794), etc.). Their main characters are no longer the 'heroes of high social rank' of the 1715 definition, but the 'other persons', the ordinary bourgeois members of society, and if the court does appear in their stories then it is placed in a critical light and very often portrayed as a threat to the virtue of the good middle-class heroine. The hero of the Rationalistic novel must use his life to put the new ideals of the Age of Enlightenment into practice, he must fight the evil in the world and do his share of enlightening or else, and this is more often the case, his stay on earth must lead to his own complete personal enlightenment. This is what is meant when contemporary theorists like Blankenburg in his *Versuch über den Roman* (1774) insist on the portrayal of *das Menschliche*; they wanted artistic expression of the gradual process of enlightenment which should take place in every human being.

One of the most representative and certainly one of the most popular of these novels was Nicolai's *Das Leben und die Meinungen des Herrn Magisters Sebaldus Nothanker* (1773–6). The scant action in the novel is focused on Sebaldus himself and his eldest daughter Marianne, who together form the two poles of the opinions given. The honest clergyman Sebaldus, a staunch supporter of the Rationalist Protestantism of the time, is dismissed from his post by the orthodox party led by Magister Stuzius and spends the rest of his life wandering around the whole country meeting various types of Protestant clergymen, discussing religion and ethics in general, and giving his opinions on the overweening aristocracy, the increasing Gallomania of his countrymen, the state of the German book trade, and other topical subjects. Marianne leaves her father and embarks on a whole series of love-affairs in the traditional time-honoured style, supplying in fact the entertaining material for Nicolai's novel of instruction; the adventurous element of the older type of novel could not yet be dispensed with and here it is represented by incidents on journeys, robber ambushes, shipwrecks, and scenes of seduction. The novel was well received by the reading public, Möser, Hamann, and Merck being amongst its most notable admirers; the first volume (1773) went through three editions in the next four years, pirated editions—a sure proof of a 'good thing' financially—appeared in Frankfurt am Main, Höchst, and Hanau, and the novel was translated into French, Swedish, Danish, English, and Dutch.[35]

Wieland writes on the task of writers during this period: '. . . man muß . . . nicht gefallen . . . man muß predigen und einschläfern';[36] the author's first duty was to instruct and only then to entertain. Perhaps the most typical novelist in this respect is Johann Timotheus Hermes (1738–1821) whose ambition was clearly to become the 'German Richardson'. He realized that the time of the all-powerful pulpit was gone, he had seen the secularized bourgeoisie turn away from the old edifying and devotional literature and knew that the flock of erring sheep was no longer to be reached from the old orthodox position. Yet to leave them to their fate would be a sin and so, like many of his fellow preachers,[37] he throws aside his cassock and as a writer, behind whose apparently secular pen no one guesses the presence of the now suspect black gown, seeks to reach his congregation by using the attractive, entertaining form of the novel. A theologian puts it thus when writing to Hermes: 'Die Zeit naht, wo wir als Prediger den Menschen wenig werden beikommen können; alsdann wird das Wahre und Schöne eines gefälligen Gewandes bedürfen, und Sie, wenn Sie fortfahren, können dann ein deutscher Richardson werden.'[38]

Hermes was born in Petznick near Preußisch-Stargard in 1738 and, himself the son of a clergyman, studied theology at Königsberg. His first post was as a teacher, then as a preacher at Lüben, after which he became court preacher at Pleß. He next lived at Breslau, first as a clergyman and then as a university professor, and it was in Breslau as *Superintendent* and *Oberkonsistorialrat* that he died in 1821. His first novel, *Geschichte der Miss Fanny Wilkes*, appeared in two volumes in 1766 and enjoyed great success, not a little of which was undoubtedly due to its setting in England with English characters; the whole novel, in fact, was written entirely under the influence of Richardson. We are reminded of how much more the German public appreciated translations from the English than they did German originals when Hermes tells us at the beginning of his novel how first he wished to put on the title-page 'translated from the English'; this was too much to have on his conscience, however, and so he added—in very small print—'as good as . . .', hoping that prospective buyers would say: 'Ey das ist ja schön, daß man einmal wieder was druckt, das im Geschmack eines Grandisons . . . geschrieben ist.'[39]

It was, however, an original German novel with a setting in contemporary Germany and with German characters which won fame for Hermes especially amongst the middle-class reading public. This novel, *Sophiens Reise von Memel nach Sachsen* (*Sophie's Journey from Memel to Saxony*), appeared in five volumes from 1770 to 1772, and was thereafter repeatedly reprinted, several times pirated, translated into Dutch, Danish, and French, but most of all imitated: *Anhang zu Sophiens Reise* (*Supplement to* . . .) (1780); *Reise einer jüngeren Sophie, aber nicht von Memel nach Sachsen* (*Journey of a Younger Sophie but not from Memel to Saxony*) (1780) and many others.[40] Brüggemann suggests[41] that much of the success of the novel may be ascribed to the fact that many readers saw themselves, like Sophie—and Hermes himself—as the victims of a transitional period. Hermes, ten years younger than Lessing and eleven years older than Goethe, had grown up under the rule of Rationalism but he could not identify all his ideas with those of Lessing's generation nor was he sufficiently sure of himself to be able to herald a new era as did Goethe with his youthful friends. Sophie, too, could not fit in with the older generation as represented in characters like Less**, Puf, and Gros, and yet she was not strong enough to shape her own life after new ideals based on subjective emotions; she is not governed by feeling alone, but the sentimental element in her is strong enough to make her reflect on her feelings and make her uncertain which path to choose in life. And Hermes is sufficiently in tune with the Rationalists to condemn her attitude and recount her fate as a warning to the reading public.

Hermes would also attract many readers by his ability, somewhat rare in his day, to present native German localities and customs in sharp detail and effective language. Even the lower classes are represented in the novel and they speak their own various dialects. After the flood of translations on the German book market readers now welcomed a story with characters they understood, a setting they knew, and conditions (the Seven

Years War) they had themselves experienced. To the student of German cultural and social history the novel is a veritable mine of information. It was to this quality of Hermes's work that the reviewer in *Teutscher Merkur* drew particular attention: 'Kurz, unter unsern Romanschreibern . . . ist der Verfasser an Kenntniß der Welt und Bearbeitung deutscher Sitten der erste';[42] the review goes on to describe the author as a man of more than usual talent who, in a constant alternation of conversations, stories, and monologues, informs us of everything in his heart and in his head that he considers worth communicating, especially concerning his system of ethics and religion.

There are two reasons for the inclusion in the novel of these lengthy discussions on varied subjects. In the first place the taste of serious-minded readers demanded it, for in this way they could keep themselves up to date on the latest views on education, social reforms, divorce, duelling, fashions, etc., just as in the later nineteenth century ancient history was learnt from Ebers (1837–98) and Dahn (1834–1912), and politics from Spielhagen (1829–1911); and, secondly, Hermes was above all a theologian, a clergyman worried about the spiritual welfare and intellectual enlightenment of his fellow humans. His attitude here is most typical of the Rationalist novelists.

Hermes never tires of declaring that he is not writing merely to fill up his leisure hours, nor out of any literary ambitions; he is not inspired by a *furor poeticus*. In fact, no one would be more pleased than he himself if he could with a clear conscience give up his activity in this field but he finds he must 'instruct, improve, at least warn'. He chooses the novel to do this since it is by now the most popular reading material on the German book market and therefore his preaching would be most effective in this form:

. . . so frage man die Buchhändler; so untersuche man die Toiletten! Ich kenne den Werth der Morgenstunden. Ein Frauenzimmer welches sich erbauen will, wird sie gewiß zur Lesung eines ernsthaften Buchs anwenden. Jede andere lieset dann einen Roman. Sollten wir Schriftsteller . . . diese Romanleserinnen nun ihrem gefährlichen Schicksal überlassen?[43]

Hermes realizes that by putting his sermons in the form of a novel, by interspersing a few exciting tales and piquant situations amongst his instruction, he will reach not only the most readers but also those most in need of attention. Stories, hardly the sort expected from the pen of a clergyman, are told and the moral quickly pointed, and in this way the novel proceeds, each chapter outdoing its predecessor so that interest may not flag. He would be very pleased if he could drop the 'entertaining cloak'—what he terms the *Puz*—and deal straightforwardly with his subjects, truth, virtue, and piety, and continues: 'Wer alle drei entweder ohne Schmuck lieben kann, oder wer . . . Holz an meinem Scheiterhaufen legen will; der kann sein Exemplar verkaufen; denn für ihn schrieb ich nicht.'[44]

With such writers as Hermes we cannot begin to speak of artistic aims and achievements, not only because they themselves deny these but also because the material and problems dealt with preclude these. The stories themselves rarely rise above the trivial, the most material realities, and most time is spent in talking over the problems of middle-class and aristocratic life with their everyday psychological situations. But this humdrum element is intended and consciously cultivated, on the one hand because truth is being reported, or supposedly so, and on the other to counteract the exoticism of the baroque novel; everything which might divert attention from the lesson in hand is most carefully avoided. The novelist has now become a preacher and instructor in ethics, his public are eager pupils, simply devouring these disguised sermons as they might swallow sugared pills. Writers deal with all problems ranging from the correct interpretation of the Christian doctrine to instruction in hygiene, hints on child-rearing, cures for measles, ideas on school reforms, etc.; Hermes, ever original in this respect, even manages to instruct true Christians to cough and clear their throats in church only in between sentences or at least during marked oratorical caesurae.[45]

By maintaining the close connection between the new middle-class family novel and the older devotional literature Hermes and his contemporaries in the Age of Enlightenment played a vital part in the creation of a wider novel-reading public. In seeking especially to instruct that section of German society which they felt was most in need of instruction, that is, those readers who could no longer stomach the straightforward, undisguised religious works for the layman, these writers in fact made fiction ever more attractive to serious-minded bourgeois circles, winning over an increasing number of readers as the century proceeded. We see the vicious circle: authors have to present their material in an entertaining manner so as to reach the 'erring sheep', yet in so doing they rob the devotional and practical books of still more readers, thus swelling the numbers of the weaker brethren and increasing the need for more enlightenment—effective only in the form of the novel. We have already seen this development mirrored in the Leipzig book-catalogues of the period which show a continuous decline in the production of religious literature for the layman and a steady and very nearly proportionate increase in the production of imaginative literature.[46]

It will be clear from much that has already been said on Hermes and his work that he and his colleagues made the wives and mothers of Germany their special concern; the subject-matter they choose, centred on everyday family life, the characters they portray, and the problems they discuss and advise on are obviously aimed primarily at interesting and enlightening the female members of the German novel-reading public for, like the editors of the moral weeklies before them, they realized firstly, that women as a rule had more leisure time at their disposal in which to indulge in reading, and secondly, that through women they could achieve both a wider and more effective dissemination of their ideas—the woman, in her capacity as mother, held the key to future generations. It is self-evident that this attitude led directly to a further widening of the novel-reading public. As long as narrative literature had concerned itself with the masculine world of brave deeds and exciting incidents, with the strange adventures of the heroes of the baroque age, so long did women remain aloof from imaginative literature; their reading material had consisted of the old-established edifying and religious literature, and their main emotional outlet had been in the Pietist movement. It was the Age of Enlightenment that saw the establishment of a feminine public for secular literature. Again the book-catalogues of the period provide us with concrete proof of these changes: the Leipzig book-fair catalogue of 1740 still lists a large number of edifying, devotional works expressly for women, but that of 1770 contains not one representative of this branch of writing for women. The interest of the feminine reading public had been awakened when the strong, daring, aristocratic hero of baroque fiction gave way to the virtuous middle-class heroine of the second half of the century, women like Richardson's *Pamela* and Hermes's *Sophie.*

A century earlier, when novels were filled with the wildest eroticism, the few women who had read novels had tried their best to keep their pastime a secret; now, however, when most novels made at least some attempt at instruction, it was a different matter. Wieland, writing in 1791, puts the new situation convincingly:

Wo ehemals kaum in den höchsten Classen hier und da einige Damen waren, die etwas Gedrucktes, außer ihrem Gebetbuche und dem Hauskalender kannten und sich in müßigen Stunden mit *Hercules und Herculiscus,* der *Römischen Oktavia* und in der Folge mit der *Asiatischen Banise,* Neukirchs *Telemach* u. a. allgemein beliebten Büchern ihrer Zeit unterhielten — da ist jetzt das Lesen auch unter der Mittelclasse, und bis nahe an diejenigen, die gar nicht lesen gelernt haben, allgemeines Bedürfniß geworden; und gegen Ein Frauenzimmer, welches vor fünfzig Jahren ein zu ihrer Zeit geschriebenes Buch las, sind jetzt (um nicht zu viel zu sagen) hundert, zumal in kleinen Städten und auf dem Lande, wo es an der Zerstreuung der großen Städte fehlt — die alles lesen, was ihnen vor die Hände kömmt und einige Unterhaltung ohne große Bemühung des Geistes verspricht.[47]

We may say then that the novels produced in Germany during the Age of Enlightenment contributed greatly to the growth of the novel-reading habit in general and amongst women in particular. Exactly the same may be said of the literary phenomenon of Sentimentalism, tentatively suggested in Schnabel's *Insel Felsenburg* but most evident in German literature since the imitation of Richardson's novels had commenced. The importance of Sentimentalism to our present theme is that it created a body of potential novel-readers who shared a nucleus of common interests, aims, and ideals—in short, a common taste which, once writers had begun to cater for it, guaranteed a work of fiction a much wider public than had previously been possible, a public whose core was in fact all those sections of German society who had, two generations previously, shown such a lively interest in the writings of the Pietist leaders.

Feeling had played an important part in the life of the Pietist; this it was indeed that distinguished him from the orthodox Protestant. With the help of personal feeling the Pietist hoped to bring about a closer union with his God. Thus feeling was to him not an end in itself, for in God he always had a last aim, a last foothold to check the transition to aimless enthusiasm. It was, then, in religious circles that the man who was capable of the strongest emotions first won respect. Gradually, however, in the more secular atmosphere of the later eighteenth century the content of feeling becomes of no importance so long as it justifies a cult. The sentimental nature is preserved but its original religious purpose, its religious anchorage, is discarded; the younger generation of the seventies had inherited the Pietists' strength of feeling and their sensitivity, but they are too enlightened to make religion the object of their exaltation, rather do they create new Gods, modern idols—like the *Humanitätsideal*—which they can adore with all their sensitive hearts.

Whoever could intensify sentiment so as to produce a vision was once called a *Wiedergeborener*, now he is a *Genie*. This is the road which leads directly from Pietism to Sentimentalism and Storm and Stress, from Spener and Francke to Fräulein von Klettenberg, Klopstock, and Goethe. In short, Sentimentalism is Pietism diverted from the religious to the secular world of feeling.[48]

The translations and imitations of the novels of Richardson and Sterne had helped to establish the sentimental novel in Germany, but for a long time Sentimentalism was content to exist as a subsidiary element of the Rationalistic novel of the present, and in most of these novels Sentimentalism is, of course, treated as something to be avoided by the Rational being; in Gellert's *Schwedische Gräfin* (1747–8), for example, Carlson and Marianne come to a tragic end because they lack composure and are unable to control their emotions, and Hermes's Sophie, too, is condemned by Pastor Gros because of her 'reflective sentimentalism'. By the seventies, however, the new movement had gained sufficient impetus to warrant the appearance of a novel where, for the first time, subjective sentiments are treated with as much respect as virtue and morality. This was the case with *Die Geschichte des Fräuleins von Sternheim* (1771) by Germany's first woman novelist Sophie von Laroche (1731–1807). The story is of the Richardson type, telling how the heroine is persecuted by the diabolical Lord Derby, deceived by a false marriage, and finally imprisoned in a tower which she leaves only in a dying condition; through all her trials and tribulations she defends her honour and virtue with complete success.

Sophie von Laroche's novel shows most clearly the influence of Pietism on the sentimental writers of this period. Besides the fineness of feeling already mentioned we note, too, a marked hostility towards all worldly pleasures, especially dancing, gambling, fashions, and the theatre, an urgent plea for the patient bearing of all sorrow and suffering, a desperate longing for peace and friendship with all men, and a burning love towards all fellow human beings. The book gives expression to the Pietist ideal of a peaceful, personal, and comforting Christianity, laying more stress on trust in God than on dogma, and praising good deeds as better than the finest thoughts.

The new place allotted to feeling makes it clear that we now have a changed human ideal—so radically changed indeed that we are obviously dealing here not with a mere change in taste but with a change in public; for a man of the older generation to subscribe to the new ideals, which were to find even more forceful expression in the *Sturm und Drang* movement, would be a betrayal of his whole outlook on life from the religious, artistic, and social points of view. Instead of Rationalistic composure and decision, the characteristics of noblest humanity are now sensitivity, a passionate heart, and, one is tempted to add, highly efficient lachrymal glands. Two passages from representative novels of the sentimental era suffice to give us a picture of the new ideal. The first is from Hermes: 'Herr Handsom war der allerschönste, der geschickteste, höflichste, und dabey der allerfrommste Mensch in ganz Schottland . . . . Und er weinte so sanft, daß mans kaum sahe . . .'[49]—he also distinguishes himself by being apt to faint or even to become violently ill when strongly moved. Fräulein von Sternheim's ideal is personified in the person of Milord Seymour:

Ich übergehe den sanften männlichen Ton seiner Stimme, die gänzlich für den Ausdruck der Empfindungen seiner edlen Seele gemacht zu seyn scheint; das durch etwas melancholisches gedämpfte Feuer seiner schönen Augen, den unnachahmlich angenehmen und mit Größe vermengten Anstand aller seiner Bewegungen,

und was ihn von allen Männern, deren ich . . . eine Menge
geschen habe, unterscheidet, ist . . . der tugendhafte Blick seiner
Augen . . . .[50]
In his person 'nobility of mind and a philanthropic nature are
united with an enlightened intellect'.

When we compare this type of hero with his counterpart in
baroque literature we find instead of the latter's courage, decision, and strength, the qualities which we now term effeminate—beauty, virtue, tenderness, and a melancholy disposition.
The whole mood of the era was, in fact, effeminate and it
was mainly the women of Germany who fell victim to the new
'fashionable plague' of Sentimentalism. Wieland writes: 'Unsere
heutigen Mädchen sind, Gott sei's geklagt, fast durchgängig auf
Schwermuth und Empfindsamkeit gestellt.'[51] Klopstock often
read aloud passages from his *Lazarus* and *Cidli* to gatherings of
young girls and reports with satisfaction that he was 'rewarded
with tears'.[52] That this mood was not confined to literary circles
is evident from the following extract from a young girl's letter
to Gellert:

> Mein Herz ist von Natur weich, zu der feuerigsten, zärtlichsten
> und beständigsten Freundschaft aufgelegt, stets bereit, alle Ein-
> drücke des Mitleids und der Empfindlichkeit aufzunehmen, dabei
> aber so sehr zur Schwermut geneigt, daß ich öfters meine Zuflucht
> zu Thränen nehmen muß, um dasselbe zu erleichtern.[53]

J. G. Jacobi's circle of friends were ardent admirers of the
English Sentimentalists. In a letter to Gleim he describes a
communal reading of Sterne's *Sentimental Journey* and tells how,
on coming to the death of the monk Lorenzo, each one looked
mournfully into the eyes of his neighbour and was pleased to
find tears there also. 'Lorenzo snuff-boxes' became the order of
the day and served, as it were, as a badge of 'The League of
Virtue'; even ladies were expected to have such a box at their
bedside.[54]

Just as it was amongst the bourgeoisie that Pietism had sought
and found most of its supporters so, too, was Sentimentalism
most widespread in middle-class society. A glance at the
Darmstadt court in the seventies, however, proves that not all
aristocratic circles remained aloof from the new movement; those
courts which had opened their doors, and hearts, to Pietism fell
victim also to the prevailing sentimental mood. But most of the

nobility were too intent on aping the Parisian 'man of the world' to pay any attention to the wave of sentimentalism sweeping over the land. Aristocratic circles found more pleasure in frivolous wit, fineness of form, and clever rhymes, than in enthusiastic sensitivity. In such society the unashamed adoration shown for the sentimental novelists was regarded as a deplorable lack of decorum; sympathy with the fashionable tear-cult was, in their eyes, a contemptible bourgeois disposition.

Musäus puts the point of view of these people when writing on Richardson's novels:

Wie die beyden Extremen Werther und Siegwart nebst allen dazwischenliegenden Mittelstimmen des empfindsamen Akkords, auf unsere gegenwärtige Generation gewirkt haben: wie sie die Schnellkraft der Seele gehoben, alle Nerven gespannt, die Sinne bezaubert, das Herz geschmolzen, die Thränendämme der Kontenanz durchbrochen, Seufzer erpreßt . . . haben, eben so wirkten bei der nächst-vorhergehenden diese ausländischen Droguen [Richardsons Romane] auf Geist und Herz.[55]

There were also some sections of bourgeois society which did not sympathize with the Sentimentalists. Nicolai's circle in Berlin for instance remained true to its Rationalistic ideals of reason, decision, and composure. Similarly, Rationalistic theology, which banished feeling from the realm of Christianity, also condemned exuberant enthusiasm in the field of ethics; it is not surprising then when we find the Lutheran minister Hess of Altstetten writing as follows on Klopstock's *Messias*: 'Mir gefällt nicht, daß mein Dichter so gar viel auf das Weinen hält. In der That, er weint nicht nur selbst bei allen Anlässen, in der Freude und im Leid, sondern er läßt auch alles weinen, was ihm vorkommt: Gott, Engel, Menschen, Teufel u. s. w. . . .'.[56] Again, the safest conclusion is that Sentimentalism reaped its greatest harvest in those bourgeois circles where the ground had been prepared by Pietism. It was in these circles that writers like Sophie von Laroche found most of their admirers.

The warm reception accorded in 1771 to *Die Geschichte des Fräuleins von Sternheim* bears witness to the presence in German society of a considerable body of readers who were simply waiting for novelists to depict in their stories the new ideals of what we now call the Age of Sentimentalism. Pirated editions of Sophie von Laroche's novel soon appeared on the market and the novel was translated into Dutch, English, and French.[57] Herder was so inspired by *Sternheim* that he made it the subject of a number of sermons.[58] Ridderhof implies that Sophie von Laroche's first novel brought her immediate European fame;[59] but this is hardly correct, for neither the original nor any of the translations bore her name. It was still considered undignified for a woman to be connected with the creative side of literature. Wieland had prevailed upon Sophie von Laroche to publish her work and it was his name that appeared on the title-page.[60] As soon as the real author became known there was naturally quite a stir in German literary circles; to many friends and admirers Sophie von Laroche became simply *die Sternheim*. She followed up the success of her first novel with a whole series of stories in similar vein (e.g. *Der Eigensinn der Liebe und Freundschaft* (1772); *Rosaliens Briefe* (1779–81); *Geschichte von Miss Lony* (1789); *Fanny und Julia* (1802), etc.), and, naturally enough, the commercial possibilities behind the exploitation of this taste for sentimental fiction did not escape the attention of other writers, both men and women. Laroche had shown the way, others followed her example and the ranks of novel-readers were swelled still further. A detailed consideration of the tremendous success enjoyed by Goethe's *Werther* (1774) lies beyond the scope of this present study, but it should be noted here that to the wider reading public Goethe's novel was merely the gripping story of an unhappy love-affair; it was not Werther the 'Titan' but Werther the sentimental lover who appealed to the vast majority of readers, and it was a novel inspired by this side of Werther (J. M. Miller's *Siegwart, eine Klostergeschichte* (1776)) which came most near to emulating the success of Goethe's work.[61]

An important factor helping in the growth of the reading habit was the large number of newspapers and journals on the book market; this journalistic literature offered a reading material so cheap as to suit everyone's purse and so varied as to cater for the most diverse tastes. The popularity of the moral weeklies and historical journals earlier in the century has already been mentioned.[62] The situation at the end of the century was such that the Helmstedt professor, Bischoff, could write in 1792: 'Zahllose Tagblätter und Monatsschriften befrachten posttäglich die Felleisen, sind auf Toilette- und Arbeitstischen, in Klubsälen, Gasthöfen und Dorfschenken verbreitet.'[63] In the

Vorspiel to Goethe's *Faust* the Theatre Manager advises the Poet to remember always that of the people in a theatre audience 'Gar mancher kommt vom Lesen der Journale' ('so many come to us from reading weeklies'), and we may be sure that this is the reading material in the Manager's mind when he says: 'Allein, sie haben schrecklich viel gelesen.' ('Take care, because they've read an awful lot.')[64]

All classes of German society were to be found in the reading public served by the journals and newspapers. Lichtenberg writes as early as 1774: 'Leute, die in 10 Jahren keine Geistesspeise zu sich genommen, außer ein paar Journal-Krümmchen, gibt es selbst unter Professoren, und [es] ist gar keine Seltenheit.'[65] One of the duties of the court secretary at the court of the Prince of Wallerstein was to give a résumé of the latest newspapers at the prince's breakfast-table.[66] The *Deutsches Museum* suggests that the only way to purge the lower classes of their silly superstitions is to introduce an entertaining and instructive newspaper 'for the ordinary man'; that he would read such a paper is certain: 'Kaufte der gemeine Mann doch sonst bey uns den *Wandsbeckermerkur* und man las ihn mit vielem Vergnügen in allen Schenken.'[67] Just as the middle class could read the latest journals in their coffee-houses and reading societies, so could the lower classes do the same in their taverns.

Different journals appealed, of course, to different classes of readers. The Karlsruhe reading society, for example, declared it would subscribe only to the better type of periodical; their list gives us some idea of which papers fell into this category: *Allgemeine Deutsche Bibliothek*; *Journal von und für Deutschland*; *Bibliothek der schönen Wissenschaften*; *die Göttinger, Gothaischen, Hallischen, Jenaischen, Leipziger und Tübinger Gelehrten Zeitungen und Anzeigen*; Schlözer's *Staatsanzeigen*; *Magazine aus Hannover und Hamburg*; *Berliner Monatsschrift*; *Deutsches Museum*; *Teutscher Merkur*; *Wiener Realzeitung*.

This type of journal was for the reader of good education; a typical example of these journals is the *Deutsches Museum*.[68] Amongst the regular contributors to the *Deutsches Museum* (1776–91) we find such men as H. C. Boie (Editor 1779–91), C. W. Dohm (theology, law, politics), G. A. Bürger (poet), F. L. Graf zu Stolberg (poet and anti-rationalist), J. G. H. Feder (philosophy, pedagogy, ancient languages), A. G. Kästner (mathematics), J. M. R. Lenz (poet), J. J. Eschenburg (theology and literary history), J. G. Schlosser (law), G. C. Oeder (medicine), J. H. Campe (pedagogy), J. H. Voß (theology and philosophy), and Lavater. The main contributors are, without exception, university graduates, and most of them held university teaching posts. An analysis of the contents of this journal for the year 1779 shows the following allocation of space: (1) entertainment 42 per cent, (2) literature, language, and theatre 27 per cent, (3) politics and economics 11 per cent, (4) philosophy, psychology, natural science, and medicine 6·5 per cent, (5) foreign news 6·5 per cent, (6) ethics and pedagogy 4 per cent, and (7) art and music 3 per cent.

The public of such a periodical was bound to be limited to well-educated readers; English, French, Latin, and Greek quotations are given without translation into German. Contributors often refer to their public as 'thinking readers', and we may well believe the editor when he speaks with pride of his public, 'das wir kühn das edelste in Deutschland nennen können'.[69]

Other tastes were catered for by such journals as Bertuch's *Journal des Luxus und der Moden* which blossomed for forty years (1786–1827) bringing the latest news in the world of fashion, details of foreign novelties, reports from the salons of Paris, London, Vienna, and Berlin, descriptions of the latest events in 'high society', and information on, and reviews of theatre performances, concerts, and other amusements. Lighter reading material, aimed primarily at entertaining the reader, was to be had in magazines like Becker's *Erholungen* and in *Straußfedern*, a collection of tales and anecdotes edited first by Musäus, then J. G. Müller, and later Tieck.

Only the more widely read newspapers and journals were printed in editions of over 1,000 copies. The first edition of Wieland's *Teutscher Merkur* in 1773 sold in 2,500 copies, a glorious success in those days, but between 1774 and 1798 sales decreased from 2,000 to 800 copies per edition. R. Z. Becker said himself that his weekly newspaper, *Die Nationalzeitung der Deutschen* (1784–1830), was worth 100,000 francs to him and brought him an annual income of 4,000 to 5,000 francs; editions of this newspaper were between 3,000 and 4,000 copies. Further examples of the size of the editions enjoyed by the most popular journals are: Schlözer's *Staatsanzeigen* 3,000 to 4,000 copies; Archenholz's monthly historical and political magazine *Minerva* sold in editions of 3,000 to 5,000; the *Wöchentliche Ostfriesische Anzeigen und Nachrichten* printed over 1,500 copies per edition in 1800; the *Berliner Intelligenzblatt*, 2,000 copies per edition in the nineties; the *Hamburgische Adreß-Comptoir*, 2,500 to 3,000 copies per edition; the *Erlanger Realzeitung*, 4,000 to 5,000 copies per edition; away above the rest stood the *Hamburgische Correspondent* which, at the turn of the century, had a circulation of 28,000 to 30,000.[70]

The journalistic literature, particularly the literary journals with their reviews of contemporary literature, played a big part in creating a literary-minded audience amongst the better-educated members of the reading public. With their letters, essays, and fragments on literary matters these journals helped to free criticism from the restraints of the moral periodicals. The main objectives of the new type of criticism seem indeed to have been to take literature away from the over-moral, over-academic atmosphere, in which in Germany it had lived for so long, and to give it that connection with real life so important for its development.[71]

Literary criticism is, then, still in its beginnings in our period, and one of the most important factors affecting its development was the great change which had occurred in the writer's conception of his public during the previous four or five decades. Throughout the age of scholarly-courtly poetry Ziegler's image of his public had kept its validity: 'Endlich erkühnet sich meine *Asiatische Banise* . . . sich auf dem schauplatz der schrifft-ekeln welt vorzustellen.'[72] and, 'Da die super-kluge Welt Schritt und Blick ihres öfters untadelhafften Nächstens auffs schimpflichste durch-zeucht . . . Wievielmehr hat sich der zu befürchten welcher sich der gantzen Welt durch die Feder auff einem Theatro vorstellig machet.'[73] The public is seen as a theatre audience who show either pleasure or displeasure at a piece without criticizing in any detail. There is no sign of the writer having any trust in the competence of his public or audience to form an opinion. Gradually, however, the new spirit of criticism of the Rationalistic age began to show itself in the literary sphere, the writer of the 1730s and 1740s saw his public as an unbiased court of law: 'Man muß dir . . . von gegenwärtigen Blättern

Rechenschaft geben, vernünftiger Leser! Ich weise mich dir, als einem Richter, vor dem ich mich verantworten soll, dessen Urtheil ich jedoch . . . mich gerne unterwerffe.'[74] Writers now began to look to criticism for help and guidance in their work, and though admittedly it was the experts who were at first asked for suggestions, there appeared in time a new confidence in the whole reading public, in the whole firm community of the educated classes of the towns, where both expert and amateur reader were to be found—and to help set the foundations on which the reader could base his criticism writers now began to use the preface to give a short historical and literary introduction to the work with a special mention of its predecessors in material or in genre. Most typical of the new attitude is the crystal-clear, unadorned style of Gellert in the introductory remarks to his works, most of which were directed to the middle and lower classes. In the Preface to his *Geistliche Oden und Lieder* (1757), for example, he quotes a few lines of a hymn and then asks in friendly schoolmasterish manner: 'And why is this passage so beautiful?'

By about the 1770s the next stage of development had been reached. The reading public had by that time served its period of literary apprenticeship and now emerged as the new and all-powerful master of the writer, and their advocate, their 'mouthpiece', representing their rights and putting forward their claims for an art based on the realities of life, was the literary critic. E. T. A. Hoffmann's reply to the offer of a job as critic for a journal illustrates the relationship: 'Insofern ich mich selbst in jenem Aufsatz berühre, werde ich mich treu und gewissenhaft an das Urteil des Publikums halten und so mir selbst nur das Organ der öffentlichen Meinung sein.'[75] Critics were in close contact with the educated reading public, and when they continually praise a writer we may be sure that he is popular at least with a large section of the public; the same cannot be said, for example, about the end of the nineteenth century when critics took on the role of high priests in the service of an art which revealed itself only to themselves and to poets—this is seen especially in the theatre criticism of that time when critics write with contempt: 'Das Stück hatte einen Publikumserfolg' ('The piece was a box-office success') or 'äußeren Erfolg' ('superficial success'), an attitude which led eventually to the Nietzsche paradox: 'Sie klatschen Beifall, welchen Unsinn habe ich gesagt?'[76]

During our period it was more a case of public and critics versus writers. The battle went on unceasingly; in the writer's eye, the critic was out to condemn and destroy everything he possibly could. The case of the writers could not perhaps be put more poignantly than does Lichtenberg: 'Wenn ein Buch und ein Kopf zusammenstoßen und es klingt hohl, ist das allemal im Buch.'[77] The critics, of course, had their answers: 'Die schlechten Schriftsteller (ihre Zahl ist Legion) sollten am wenigsten gegen die *Allgemeine Deutsche Bibliothek* schreyen. Sie erhalten dadurch doch eine Art von Unsterblichkeit, die ihnen ihre Werke nicht geben konnten.'[78]

In any case it was by now clear to those writers who wished to earn their bread by their pens that they must fall into line with the demands of the wider reading public. When writers had depended on aristocratic patrons for their living, the verdict of the greater public had carried no weight, but now this verdict, spoken by the literary critics on behalf of the public, was all-important. Lichtenberg puts it thus: 'Ich sehe die Rezension als eine Art von Kinderkrankheit an, die die neugeborenen Bücher mehr oder weniger befällt . . . man hat häufig versucht, ihnen durch Amulette von Vorrede und Dedikation vorzubeugen oder sie gar durch eigene Urteile zu inokulieren; es hilft aber nicht immer.'[79]

Writers were obliged to recognize their master in the wider reading public. It was now possible, however, to earn a comfortable living by serving this master well. The profession of letters was at last established in Germany.

By the end of the eighteenth century Germany was in this respect in a situation comparable to that of England as described by Goldsmith in 1760: 'At present, the few poets of England no longer depend on the great for subsistence; they have now no other patrons but the public, and the public, collectively considered, is a good and generous master.'[80] The first German poet who regarded his writing as a serious and all-absorbing calling was Klopstock but he was not in the strictest sense a professional writer, for he still required a patron, and found one in the King of Denmark. From 1750 onwards, however, the number of writers who supported themselves at least for lengthy periods solely by their pens increased; Lessing, Wieland, and Knigge were amongst the first to do this.

The possibility of earning a living by writing obviously depended in the first instance on the existence of a public willing and able to buy books. Such a public did, as we have seen, exist in Germany in the second half of the century; after 1770 references in contemporary newspapers to the *leselustige Publikum* ('public of avid readers') are innumerable, the phrase being applied most often to the novel-reading public. In 1774 Nicolai's Magister in *Sebaldus Nothanker* could, then, speak of writing as a full-time and often most profitable profession, 'just like wallpaper designers and guild pipers';[81] he sees authors as human factories turning out mass-produced goods for the Leipzig book fair. As in every other trade, so do we find bargaining here, too; the author wants as much money for as few pages as possible whilst the publisher wants to buy as much manuscript as cheaply as possible which he will sell again as dearly as possible. Like any other 'factory owner', the publisher also has frequent conferences with his workers, the authors, when he tells them exactly what he wants: stories, novels, murder mysteries, ghost thrillers, accurate reports on things the poor authors have never seen, irrefutable proofs of things they do not believe, and thoughts on things they do not understand. The authors are then left to it, and it is the fastest writer, not the best, who earns the most. The publisher with the worst books is, after all, always best off at the fair; when products are exchanged (as they still were at this time) he is bound to get something better than his own goods, and the one who finally does get the 'bad eggs' can always find a ready public amongst his book-hungry customers.

Again, the parallel to circumstances in England twenty years previously is striking; Fielding's friend and collaborator, James Ralph, writes in *The Case of Authors* (1758):

Book-making is the manufacture the bookseller must thrive by: The Rules of Trade oblige him to buy as cheap and sell as dear as possible . . . knowing best what Assortment of Wares will best suit the Market, he gives out his Orders accordingly; and is as absolute in prescribing the Time of Publication, as in proportioning the Pay.

This will account in a good Degree for the Paroxysms of the press: The sagacious Bookseller feels the Pulse of the Times, and according to the stroke, prescribes not to cure, but to flatter the Disease: As long as the Patient continues to swallow, he continues to administer; and on the first Symptom of a Nausea, he changes the Dose. Hence the Cessation of all Political Carminatives, and the Introduction of Cantharides, in the shape of Tales, Novels, Romances, etc.[82]

With such a great demand for their wares it is not surprising that publishers made the most of translations and translators as an easy and less expensive way of meeting part of this demand. For translations publishers need pay no author's honorarium, merely a translator's fee. The Leipzig book-catalogues offered more than a fair proportion of translations during this period and not all translations proclaimed their true origin in this official publication. Goldfriedrich gives the following figures:[83]

	1765		1775		1785		1795		1805	
Percentage of translations from *living languages* in total book production	8·4%		9·4%		7·9%		5·4%		3%	
Total no. of translations from French and English	Fr.	Eng.	Fr.	Eng.	Fr.	Eng.	Fr.	Eng.	Fr.	Eng.
	31	23	59	41	70	38	..	..	46	36
No. of novels translated from French and English	5	3	7	10	7	6	..	..	9	5

He also reminds us that not all translations are named as such in the Leipzig catalogues but suggests that this could make little difference to the over-all picture. The figures arrived at by Jentzsch after his detailed analysis of three Easter fair catalogues and consultation of other sources would seem, generally speaking, to confirm this; there is, however, quite a large discrepancy in the figures for narrative literature towards the end of the century:

		1740	1770	1800
Percentage of translations from *all* languages		10·48%	14·68 %	9·48 %
Narrative literature	Total no.	20	46	300
	Translations	10 { 8 Fr. / 2 Eng.	16 { 8 Fr. / 5 Eng.	52 { 27 Fr. / 18 Eng.

Nicolai's Magister, in his discussion of the German book trade, tells us that translators were given a fixed time-limit in which to do their work, especially if it was a French work being translated since these were the most common and most marketable of all. There were different ranks in the army of translators; the English expert was superior to the French because he was rarer. The Italian had to be asked very nicely and he did not always accept the imposition of a time-limit; Spanish translators were indeed rare and thus many Spanish works had to be translated by people who did not know the language. There was no shortage of Latin and Greek translators but they were no longer needed so often.

The publisher who needed only a few more works to make up his quota for the Leipzig fair simply looked for foreign works whose titles he liked and parcelled these out to his regular translators. For theological works he required a well-known scholar to put his name to the preface as translator; any mistakes in the translation would then be ignored. Nobles were usually sought to vouch for travel books and historical works, but with novels it was different; here the translator must be really good 'denn diese Bücher kommen allzuvielen Lesern in die Hände, und die Kunstrichter sind hier gleich bey der Hand, und lassen sich selten durch einen berühmten Namen von Tadel abschrecken'.[84]

The number of writers engaged in turning out the mass of printed matter required by the reading public was, of course, large and becoming larger with every year. Lichtenberg writes in 1777 on this subject: 'Es ist zuverlässig in Deutschland mehr Schriftsteller als alle vier Weltteile überhaupt zu ihrer Wohlfahrt nötig haben';[85] Goethe waxes more poetic: 'Alles schreibt, es schreibt der Knabe, der Greis, die Matrone. / Götter erschafft ein Geschlecht, welchem das schreibende schreibt.'[86]

Working on the basis of various contemporary estimates of the number of living German writers, Goldfriedrich states that at the beginning of the period of Storm and Stress (1773) Germany had 3,000 writers.[87] Twelve years later the editor of *Das gelehrte Teutschland* (1785) estimated 'daß das deutsche Schriftstellerheer auf 5,500 Mann stark sey'.[88] These figures by no means include all the writers active in Germany but only those who had been named publicly; similarly the 3,000 items listed in the 1790 catalogues give no complete picture of their prolific output. The *Allgemeine Deutsche Bibliothek*, for example, counted as one item but writers worked in their hundreds on this one item, and this was just one of the mass of such periodicals appearing in Germany at this time. The spectacular increase in the number of men striving to satisfy the voracious appetite of the German reading public during the last three decades of the century is evident from the following estimates of J. G. Meusel: in 1771 Germany had over 3,000 writers; in 1776 over 4,300; in 1784 over 5,200; in 1791 over 7,000; in 1795 over 8,000; at the end of the century no fewer than 10,648 Germans could lay some sort of claim to the designation *Schriftsteller* ('writer'), 267 of them being engaged in the production of novels.[89] James Lackington, the London bookseller, was very impressed by, and also, it will be noted, well informed on, the size of this 'army of writers' in Germany; after remarking on how, in England, the introduction of 'romances, stories, poems etc. into [Sunday] schools has been a very great means of diffusing a general taste for reading among all ranks of people', he continues: 'I am also informed that literature is making a still more rapid progress in Germany, and that there are at this time [1791] seven thousand living authors in that country, and that every body reads.'[90]

About the year 1790 there was in Germany one writer to every 4,000 of the population; the proportion varied, of course, in different localities. The Electorate of Saxony was away above the average with a ratio of 1:2,714 in 1780; the most literary-minded towns in the Electorate were Leipzig (133 writers), Dresden (77), Wittenberg (33), and Bautzen (21), the town of Borna (near Leipzig) earning a special mention in those days by having no writers at all.[91] In the Prussian lands the ratio was 1:5,382, varying as follows for the different districts:

Minden, Ravensberg, Lingen, Tecklenburg	1:14,214
Pomerania, Lauenburg	1: 9,893
East Prussia	1: 9,400
East Friesland	1: 9,272
Silesia	1: 7,842
Brandenburg	1: 2,933
Halberstadt, Hohenstein, Quedlinburg	1: 2,699
Magdeburg, Mansfeld	1: 2,060

The most active towns in literary Germany were Göttingen; and Leipzig about 1790 Göttingen had a population of 8,000 with 79 writers (1:100), and Leipzig had 170 writers in a population of 29,000 (1:170). Berlin, with a population of 150,000 had a total of 222 writers (1:675). Most of the literary activity of Austria was concentrated in Vienna; of the 615 German writers in the Austrian Empire (1:15,000 Germans), no less than 304 lived in the capital with a population of 254,000 (1:800).

During the first half of the eighteenth century authors were, as we have seen, very poorly paid for their work;[92] most of them regarded writing merely as a secondary source of income. With the growth of the reading habit, however, they began to see the financial possibilities of their work; at any rate publishers seemed to be making a comfortable living from their business. Some writers tried to cut out these 'middlemen' by means of self-publication and subscription publication (phenomena which are in themselves indicative of the increased interest in reading and in the world of books) but these proved to be no satisfactory solution to the situation.[93] The fight for higher fees had started.

We may take Gellert's relations with his publisher Wendler as characteristic of the early years when publishers had certainly realized the commercial possibilities of popular writing but authors were as yet unaware of, or chose to ignore, the financial benefits to be had from their literary activity.[94] In his *Fabeln* Gellert created what was perhaps the most popular book of the eighteenth century and for it he received from Wendler 1 Thaler 8 Groschen per sheet—a total of only 20 Thaler 16 Groschen (about £3·15). Gellert was content to sit back in the moderate comfort of his professorship, secure in the thought that he had at least tried to do his share of enlightening. Wendler, on the other hand, became a rich man through this one book; from the profits he was able to set aside a fund of 10,000 Thaler (about £1,500) for three scholarships, found the Wendlersche Freischule for poor children and six *Konvikt-Freistellen* for young men of Nuremberg studying at Leipzig University. Gellert received only 45 Thaler (about £6·30) for his *Lehrgedichte* of which Wendler immediately issued an edition of 6,000 copies at 6 Groschen (4p) a copy, and so could expect gross takings of 1,500 Thaler (about £225) from this one edition. When the Weidmann publishing house bought the stock and copyright of Gellert's works in 1787 it cost them 10,000 Thaler (about £1,500). Gellert's was the classic example used by all authors to put their case against the publishers.

As the century proceeded conditions improved for the writers, particularly in north Germany where the Leipzig publishers, led by Reich, started to introduce higher honoraria. In the period 1749 to 1773 Klopstock's fee for his *Messias* rose from 3 to 12 Thaler (45p to £1·80) a sheet. Even authors of the middling sort were being paid 5 to 6 Thaler (75p to 90p) a sheet by Reich in the seventies, the better writers receiving as much as 12 Thaler (£1·80). Thümmel, for his popular ten-volumed novel *Reise in die mittäglichen Provinzen von Frankreich* (1791), received from Göschen the handsome sum of 5,000 Thaler (about £750). Translators were now paid 2 Thaler (30p) a sheet and in exceptional cases even more; Bode, for example, received 5 Thaler (75p) a sheet for his *Landprediger* (*Vicar of Wakefield*), and Reinhold Forster was paid 7 Thaler (£1·05) a sheet for *Cooks Reisen* (*Cook's Voyages*).

Wieland's career illustrates most clearly both the improvement in conditions for authors and the lead which Leipzig was giving the German book trade. In Zürich Wieland was paid 3 Thaler 8 Groschen (45p) a sheet for his *Komische Erzählungen,* 5 Thaler (75p) a sheet for *Agathon*, and 1 Thaler 8 Groschen (15p) a sheet for his *Poetische Schriften*. On moving to north Germany, however, Wieland commanded fees ranging from 8 to as much as 16 Thaler (£2·40) a sheet from Reich for his extremely verbose later works, such as *Sokrates* and *Lucian*. In all, Wieland received from Reich the sum of 6,700 Thaler (£1,000), enough to keep him and his family in moderate comfort for ten years.[95]

When fees began to rise so also did the number of writers, the number of books and, naturally, the number of bad books, all of which was seen by the older generation of scholarly writers as the result of 'the selling of scholarship', the outcome of the new fashion, 'sich isoliert hinzusetzen, und schriftstellerisch zu faullenzen, höchstens nebenher etwas unmittelbar für den Staat zu thun'.[96] Writing was now a main source of income and some other job provided a secondary source;[97] the situation during the seventeenth century had been completely reversed. Writers were, however, not yet satisfied; now moderately well off, they pointed to the rich publishers, and this was the case not only in Germany but in most European lands: 'Der Dichter säet und pflanzt, / Der Drucker meiht und pflückt' (*Lob der Geldsucht*—Goethe?) ('The poet sows and plants, / The printer reaps and picks'); 'Les libraires et les acteurs sont les créatures des Auteurs, et ces créatures traitent fort mal leurs créateurs' (Voltaire) ('Booksellers and actors are the creatures of authors, and these creatures abuse their creators most grievously'); 'What authors lose, their booksellers have won, / so pimps grow rich, when lovers are undone' (Pope).

4

REPERCUSSIONS ON THE GERMAN
BOOK TRADE

THE growth in the reading habit and the increased demand for works of light entertainment, particularly novels, were not without their effects on the organization of the German book trade, for obviously that trade had always depended to a great extent on the nature and size of the reading public and on the intensity of its response to events in the general cultural and specifically literary sphere. Thus we might expect that the history of the German book trade and the history of German literature are contiguous at important or crucial points, and this is indeed the case.

The history of the German book trade falls, broadly speaking, into three main periods: the first, lasting until about mid sixteenth century, was characterized by the printer-cum-publisher, by cash trading, and by the travelling book-pedlar; the second, covering the years from the mid sixteenth to about the mid eighteenth centuries, saw the predominance of the publisher-cum-bookseller, with trade being conducted on an exchange basis and entirely dependent on the dealers' personal attendance at the book fairs; the third and last period, during which the modern organization of the German book trade was evolved, began in the second half of the eighteenth century and had as its characteristic features the gradual separation of the publishing and selling sides of the business, the introduction of 'on sale or return' trading, and the appointment of publishers' agents at Leipzig to carry on business the whole year round and not just at the Michaelmas and Easter book fairs. It will be seen that these three periods coincide, in the cultural and literary sphere, with the rise of Humanism, the post-Reformation period, and the Classical Age of German literature with its more widespread interest in, and demand for, books in general and works of imaginative literature in particular. But the increased impetus behind German literary life in the last three decades of the eighteenth century led not only to major reforms in the organization of the book trade; it also ushered in a period of general upheaval in that trade—what might be termed the book trade's own period of *Sturm und Drang*—and three important facets of these boisterous years were the increased activity of pirate publishers, an attempt to enforce a more stringent censorship, and finally the establishment of lending libraries.

Author and publisher might frequently disagree on the question of fees, but in one thing they were unanimous—their condemnation of the literary pirate, for the lack of adequate copyright protection for literary property robbed both of their rightful profits. In England a copyright act had been passed by Parliament on the petition of the booksellers as early as 1710 but in Germany the lack of political unity and effective central control meant that the publishing trade, though representing one language, literature, and people, was still carried on under exclusive regulations in every individual state. As long as the demand for books had not been great, the involved system of imperial, territorial, or municipal 'privileges', whereby each separate state and large town could grant a particular book a limited copyright, had worked not too badly but as soon as it became evident that literary piracy was a most profitable business the whole complicated procedure proved totally inadequate. There was, then, no general copyright and, still worse, the practice of reprinting without acknowledgement a work which had been published in another state was not only officially tolerated in some states but even actively encouraged as a 'legitimate' source of income. Such was the case in Baden and in Vienna, for example; the Viennese censorship indeed was not even averse to pirate editions of otherwise forbidden books as long as they were 'local products' which thus brought more profits to the capital, and as long as their office was not compromised—the official formula in the 1790s for such cases was: 'admittitur absque loco impressionis.'[1]

Typical of the legislation in matters of copyright is the Würzburg decree of 1792 which declared that literary piracy was allowed 'only under one of the following circumstances': (1) if the authorized edition was too expensive and the pirate edition would be cheaper, or (2) as an act of reparation, or (3) if the book concerned would be 'gemeinnützig und wenigstens für die niedere Volksklasse besonders nützlich'.[2] It was a poor pirate indeed who could not legalize his action in Würzburg.

The bookseller Perthes points out the unfairness of piracy to honest publishers and authors; if a publisher thinks ('know he cannot') a book will be well received he accepts it from the author and publishes it, and when he is mistaken he is left with a loss and unsold copies of the book; this happens several times and then perhaps with the sixth attempt he picks a winner and makes some profit. Then along comes the pirate who pounces at once upon the popular work and prints a new edition at a cheaper price, which he can afford to do as he has neither previous losses to cover nor author to pay. The original publisher is left with half an edition on his shelves and is afraid to venture on anything else.[3]

The usual defences put forward by pirates were: (1) the practice was forbidden by neither civil nor ecclesiastical law, (2) its suppression would lead to book monopolies, (3) the very existence of *Privilegien* proved that pirating in itself was not wrong, (4) it made for cheaper prices, and (5) it was the real servant of the *bonum publicum*. An example of the application of this last 'defence' are the following words from the pirate publisher of *Erzählungen und Geschichten* by Karl von Ekartshausen: 'Die unverkennbare Herzensgüte des Verfassers und dessen aus jeder Zeile seiner Werke hervorleuchtender Wunsch, alle Menschen so viel möglich beglückt zu sehen, lassen mich hoffen, daß er selbst mein Unternehmen nichts weniger, als mißbilligen, sondern vielmehr seiner eigenen Absicht gemäß finden werde.'[4] The reviewer quotes this passage but refuses to review the work, which had been put together by the pirate from Ekartshausen's weekly contributions.

All five defences quoted above were put forward (and at once refuted) as early as 1732 in *Charlatanerie der Buchhandlung*; but it was not until the second half of the century, with the increase in the reading habit, that pirating really became a menace to the trade.

The publishers of Holland and Switzerland were amongst the first in the field but it was Austria, geographically remote, commercially isolated, and intellectually backward, which eventually became the centre of the piratical activity; and pirates found a leader in the Austrian publisher, printer, and bookseller Johann Thomas von Trattner (1717–98) who was supported in all his undertakings by the Imperial Court of Maria Theresa and Joseph II. The (by now) ridiculous system of 'privileges' let its last mask fall when imperial privileges were no longer respected in the Habsburg capital itself. The leader of the legitimate book trade, Philipp Erasmus Reich (1717–87) of the famous Weidmannsche Buchhandlung, writes in 1764: 'Gegen den nun von Kaiserl. Maj. Baronisirten Buchhändler Trattner schüzet kein Privilegium mehr! Von den Geldern des Hofes unterstüzet, überschwemmt er ganz Deutschland und scheuet sich nicht, in unserem eigenen Lande den Meister zu spielen....'⁵ Reich tried to form a protective association of dealers and he found support in most of the large towns, particularly in north and central Germany but also in Nuremberg, Munich, and Ulm too, but at their first meeting in 1765 a note from Trattner offered them—all in unauthorized editions —the complete works of Gellert, Geßner, Hagedorn, Ewald von Kleist, Klopstock, Zachariä, Haller's poems, and Rabener's satires, so much did he fear their action! Trattner even sent his publications to the Leipzig book fair and dealers, including those in the association, could not resist his cheaper prices. Nicolai, it would seem, had known what would happen for he had refused to join Reich's group because, as he said, it was his wont to keep any promises he made.

The whole of south and south-west Germany now fell prey to the pirate publishers. With the fall of the Frankfurt fair (1750) the book-dealers in this area felt themselves isolated; the journey to Leipzig was both too inconvenient and too costly for them—to travel from Munich to Leipzig in the eighteenth century involved a journey of at least four days. When Perthes, writing of the 1780s, speaks of Frankfurt in the west and Nuremberg in the south as being the last 'literary outposts' maintaining their connection with Leipzig, he is no doubt exaggerating a little, for other contemporaries tell us that dealers in Augsburg, Ulm, Regensburg, Stuttgart, Mannheim, and Karlsruhe, for example, still concentrated their trade on the Leipzig organization; nevertheless, there is plenty of evidence to prove that after 1750 very many book-dealers in

the south and south-west either could not or would not travel
to the Leipzig fairs.[6]

Yet the public in this area still demanded reading matter,
even if this too, like the book trade itself, was becoming more
north German in character. With Leipzig so far away, and
with trade there now being conducted more and more on a
cash basis, such towns as Nördlingen, Ansbach, Tübingen, Reutlingen, Worms, Speyer, Erlangen, Bamberg, etc., took up the
challenge issued by the Leipzig dealers and chose pirating as
their chief weapon. They saw it as their only means of salvation
against the book monopolies and cash deals, with the resultant
higher prices, of the Leipzig dealers. The pirate publishers
even tried organizing their own book fair in Hanau from 1775
to 1777 but it was not a success—neither, however, was it
a necessity. In reality the whole of south Germany was their
book fair; contemporaries even asserted that more pirate
editions were bought in Austria, Bavaria, Franconia, Swabia,
and Switzerland than authorized editions in the rest of
Germany.[7]

There was very little that authors and publishers could do to
right this situation without an effective and universally recognized central authority to back them up. Some authors tried
publication by private subscription, but this did not deter the
pirates. Lessing was faced with the problem when a Leipzig
pirate, masquerading under the name of 'Dodsley und Com-
pagnie', started to print unauthorized editions of his *Hamburgische Dramaturgie*; Lessing stopped the twice-weekly publication
of the individual sections and tried issuing the work in volumes
at irregular intervals but the pirate edition still appeared. All
Lessing could do was to appeal to the public to buy only the
Bode edition. Not until the very end of the eighteenth century
do we see any sign of government intervention on behalf of
writers and legitimate publishers. The lead came from Prussia
in 1794 but clearly it required not one but all the leading German states to participate before effective protection and control
could be guaranteed, and it was well into the nineteenth century
before this was achieved. The first work granted full copyright,
recognized throughout all Germany, was Cotta's definitive
edition of Goethe's works in forty volumes (1827–30). Until then
the only counter-measure available to publishers was to issue

special cheap editions in the almost forlorn hope of underselling the pirates.

In this connection, there is no doubt that the pirate publishers did a lot to make reading a cheaper and therefore more general pastime. Even some writers admitted this; the north German Knigge saw in literary piracy the means of educating and entertaining the whole nation, all humanity, and, he continues, 'wahrlich in einer Wagschale, worin dieser Preis liegt, spielt ein Louisdor eine demüthigende Figur'.[8] In the same vein we hear from the pirate publisher Beecke of Mannheim: 'Denken Sie sich einmal den Nutzen, der in Deutschland entsteht, wenn die besten Schriftsteller künftig nicht nur in den Bibliotheken der Reichen, die sie mehrentheils nicht lesen, zum (sic) Pracht da stehen, sondern in den Häusern der Bürger, in den Händen eines jeden seyn werden!'[9] More will be said later on the subject of book prices[10] but it is important in the present context to note that, according to Goldfriedrich,[11] whereas prices in the legitimate book trade had increased fourfold in the course of the second half of the eighteenth century, pirates (paying no authors' fees, printing only proven works, and quite often using the cheapest paper) were able to maintain throughout the whole period the same low prices that had prevailed in the days of Gellert—prices that must have been tempting to even the most honest of men.

Besides making for cheaper books, literary piracy helped in enlarging the reading public in another way. In 1773 the sale and distribution of unauthorized editions at the Leipzig book fair was forbidden, and so pirates had to find a new means of getting their books to the public. This they did by using travelling salesmen and door-to-door pedlars, who visited small towns and villages where books had once been a rarity and made regular customers of the inhabitants, and, in many cases, local agents of the country preachers and teachers; a contemporary observer writes in 1795:

Dies gelang ihm [dem Hausierer] bekanntlich nur zu gut; und so drangen die Nachdrucke in wenigen Jahren bis in die entferntesten Winkel aller Provinzen, wohin nie ein Buchhändler mit aller Mühe gekommen war, und mit dem besten Willen nicht kommen konnte. Der wohlfeile Preiß, und die Auswahl der besten Bücher, lockten die Liebhaber herbey, und Mancher dem es sonst in seinem ganzen

Leben nicht eingefallen seyn würde, ein Buch zu kaufen, schafte sich nach und nach eine kleine Sammlung an.[12]

From the cultural point of view, however, the pirating of books had one big disadvantage; only books sure to enjoy good sales were printed. Formerly, honest publishers had used the surplus from popular works to finance the publication of important learned works, but now they could not afford it. The bookseller Ganz puts it thus: 'Was am leichtesten abgefaßt, was am geschwindesten abgesetzt, wobey der geringste Verlust ist— das müssen Schriftsteller schreiben, und Buchhändler verlegen, so lange die Pest des Nachdrucks fort dauert.'[13] We get some idea of the general standard of the pirate's stocks when we hear that Trattner, on submitting to Joseph II a 'draft plan for the dissemination of reading material throughout the Imperial lands', had *not* included the following in his suggested list of 'victims': Bürger, Gellert, Gleim, Goethe, Hagedorn, Haller, Hölty, Jacobi, Ewald von Kleist, Klopstock, Lessing, Nicolai, Rabener, Schlegel, Stolberg, Uz, Voß, Weiße, Wieland, and Zachariä.[14] In conclusion it may be noted that, in face of the uncertainty surrounding the term *Auflage* (edition) in the eighteenth century, the activity of the pirate publishers is one of the few sure means we have today of learning the most popular books of that period; Jean Paul puts it thus: 'Ein elender Ladenhüter wird so wenig auf einem Nachdruckerlager angetroffen, als unter den von Eichhörnchen gestohlenen Nüssen eine hohle.'[15]

Another foe of the book trade—one which had threatened the trade since its beginnings but never with such rigour as in our present period when reading became so widespread a pastime— was censorship.[16] Originally a privilege of the Church, the right of censorship had by the eighteenth century passed mainly into the hands of each individual state and town; in some districts it was practised by both state and Church simultaneously. Once more the political condition of the Holy Roman Empire, that complex patchwork of independent and semi-independent territories, made matters even more involved; enmity and rivalry between rulers, lack of uniformity, and lack of effective central control meant that works were frequently forbidden in one state, yet allowed in the neighbouring ones. Where a book was to appear could therefore be a matter of some concern to an author; thus do we find Schiller, for example, requesting Göschen to have his *Geisterseher* printed not in Leipzig, where Schiller had found the censorship particularly restrictive in certain points, but in Rudolstadt, Jena, or Weimar.[17] The strictness of the censorship, in fact, varied according to the state concerned, the political situation at any given time, and also the attitude of the person heading the censorship committee; it was most severe in Austria and south Germany, where both State and Church united in the banning of Protestant works.

Censorship in Austria had been exclusively in the hands of the Jesuits until 1753 in which year it was made the responsibility of a secular authority, the Wiener Zensurhofkommission; the rulings of this commission were published in various editions of the *Catalogus librorum prohibitorum* together with frequent supplements during the period 1754 to 1780. The 1765 catalogue provides a fair indication of the nature and scope of its work; the catalogue comprises 184 pages printed in small octavo and lists about 3,000 books considered unsuitable for the Austrian reading public. Amongst the authors of proscribed political, philosophical, and theological works we find: Basedow, Bayle, Böhme, Frederick the Great, Helvetius, Hobbes, Hume, Lavater, Locke, Mosheim, Samuel von Pufendorf, Rousseau, Spener, Christian Thomasius, Voltaire—but also Cardinal de Bernis, Bossuet, Pater Martin Cochem, and Thomas à Kempis. The more piquant works of world literature are, of course, well represented: Boccaccio, Brantôme, Crébillon, Grécourt, Rabelais, and Sansovino. Of English authors the works of Fielding, Sterne's *Tristram Shandy*, and Swift's *Tale of a Tub* are forbidden. And finally, amongst the German works banned are, for example: Grimmelshausen's *Simplicissimus* and *Vogelnest*; three volumes of Lessing's works; one volume of Gottsched's poems; Haller's *Kleine Schriften*; *Philander von Sittewalds Gesichte* (Moscherosch); Gryphius's *Säugamme oder das untreue Gesind*; Reuter's *Schelmuffsky*; Zachariä's *Schöpfung der Hölle*; Lohenstein's *Agrippina*; and also numerous 'Robinsonades' and many of the popular chap-books, including Gottsched's edition of *Reineke Fuchs*.

By the late 1770s, of course, the list had lengthened considerably and now included, amongst others, works by Abbt, Goethe, Jacobi, Leisewitz, Mendelssohn, Nicolai, Wieland, and Voß.

But perhaps even more deplorable than the actual banning of such authors was the way they were lumped together in these catalogues with the absolute dregs of the writing profession, for the vast majority of the items listed here consists of books of the most worthless kind, fiction of the lowest type—the *Amours, Amusements, Deliciae, Facetien, Galanterien, Mémoires,* and similar products. With the accession of Joseph II in 1780 there came some improvement; most of the better German authors were removed from the catalogue and a further concession came in the introduction of four exceptional categories: (1) *Erga schedam* (only with special permission), (2) *Eruditis* (only for scholars), (3) *Acatholicis* (only for non-Catholics), and (4) *Continuantibus* (only for subscribers to longer works); and the publication of the catalogue ceased, the list being kept henceforth in manuscript form by the appropriate authorities. Needless to say, events in France in 1789 led to a further tightening of the political censorship, and not only in Austria but in most of the German states.

In Bavaria in the nineties, for example, anything connected with the French Revolution and 'the rights of man' was banned, even novels that used the Revolution merely as a background to the story, like *Begebenheiten eines Hofmeisters in Paris während der Revolution* (*Adventures of a Court Steward in Paris during the Revolution*). Also forbidden were 'all plays having any bearing on our country's history', all religious works not specifically Catholic, and all the works of Burke, Campe, Erasmus, Frederick the Great, Kant, Kotzebue, Montesquieu, Rousseau, Schiller, Spalding, Spieß, Spinoza, Swift, Voltaire, Weckherlin, Wieland, further the *Allgemeine Deutsche Bibliothek, Deutscher Zuschauer, Berliner Monatsschrift,* Goethe's *Werther,* Musäus's *Volksmärchen, Eulenspiegel,* Klinger's *Faust,* Knigge's *Umgang mit Menschen,* Ovid's *Metamorphoses,* and Virgil's *Aeneid.* The Bavarian catalogues of 1790 to 1793 list a total of 214 items, but it must be remembered that one 'item', either in the catalogue or the subject of a special decree, might cause the proscription of the whole of an author's work or a whole series or group of novels; the three book-dealers of Munich, for example, were forbidden to sell *Liebesromane* (love-stories); similarly, in 1802 an Austrian decree made the selling of *Hexen- und Gespensterromane* (tales of witches and ghost-stories) illegal, whilst a further decree of 1806 added to the proscribed list *Genieromane* (stories of men of genius), *Räuberromane* (robber novels), *Ritterromane* (romances of chivalry) and just to be on the safe side, 'die ganze Gattung, welcher man im verächtlichen Sinne den Namen Roman beilegt'.[18] In Würzburg Nicolai's novel *Sebaldus Nothanker* was forbidden to all except qualified theologians. And so each state went its own separate way, making or marring its own reputation; Trier was regarded as strict, Mainz as relatively slack, Augsburg as reactionary, and Salzburg as tolerant.

The only northern state which approached the severity of Austria and Bavaria in censorship was Prussia under Frederick William II who determined immediately on accession to make up for his great predecessor's laxity 'da ich vernehme, daß die Preßfreiheit in Preßfrechheit ausartet und die Bücher-Censur völlig eingeschlafen ist'.[19] Henceforth, for example, the *Gothaische Gelehrte Zeitung* and the *Allgemeine Literatur-Zeitung* (Jena) were forbidden in the Prussian realm. In general there was considerable freedom in the smaller northern states; a contemporary author writes of the very liberal authorities in Brunswick and Hanover: 'Von Beschränkung der Preßfreiheit, von verbotenen oder konfiszierten Büchern . . . habe ich in den beiden Staaten, so lange ich Mitbürger derselben war und bin, nicht einmal reden hören.'[20] This is not, of course, to be taken literally, but the freedom there is often spoken of by contemporaries.

There were, however, too many small states, political systems, and responsible authorities to make the censorship of writings in eighteenth-century Germany workable and, after all, the only result of banning any work was, as it still is, an increase in its attraction and market-value; the authorities, too, seemed to realize this, for heading almost every list of forbidden books was the *Catalogus librorum prohibitorum* itself, so that, as Nicolai says, 'die schlechten Leute nicht die schlechten und die klugen Leute nicht die klugen Bücher aus demselben kennen lernen'.[21] There were booksellers indeed who dealt only in those books which had been 'recommended' in such catalogues and at least one of them, named Binz, is said to have made a fortune from such wares.[22] Goethe tells us how the public burning of a French novel proved to be excellent publicity for the publisher, everyone wishing to have a copy of such a dangerous work;[23] but the ultimate futility of censorship in eighteenth-century Germany is perhaps best illustrated by the oft-repeated instruction issued to his army of writers by the Gotha publisher, Ettinger: 'Schreiben Sie doch etwas für meinen Verlag, was confiscirt wird.'[24]

One would expect that in view of the increase in the reading habit, the booksellers of Germany would now be enjoying a brisk trade, huge profits, and expressing satisfaction at the new developments in the book-world since mid eighteenth century; but this was not the case. When reading did become a more general pastime, sales, of course, increased but the increase was by no means in proportion to the increase in the reading habit. The pre-1740 reading public had consisted mainly of scholars and these were the best customers of the booksellers; after 1740 every class of society, from the aristocrat to the peasant, was represented in the German reading public but scholars were still the dealers' main customers. A book-dealer writes in 1781:

> Bibeln, Gesangbücher, Calender, und politische Zeitungen abgerechnet, sind ganz gewiß gerade die Gelehrten, ohne allen Vergleich mit den anderen Ständen im Staate, die stärksten Bücherkäufer, und die eigentlichste Stütze alles Buchhandels, ohne deren Kundschaft es um jeden Buchhändler, dem sie fehlt, mißlich steht.[25]

On the other hand, Nicolai's bookseller Hieronymus, when he took Bibles, hymn-books, almanacs, and journals into account could say: 'Meine besten Kunden sind Schulknaben, Handwerksburschen, Bauern, und gute Mütterchen.'[26] It will be noted that the middle-class and better-off lower-class readers, the backbone of the novel-reading public, are both missing from these two statements; they were not good customers of the bookdealers for the simple reason that they had another means of obtaining their reading material—in the newly established reading societies and lending libraries.

The seventeenth century had seen the age of the great private and court libraries, when books were regarded as precious possessions, the pride of their owners, and the objects of respectful, almost childish worship of collectors. Even the external form of books at this time symbolizes their great worth and exclusive nature; most of them were of the unappetizing folio size and of such length and content that we would today certainly be most pleased to leave them on their shelves. There were indeed, even in the seventeenth century, libraries which called themselves public but they were rare, badly stocked, and in reality anything but public. Bremen town library, for example, was from 1660 onwards open to the public only on Wednesdays of every other week ('es wehre denn daß der Bibliothekarius durch Erheblichen verhindert, und es zuvor per scedulam notificirt').[27] In the 1730s Königsberg citizens could read the books in their town library only on Monday afternoons; books could be taken home for eight days but only as a special privilege.

The second half of the eighteenth century saw a few improvements in this state of affairs but facilities for the use of public libraries were nowhere near those of today.[28] The extent to which a library really was public depended all too frequently on the character and opinions of the librarian. Up to the 1740s, for example, the ducal library at Gotha was open five hours daily to the public; in 1746 a new librarian was appointed and thenceforth the public was allowed the use of the library for two hours on only three days a week. Characteristic of these libraries is the following proclamation of the same librarian in the regulations of 1774: 'Wer ein Buch näher ansehen will, muß es sich vom Bibliothekar ausbitten, der es ihm dann vorzeigen, allenfalls auch darin zu lesen verstatten wird.'[29] To such a man books were still things to be admired rather than read.

Conditions were not much better even in university libraries, which were long regarded as for the exclusive use of members of the academic staff who would then, it was argued, pass on all the necessary information to their students.[30] It was considered a great novelty when Göttingen, on its foundation in 1734, opened its library every day for both staff and students—the latter could even borrow books too! Halle, one of the most popular German universities of the eighteenth century, did not even have a building for its library until 1778 (up to then it had been accommodated in a few rooms of the municipal weighhouse); it was open for only four hours weekly, and the same was the case at Leipzig. In Marburg the librarian closed the library for ten consecutive winters so as to spare his health. The four public libraries at Liegnitz regarded their contents as precious exhibits even at the close of the century, and Goethe tells us of the chaos reigning in the Jena library where the location of each book was 'secret information, known exclusively to the library attendants rather than to the higher employees'.[31] But even if these libraries had been more accessible to the public they would have held but little attraction for the average reader in eighteenth-century Germany who wanted light reading for his leisure hours. Up to mid nineteenth century the German public libraries were intended for the most part to serve scholars and research workers, and were used only by learned members of the reading public. The librarian Friedrich Adolf Ebert, writing in 1811, gives the following picture of these libraries: 'Staubigte, öde und unbesuchte Säle, in denen sich der Bibliothekar wöchentlich einige Stunden von Amts wegen aufhalten muß, um diese Zeit über allein zu sein. Nichts unterbricht die tiefe Stille, als hier und da das traurige Nagen eines Bücherwurms.'[32]

Of interest at this point is a reader's letter published in the *Allgemeine Literatur-Zeitung* in 1785 telling of a regimental library founded shortly after the Seven Years War in Insterburg (Prussia) and containing, in addition to military works, a good selection of biographies, travel-descriptions, and 'the most instructive novels' ('especially those of ethical substance'); the letter continues: 'Auch hatten Sr. Excellenz General-Leutnant von Platen für das lesende Publikum der Stadt die Gefälligkeit zu erlauben, daß dasselbe für einen kleinen monatlichen Beytrag, gleichfalls an diesem nützlichen Institute Theil nehmen konnte.' The subsequent developments illustrate not only the increased demand for reading material over the previous twenty years and the difficulty in some regions of obtaining it but also one method of self-help open to readers:

> Es sind aber seit kurzer Zeit die Anzahl der Lesenden in der Stadt sehr angewachsen, und die Herrn Officiere, zu deren besten eigentlich diese Bibliothek errichtet worden, würden nicht immer die verlangten Bücher erhalten können, wenn man den Lesekreis zu sehr erweiterte, daher ist die Stadt seit einigen Jahren vom Antheil an den Büchern des Regiments ausgeschlossen worden, und haben sich in derselben nunmehro viele Einwohner vereiniget, die sich Bücher und Journale verschreiben, wodurch der Geschmack sehr gebildet und die Liebe zur neuesten Literatur vermehrt werden wird.[33]

The good citizens of Insterburg, excluded from the regimental library by official regulations and from any near-by public libraries by their very nature, had in fact formed their own reading society as had many of their countrymen in all parts of Germany. And it was the immense success of these reading societies, together with the newly established lending libraries, that led the book-dealers of the period to complain that sales were not as good as one would expect in such a book-hungry land; books, they complained, were now 'often read but rarely bought'.

The reading societies catered for the better-educated members of the middle class, for teachers, ministers of religion, state and town officials, and the like.[34] The earliest known to us is that founded in Stralsund in 1779 but it is possible that there were earlier ones; in any case, from 1780 onwards they are one of the characteristic symptoms of that age which contemporaries labelled *das papierene Zeitalter* ('the Paper Age'). The high social level of the reading societies becomes clear when we hear that the Mainz society had Hofrat Bentzel as its secretary in the 1780s, in Glückstadt in the same period the society was led by a *Direktor des Intelligenzcomtoirs*, a *Konsistorialrat*, and a *Rektor*, the chairman of the Köthen society in 1800 was the headmaster of the grammar school; most of the members of the Hermannstadt circle were ministers of religion, whilst the chairman of the Mühlbach society was the town preacher and its meeting place the vicarage.

The aim of the reading societies was to give members the opportunity for reading at as small a cost as possible. Reading material was either circulated amongst members or else put at their disposal in a common reading-room, and sometimes a combination of both methods would be used. Books and journals were bought from a common fund and if the society had no standing library, they were usually auctioned to members after all had read them; often, in return for a society's custom, a bookseller would promise to lend out books to its members for a limited period. The societies were as a rule organized to the last detail; the Ulm society had in the nineties a secretary, a librarian, a treasurer, an *Ökonom* (steward or manager), each with an assistant, and finally an auditor. Great pride was taken in being a member of such a literary organization; the patricians of Ulm, for example, tried to exclude the ordinary *Bürger* from their society and when they failed to do this, they themselves stayed away 'to avoid contact with the bourgeois rabble'.[35]

The number of members varied, of course, with each society but the average was comparatively high. Stralsund started with only twenty members, Köthen, however, with seventy, Bernburg with 120, and Frankfurt am Main with 140. Members were found not only in the town concerned but also in the surrounding country areas; of Köthen's seventy members, seventeen lived outside the town.

The reading material, too, varied with the different societies, but popular with all of them were the journals and newspapers of Germany and in some cases of France and England too. Glückstadt and Stralsund are typical of the two main types of reading societies. Glückstadt kept the most important journals and newspapers, books of general interest (geography, history, science, statistics, etc.), pamphlets, and the best almanacs; Stralsund specialized in lighter reading material, novels, dramas, and poems. Larger towns eventually boasted two or more such societies, each with its own speciality; the *Allgemeine Literatur-Zeitung* reports the existence of no less than four in Frankfurt an der Oder in the eighties, each led by an 'expert': one for philosophy, history, and belles-lettres, one for general periodicals, one for theological works and scholarly journals, and the last for 'miscellaneous works'—the expert in the latter field was apparently a book-dealer.[36]

We may say that the reading societies are a proof of the increased desire to read amongst those members of society who had for long formed the backbone of the German reading public—the landowners, professors, teachers, preachers, lawyers, doctors, officials, etc. The founding of lending libraries, however, is a proof of the spreading of the pastime of reading to those classes which had formerly shown little or no interest in books; James Lackington, the first remainder bookseller in England, was one of the very few members of his profession who were willing to recognize and defend this positive aspect of the new establishments which could lead eventually to increased sales: 'The sale of books, so far from being diminished by them, has been greatly promoted, as from these repositories many thousand families have been cheaply supplied with books, by which the taste for reading has become much more general, and thousands are purchased every year, by such as had first borrowed them at those libraries.'[37]

The first German lending library was founded as early as 1704 in Berlin and the second one followed in the same year, but it was not until the second half of the century that they really became common throughout the land.[38] In Leipzig at the end of the sixties the lending library was still looked on as something quite special, yet by the end of the century almost every German town boasted at least one such library; in most cases they were established first as an integral part of a bookshop, just another means of making more money from the stock in hand, and not as a separate library, and it would seem to have been the bookbinders more than anyone else who first saw the financial possibilities behind the new service—the German bookbinder had in fact always been more in touch with the ordinary reader and his tastes than had his colleague, the publisher-cum-dealer. A lending library was founded in Brunswick in 1767, in Hanau in 1774 (a second in 1777), Munich in 1774, Hermannstadt in 1782, Schwäbisch-Hall in 1784 (a second in 1792), Gießen in 1785, Solothurn in 1788, Stuttgart in 1791, Bamberg in 1795, Breslau in 1800, etc. Hanover had four lending libraries of considerable size, but the largest were probably the three in Dresden with 8,000, 18,000, and 30,000 volumes. For comparison, a few dates from contemporary Britain may be given: Edinburgh 1725, Bristol 1728, Bath 1735, London 1740, Cambridge 1745, Newcastle upon Tyne 1746, Birmingham 1751, Manchester 1757, Liverpool 1758, Rochdale 1770, and Exeter 1780.[39]

Before starting a lending library permission had, in the interest of the nation's morals, first to be obtained from the local town-council, who were in many cases not slow in pointing out the damaging effect the modern craze for reading, especially for reading novels, could have on the nation's well-being. We may be sure that the town-council of Oschatz (near Leipzig) were thinking mainly of the many and widely popular lower types of fiction when they refused a printer's request for permission to open a lending library; they would wish rather: 'daß das hiesige, und benachbarte hohe Publicum auf dem Lande, bis zur niedrigsten Volks Classe, seine Berufs Arbeit und höhern

Pflichten der Lesesucht und dem Gängel Bande einer modernen und, größten Theils, ganz zwecklosen, Zeit und Charakter verderblichen, Lectüre nicht länger aufopfern möchte.'[40] Permission was granted in Amberg (Bavaria) in 1800 only on condition 'that diversion be offered only in the form of useful and instructive books . . . and that particular care be exercised when issuing books to young persons and students'.[41]

Lending libraries were opened even in the smaller towns, since they made no great demands on either the energy or the purse of the owner. One enterprising Leipzig book-dealer (Sommer) started to sell libraries of 330 and 504 volumes for 77 and 137 Thaler respectively (£11·55 and £20·55)—the shop price was 253 and 407 Thaler (£38 and £61)—for anyone wishing to start a lending library; he thought it a pity that some members of the public had to go as far as twenty miles to the nearest lending library and, he assures us, there is scarcely a more profitable investment for our money. So encouraging was the response to his offer that he later extended his invitation to cover even smaller libraries at 25 and 50 Thaler (£3·75 to £7·50).

As to the type of book which was most popular in these libraries, a Berlin critic writes in 1780 of one of them: 'Nützliche Bücher sind hier diejenigen, die fast immer zu haben sind, man erkennt sie an dem neuen Deckel, bisweilen sind sie schon durch viele Hände gegangen und noch unaufgeschnitten; Liebes- und Rittergeschichten sehn dagegen sehr abgenützt aus.'[42] Further information on this subject, on the type of customers of the lending libraries and, incidentally, on the reactionary attitude of the Bavarian authorities, is given by the following extract from a letter from Heinrich von Kleist to his fiancée Wilhelmine Zenge in 1800; he is describing a visit to the lending library at Würzburg:

Höre was ich darin fand, und ich werde Dir ferner nichts mehr über den Ton von Würzburg zu sagen brauchen.
,Wir wünschen ein paar gute Bücher zu haben.'
Hier steht die Sammlung zu Befehl.
,Etwa von Wieland.'
Ich zweifle fast.
,Oder von Schiller, Goethe.'
Die möchten hier schwerlich zu finden sein.

‚Wie? Sind alle diese Bücher vergriffen? Wird hier so stark gelesen?‘
Das eben nicht.
‚Wer liest denn hier eigentlich am meisten?‘
Juristen, Kaufleute und verheiratete Damen.
‚Und die unverheirateten?‘
Sie dürfen keine fordern.
‚Und die Studenten?‘
Wir haben Befehl ihnen keine zu geben.
‚Aber sagen Sie uns, wenn so wenig gelesen wird, wo in aller Welt
sind denn die Schriften Wielands, Goethes, Schillers?‘
Halten zu Gnaden, diese Schriften werden hier gar nicht gelesen.
‚Also, Sie haben sie gar nicht in der Bibliothek?‘
Wir dürfen nicht.
‚Was stehn denn also eigentlich für Bücher hier an diesen Wän-
den?‘
Rittergeschichten, lauter Rittergeschichten, rechts die Ritter-
geschichten mit Gespenstern, links ohne Gespenster, nach Belieben.
‚So, so!‘[43]

The Solothurn lending library is the exception which proves
the general rule; its first catalogue of 1788 lists 697 items including novels, dramas, anthologies, geographical, theological,
pedagogic, and philosophical works. Amongst the writers represented in the section headed 'Belles-lettres' we find Bacon,
Herder, Kant, Lessing, Mendelssohn, Montesquieu, Racine,
Rousseau, Shakespeare, and Sulzer. More typical is the catalogue of the lending library at Amberg which lists 137 periodicals, 91 novels, 51 'other poetical works', 46 dramas, 26 travel
books, 23 of miscellaneous content, and 21 anthologies of poetry.

It was not unknown for lending libraries to specialize in
certain types of literature. In Liegnitz, for example, there were
two lending libraries. The larger and more used of the two was
owned by a bookbinder and catered for readers looking purely
for entertainment, for satisfaction for their feelings, phantasy,
curiosity, and romanticism; its stock consisted largely of novels,
and its customers, over half of them women, were of the lower
classes of the town and neighbouring countryside. The second
Liegnitz lending library was run by a tax-collector and kept
only a few, 'but good', novels (by Lafontaine, Becker, Rochlitz, and J. G. Müller), also books and journals by Archenholz,
Wieland, and Bertuch, and works for 'serious entertainment'
particularly on geography and politics; this library was used

mostly by male members of the upper-middle class who also
organized a 'reading circle' in conjunction with the library.[44]
Complaints against the harmful influence the lending libraries
had on morals were unceasing. Here, as an example of the most
popular wares to be had in what one contemporary called *diese
moralischen Giftbuden* ('these booths full of ethical venom'), is an
advertisement from the Leipzig newspaper *Reichsbote* (1805):

In allen angesehenen Lesebibliotheken findet man nachstehende
äußerst unterhaltende Schriften:

Cölestinens Strumpfbänder (3. Aufl.) .	8°	10 gr.
Corona. Der Geisterbeherrscher . .	8°	18 gr.
Der Geist meines Mädchens; ihre Erscheinung und meine Hochzeitfeyer .	8°	8 gr.
Geisterbibliothek 1. Bd; Die schrecklichen Gemächer, Geistergeschichte .	8°	1 Thlr 4 gr.
Kunigunde oder Die Räuberhöhle im Tannenwald	8°	10 gr.
Lisara, Die Amazone von Habyssinien, Ein romantisches Gemälde . .	8°	20 gr.
Sagen aus der Geister- und Zauberwelt (neue Aufl.)	8°	16 gr.
Der Selbstmörder, eine Schauder- und Wundergeschichte . . .	8°	1 Thlr 4 gr.
Zauberstreiche, eine komische Geschichte	8°	14 gr.
Der Alte im Walde oder die unterirdische Wohnung	8°	20 gr.
Wunderbare Begebenheiten eines Engländers in Amerika . . .	8°	1 Thlr 16 gr.
Kreuzhiebe und kurzweilige Anekdoten zur Erschütterung des Zwergfells, von G. C. Cramer . . .	8°	8 gr.[45]

It will be noted that only in one case is the author named;
writers catering for this section of the reading public clearly
relied more on 'promising' titles than on reputation to attract
buyers.

These were by no means the very worst type of novel on the
German book market; they were still a few stages above such
works as *Auguste, oder Geständnisse einer Braut vor ihrer Trauung*
(*Augustina, or Confessions of a Bride before her Wedding*) by 'Freiherr von Dankelmann', or *Gustchens Geschichte, oder, eben so muß
es kommen um Jungfer zu bleiben* (Stambul and Avignon 1805) (*The*

History of Gussy, or That's the Way it goes if You want to remain a Virgin) by C. Althing, or *Das galante Sachsen* (*The Gallant World of Saxony*) and the rest of the so-called *heimliche Bücher* ('clandestine literature'), which made up most of the stocks of the travelling book-pedlars who carried their wares to the small towns and villages of all parts of Germany. With such products still on the market it is not surprising that the old complaints against fiction were still being heard at the close of the eighteenth century.

Far above the average lending libraries were the so-called *Lesekabinette*, founded in most cases by well-respected publishers and book-dealers. Several such libraries existed in the last decade of the century in the larger German towns; even the pirate publisher Trattner had his *Lektür-Cabinett* in Vienna. Only the best type of literature was kept in such collections; the Leipzig *Museum*, founded in 1795 and receiving from 1799 onwards a state grant of 100 Thaler annually, boasted of its lack of licentious literature and abundance of scientific learned works and of the really great imaginative literature. The 1799 catalogue of the Leipzig *Museum* lists 2,454 items (not volumes) under the rubric 'novels', 1,663 under French literature, 325 under English literature, and 105 under Italian literature out of a total of 11,977 items (about 37 per cent of the collection, therefore, were works of imaginative literature).

As long as the demand for reading material had remained comparatively slight the organization of the German book trade, as established in the course of the sixteenth and seventeenth centuries, had proved perfectly adequate—indeed it is doubtful whether any system of trading other than on an exchange basis could have functioned at all amidst the economic and fiscal chaos of Germany in that period. But by the second half of the eighteenth century the disadvantages and ultimately the impracticability of the old system were becoming clear to all. Under the exchange system of trading the publisher who took the best works to the fair was bound to come off second best; there was no incentive towards lowering the prices since this would not result in more 'sales' but simply in the devaluation of one's own goods on the exchange mart; publishers were forced by this system to use all methods to get rid of their wares, so that they might have something to offer their customers in their capacity as book-dealers—the changing of titles and years of publication was not infrequent; there was no opportunity to specialize in any branch of the trade when everyone had to be publisher, seller, and second-hand dealer combined. Reforms in trade organization, then, were, at the very least, desirable and with the increase in book production making the system of exchange trading all but unworkable, they began to make their appearance in the last few decades of the century. When Friedrich Perthes, later one of the most famous booksellers in Germany, entered on his apprenticeship in 1787 the old organization was still in force, but by the end of the century a new system of trading, the basis of the modern German book trade, had been established in almost all the German states.[46]

The first publishing houses to drop the selling side of the business appeared about mid century, the first one in Leipzig in 1735, and as their numbers increased, the introduction of cash dealings became inevitable, since these firms could no longer participate in exchange trade. In time the new method was adopted universally (the book-dealers of south Germany were the last to be converted) and henceforth at the end of each fair all outstanding balances were paid in cash. Thus every bookseller whose purchases exceeded his sales required a supply of ready money—a source of great anxiety to many of them; on the other hand, the bookselling business now found itself at last in a position to assume a separate and independent form; Perthes was, as he himself says, der erste reine Sortimenter ('the first purely retail bookseller'). To facilitate the payment of both outstanding debts and recent purchases the Leipzig book-dealers Kummer and Horvath organized in the course of the last decade of the century the Buchhändlerbörse, superseded in 1825 by the Börsenverein, where publishers were represented the whole year round by their agents. Trade, therefore, was no longer confined to the times of the book fairs and no longer dependent on the personal attendance of publishers and dealers at the fair.

If the introduction of trading on a cash basis had threatened many booksellers with ruin, one further change in trade organization which gradually came into operation during the last two decades of the century gave an extraordinary impulse to the bookselling department. Formerly no bookseller could return books which he had once taken from the publisher; if they remained unsold he was obliged to keep them himself, and so great caution was exercised by dealers when making purchases. Publishers, however, now realized that the sale of their works might suffer owing to the early exhaustion of the bookseller's limited stock and so, by way of experiment, they gave to the latter, over and above the copies bought by him, a certain number on commission. These the bookseller was to try to sell but if he failed to do so they were to be taken back by the publisher. This system of trading ('on sale or return') had first been practised most widely in south Germany from about 1780 onwards but it soon became more general and eventually the purchase of copies by the bookseller was almost entirely discontinued; every new work, as it appeared, was sent by the publisher to all active and solvent houses, and the unsold copies were returned at the next fair as *Remittenda*. All risk of loss was thus shifted to the shoulders of the publishers.

The comments of contemporary observers, the rise of the profession of letters, the mass of publications on the German book market, the increasing activity of pirate publishers, the establishment of reading societies and lending libraries, and the upheavals in trade organization all demonstrate the increased impetus and intense vigour behind the literary life of Germany and the increase in the reading habit. By the end of the century reading was a favourite pastime of broad sections of the German community, irrespective of social class. As one contemporary observed, the situation in Germany was now such 'daß der Gelehrte, der nicht zurückbleiben will, jetzt fast nichts mehr thun kann als lesen'.[47]

Professor Bruford sums up the development during these years as follows:

Between 1740 (the year selected by contemporaries as the turning point) and 1800, Germany had changed from a country so unproductive of native literature that every educated man had depended on foreign writings for his culture to a land of 'poets and thinkers', amongst whom the few known to history were the apex of a pyramid firmly based on a countless mass of pedants and scribblers. It had developed a classical literature, and also something very like an intellectual proletariat.[48]

5

NOVEL AND PUBLIC IN 1800

DURING the age of literary patronage the writer's task had
been to please his generous master. His public had consisted to
all intents and purposes of one man whose interests and prejudices, likes and dislikes, political opinions, and literary taste
were fully known to him. He knew exactly what to write and
how to write it if he was to please his public.

When, during the second half of the eighteenth century, the
age of patrons came to an end and it became the new ambition
of writers to reach a wider circle of readers, the same might
have held true, if Germany at that time had possessed what we
might term 'a general public', a reading public whose members
had a uniform standard of culture, common interests, and
similar literary tastes, irrespective of social rank, religious
beliefs, and geographical location. Such a public, however, did
not exist in Germany at the end of the eighteenth century, and
could never exist as long as the political system of particularism
and the social system of scrupulous class distinction persisted.
In the question of literary taste, state differed from state, and
class from class.

It is important to remember that Germany was at this time
a nation in name only. In reality it consisted of a loose confeder-
ation of over 300 states, each with its particular governmental
system, special privileges, and allegiances. The Holy Roman
Empire as a political reality had long ceased to function. To
contemporaries the term *Reich* was applicable only to south and
south-west Germany, whilst only the inhabitants of the free
towns called themselves *deutsch*; the rest thought of themselves
primarily as Österreicher, Bayern, Sachsen, Preußen, etc.,[1] just
as in the sphere of European diplomacy we can talk of an
Austrian policy or a *Prussian* policy, but not yet of a *German*
policy. Thus do we find, for example, lines such as the following

in the *Xenien* of Goethe and Schiller: 'Deutschland? aber wo liegt es? Ich weiß das Land nicht zu finden' ('Germany? But where is it? I can find no such country'); and when it is suggested to Nicolai's hero, Sebaldus Nothanker, that he preach on the subject 'Death for the Fatherland', his bewilderment, though aggravated by the vagaries of politics at the time of the Seven Years War, is typical of the many contemporary witnesses to the lack of any sense of belonging to a major national unit:

> Und wo ist in unserm unter Krieg und Verheerung seufzenden Deutschlande jetzt wohl das Vaterland zu finden? Deutsche fechten gegen Deutsche. Das Kontingent unsers Fürsten ist bei dem einen Heere, und in unserm Ländchen wirbt man für das andere. Zu welchem sollen wir uns schlagen? Wen sollen wir angreifen? Wen sollen wir verteidigen? Für wen sollen wir sterben?[2]

If the inhabitants of Germany at this time were capable of any feelings of patriotism at all, then it was towards their own little states rather than towards any national union of states. With no national capital to take on the role of Paris in France, and no national history to give men a feeling of common purpose, most people were content to follow the interests and accept the views (and prejudices) of their own province or town; Wieland complains in the Foreword to *Teutscher Merkur* (1773): 'Wir haben keine Hauptstadt, welche die allgemeine Akademie der Virtuosen der Nation, und gleichsam die Gesetzgeberin des Geschmacks wäre.'[3] Literary affairs, then, as well as political were characterized by a pertinacious adherence to the provincial or local. How different was the task of the French writer whose public comprised one nation and whose capital city furnished a sort of literary barometer in matters of taste, from that of the German who had, as Knigge points out, to try to appeal at once to 'the good-natured, naïve, sometimes rather materialistic Bavarian, the refined, smooth-tongued Saxon, the heavy Westphalian, the polite Frenchified Rhinelander, the blunt North Saxon'.[4] Faced with this almost impossible task, Knigge, no doubt expressing the sentiments of many of his colleagues, calls out in desperation: 'Herrscht wohl auf zehn Meilen Weges in Deutschland einerlei Geschmack, und bleibt dieser Geschmack sich wohl zehn Jahre hindurch gleich?'[5]

In surveying the predominant tastes of the German novel-reading public at the end of the eighteenth century, then, we must always keep in mind the religious, cultural, and intellectual differences of the various provinces. Important to remember is the fact that Austria and southern Germany, once the leaders of cultural life, were in the eighteenth century far behind northern and particularly central Germany as far as the 'march of culture' was concerned. Hamburg, Leipzig, Göttingen, Berlin, and many of the smaller towns of Protestant north and central Germany were now the focal points of Germany's intellectual and literary life. The Catholic south played but a small and unimportant part in the great intellectual and literary developments which took place in Germany during the century, whilst to be a Protestant was almost synonymous with being 'intellectually progressive'.

Even the Catholic Sonnenfels, writing in Vienna in 1782, ascribed the lead of the north to the impulse given to intellectual life by the Reformation, whilst a Lutheran minister of Augsburg is even more outspoken: 'Mit unseren Katholiken ist wenig anzufangen; die meisten bleiben dumm und grob.'[6] Learned Catholics, it is true, kept themselves well informed on the latest ideas; Jesuits were to be found amongst the followers of Wolff, seeing in his philosophy the means of combating the English free-thinkers; the monastic libraries of this period all include a selection of the works of Voltaire, Mosheim, Jerusalem, Baumgarten, and the *Wolfenbütteler Fragmente*; many Protestant teachers were called to southern universities and Catholic scholars often studied at Göttingen.

The middle and lower classes of south and south-west Germany, however, were little affected by the great intellectual forces at work during the century. The reactionary attitude of the Bavarian and Austrian censorship has already been noted,[7] but mention must be made here of the ignominious part played by the lower Catholic clergy, who were always in close touch with the people and whose duty it would seem to have been to foster the silly superstitions and encourage the uncompromising conservatism of the simple folk both in the towns and in the countryside; one unfortunate village priest, for example, was imprisoned by the Bavarian authorities because he denied the existence of witches in his *Lesebuch für das Landvolk* (1791).[8]

Wilhelm Heinrich Riehl (1823–97) writes as follows about

the lower Catholic priests and the effect which they had on the population of Bavaria:

Diesen Priestern aus der guten alten Zeit machte die Wissenschaft in der Regel nicht viel Beschwerde, sie waren kapuzinerhaft volkstümlich, Bauern, die geistlich studiert hatten, und deren höchst handfeste Auffassung des priesterlichen Berufes vortrefflich zu der handfesten Natur ihrer Beichtkinder paßte. Diese merkwürdigen Leute waren es, welche zumeist dafür sorgten, daß das bayrische Volk vom 17. Jahrhundert ins 19. herüberging, ohne etwas vom 18. gemerkt zu haben.[9]

The effect that all of this had on the book trade is indicated when we find that Nicolai, when discussing the book-catalogues and sales of dealers in Catholic regions of the country, gives representative titles of works on religious themes, collections of sermons, prayer-books, life-stories of the Saints, and other devotional literature, but does not find it necessary to mention imaginative literature and works of light entertainment in this context.[10] With the vast majority of the population of south and south-west Germany living in villages and small towns and thus entirely under the influence of the priests, these areas are of minor importance in a study of the novel-reading public.

Even the educated classes of southern Germany could not keep pace with the swiftly moving events in literary-minded Saxony. The ideas and works of men like Gottsched and Gellert were very late in gaining influence in Bavaria and Swabia and attempts to right the situation, like the founding of the Gesellschaft der Vertrauten Nachbarn am Isarstrom, met with only moderate success; the year 1759 had, it is true, seen the founding of the Bayerische Akademie der Wissenschaften but it confined its activity to research in Bavarian history.

In Austria the situation was very much the same. Excelling in music—at this time still very much an 'aristocratic art'—Austrian culture had, despite the strivings of Maria Theresa and Joseph II for reforms in education, won very little ground from the Frenchified aristocracy and the backward Catholic clergy. Vienna in 1770 was still mustering considerable support for the by now unfashionable Gottsched, and Austrians were reading Gellert until well into the nineteenth century. North-German contemporaries were all too well aware of the situation in Austria. The *Bibliothek der schönen Wissenschaften*, for instance, greets the appearance of a new journal, *Oesterreichischer Patriot*, in 1757 and states that such a publication will be especially welcome in Austria 'wo die Wahrheit und der gute Geschmack noch mit Aberglauben, Vorurteilen und Barberei zu kämpfen hat, wo von Zensoren und Aufsehern, aus Dummheit oder Bosheit solche Schriften verdrängt werden, weil deren Gebrauch ein Licht verbreiten könnte.'[11] Similarly, the editors of *Deutsches Museum* ask their readers in 1777 for any literary news they may have of those districts 'little known to us in the north, i.e. Swabia, Bavaria, Austria, Bohemia, etc.'.[12]

The attitude towards writers in Swabia gives us some idea of the situation there as regards literary matters. Wieland writes: 'Einen Poeten hält man da für einen Zeitverderber und unnützen Menschen';[13] Wieland's first move on deciding to make writing his career was, therefore, to sever all his connections with Swabia and the rest of south Germany. Schubart, Wieland's Swabian antipode, draws poetic inspiration not from Danaë or Musarion but from Swabia's illiterates:

> Ich Mädchen bin aus Schwaben
> Und braun ist mein Gesicht;
> Der Sachsenmädchen Gaben
> Besitz' ich freilich nicht.
>
> Die können Bücher lesen,
> Den Wieland und den Gleim:
> Und ihr Gezier und Wesen
> Ist süß wie Honigseim.
>
> Das Tändeln, Schreiben, Lesen
> Macht Mädchen widerlich;
> Der Mann für mich erlesen,
> Der liest einmal für mich. . . .[14]

Even Protestant Swabia–Württemberg had very little to offer its men of intellect; both Schiller and Hegel, it will be remembered, found fame in more northerly climes. In a survey of books in the possession of the citizens of Tübingen in the period from 1750 to 1850 we find that 80 per cent of the items listed are works of a religious nature, the rest consisting largely of almanacs and collections of fables—imaginative literature is represented only by Gellert and Rabener.[15]

Lower down the Rhine, too, in areas where the influence of

the clergy was still supreme, conditions still left much to be desired, though they were not quite so bad as in the extreme south. When J. H. Faber, a professor at Mainz University, published in the sixties a book on aesthetics, one reviewer expresses his surprise on seeing the place of publication of the book (Mainz): 'Wie? dachten wir, ein großes, dickes Buch über die schönen Wissenschaften aus einer Gegend, deren Bewohner und Nachbarn kaum wissen, ob auch Deutschland Klopstocks und Utze besitze?'; he goes on to praise the book, but Faber had to give up his university post on refusing to promise never to have another book published.[16]

Of the rest of Germany, the north-west was only moderately active in the literary world, whilst the land east of the Oder, with the exception of Danzig and Königsberg, was as intellectually backward as was, say, Bavaria. Once the writer, as a learned man, had enjoyed at least a little respect in those areas, but that was no longer the case; Hippel, for instance, speaks in his novel *Lebensläufe nach aufsteigender Linie* (1778–81) of a 'Litteratus, welches in Curland eben keinen Gelehrten sondern ein unselig Mittelding von Edelmann und Bauer bedeutet'.[17]

The geography of the German book trade confirms the above remarks on the cultural contrasts in the various provinces. The bookseller Perthes tells us in his *Memoirs* that for most of the eighteenth century the book trade was confined to northern and central Germany. In the south, from Vienna to Regensburg, there was, with the exception of a few publisher-dealers in Catholic works, no bookseller; and from Regensburg to the Tyrol only one—and he in Augsburg. The booksellers of Nuremberg were able to satisfy the trifling demands of this vast tract of country. In Tübingen and Heidelberg there were indeed flourishing houses, but the whole north-west, taking Münster as the most advanced literary outpost, was dependent on the scanty supply which Frankfurt could furnish. Perthes was forced to the conclusion that the whole of Austria and, with the exception of Württemberg, those parts of Germany south of Nuremberg and Dresden, and west of Frankfurt and Heidelberg were totally dead to literature. It should, however, be remembered that, firstly, Perthes was thinking here exclusively of the legitimate book trade of Leipzig and, secondly, in his enthusiastic advocacy of that organization he may have been inclined to overstate his case somewhat; nevertheless the general picture he paints cannot have been far from the truth. A rough measure of his enthusiasm may be got from my own finding that of 617 books reviewed in the *Allgemeine Literatur-Zeitung* from 3 January 1785 to 30 June 1785 with German, Austrian, or Swiss places of publication, 116 (18·8 per cent) appeared south of 'the Perthes Line'; twenty-two of these (about 1 in 5) come under the rubric *Gottesgelahrtheit*. If we apply Perthes's phrase 'with the exception of Württemberg' the figure is 105, i.e. 17 per cent. Leipzig (151), Berlin (84), and Hamburg (32) together account for 43·27 per cent of the total. Just over 15 per cent of the books published in the north are found under the heading *Gottesgelahrtheit*.

But the situation in the south was not entirely devoid of hope. During the last decades of the century the activity of the pirate publishers of Austria and south Germany did much, as we have seen, to spread the reading habit and an interest in imaginative literature, particularly in novels, in these areas. Though they may have had no traffic with the legitimate book trade of Leipzig, still the book-dealers of the south were anxious to create a literary public, as shown by the following advertisement issued by the firm of Jacob Ulrich Mäcken & Co. on opening up in Reutlingen:

> Reutlingen im Oktober 1798. E. E. zeigen wir hierdurch an, daß in unserer Handlung alle-möglichen Nachdrücke von hier, Tübingen, Stutgardt, Carlsruhe, Frankenthal, Bamberg, Augsburg, Bregenz, Neuwied und Wien unter den billigsten Bedingnissen und in den wohlfeilsten Preisen gegen ½-jährliche Zahlungs-Rechnung zu haben sind. . . . Unser Fond ist so beschaffen, daß wir im Stande sind, alles Vorzügliche, was in der litterarischen Sächsischen Welt erscheint, sogleich in einer wohlfeilen geschmackvollen Ausgabe zu liefern, und dadurch dem Unwesen der enormen, Sächsischen Bücher-Preise zu steuern, und die Wünsche vieler Tausende zu erfüllen. . . .[18]

Writing in the 1820s Perthes draws attention to the great changes that had occurred in the geography of the book trade during the previous half-century. The Rhine provinces, now under Prussian rule, Austria, and Bavaria had identified themselves more with German intellectual and literary life, and the book trade's connections with these areas had greatly increased. Forty years previously, Perthes continues, almost all southern

Germany, the Rhine provinces, and Westphalia had had little correspondence with the book trade in the rest of Germany, but now that same book trade had depots in all Westphalia, on the Rhine as far as Aachen and Trier, in all Bavaria, in the Tyrol as far as Bozen, and in Switzerland, and the prosperity of these establishments was a proof of the extent to which German literature had become 'common property and a necessity of life'.[19] The reading public in these areas was soon to reach its literary maturity with the appearance of Grillparzer in Austria, Mörike and Uhland in southern Germany and Annette von Droste-Hülshoff in Westphalia.

Great as were the regional differences in Germany at the end of the eighteenth century, much more fundamental were the differences in culture, education, and literary taste amongst the various social classes. The meticulous class distinction between the medieval estates still persisted and although efforts were made later in the century to right the situation (following the events in France in 1789), men were in 1800 still acutely conscious of their social origin. The legal distinctions between nobleman and commoner were, it is true, gradually abolished, but society continued for long to judge a man by his rank and possessions rather than by his ability and achievements. There was even discrimination within the separate classes; within the aristocracy careful distinction was still made between the higher nobility (*der hohe Adel*) and the lower nobility (*der niedere Adel*), within the middle class between the university-trained town officials and professional men (*Honoratioren*), the wholesale merchants (*Kaufleute*), and the retail merchants (*Krämer*).

So great indeed were the differences between the various social classes in standard of living, social customs, and moral code, in education and taste in art and literature that a survey of the predominant types of fictional literature and their public at this time can be effectively presented only if based on social rather than, say, regional or purely literary considerations. It is of little use, for example, to arrange such a survey on the basis of the writers themselves, that is classification according to author, not only because there are so many of them (and most of them were in reality nothing more than mercenary 'pen-pushers') but also because their works were expressions not of their own personality but of their age in general; the stress must,

almost of necessity, move from author to public, from book producers to 'book consumers'.[20]

During the seventeenth century, the age of baroque literature,
the courts had been the home and inspiration of German art
and literature; no other class was at that time in a position to
challenge the superiority of the aristocracy in cultural life. By
the end of the eighteenth century, however, every aspect of
culture, with perhaps the exception of music, was dominated
by the middle class of German society. We have seen in previous
chapters how the bourgeoisie had regained its confidence, first
in religious life through the Pietist movement, then in the realm
of philosophy and ethics through the teachings of Wolff, and how
its interest in imaginative literature had been awakened by the
works of men like Defoe, Schnabel, Gellert, Richardson, and
Hermes, all of whom were writing expressly for the serious-
minded middle-class reader who demanded first instruction,
then entertainment, from his reading material.

In contrast to the baroque age, literature in 1800 was a
predominantly middle-class art. It is no mere concidence that
the areas found by contemporaries to be most active in the book
trade at this time were those where a strong bourgeoisie prevailed—northern and central Germany. The centres of German
literary life were now the large commercial towns like Hamburg,
Leipzig, Berlin, and Königsberg, and no longer the courts of
the aristocracy.

German eighteenth-century literature saw very little actual
creative work by the aristocracy, nor was it so fashionable as it
had once been to encourage the work of others in this field. The
hallmark of the German aristocracy during the first half of the
century seems indeed to have been ignorance and indifference,
and this is the opinion not only of contemporary bourgeois
critics but also of the more honest members of the nobility.
Johann Michael von Loen, for example, writes in 1740 of his
own class: 'Wenn man den heutigen Adel beschreiben wollte,
so würde es vielleicht ein Gespötte heißen; man müßte ihn
lächerlich abmahlen, und die Wahrheit würde manchen allzu
natürlich treffen: Wir wollen lieber schweigen, unsere Schande
bedecken, uns rathen lassen und uns bessern.'[21] Loen writes
elsewhere: 'Die Unwissenheit ist beinahe das Kennzeichen einer
vornehmen Geburt';[22] and Goethe puts the following words into

the mouth of the 'Schöne Seele', speaking of the boredom she suffered amongst the nobility: 'Nicht einmal der geliebten Bücher wurde gedacht. Die Leute, mit denen ich umgeben war, hatten keine Ahnung von Wissenschaften; es waren deutsche Hofleute, und diese Klasse hatte damals nicht die mindeste Kultur.'[23] The second half of the century saw only little improvement in aristocratic attitudes, and that very largely confined to those court circles which, consciously or unconsciously, were striving to follow the example of the German middle class; the atmosphere of the court at Weimar in 1775, for instance, drew the following phrase from Goethe: 'Gutmüthige Beschränktheit, die sich zur wissenschaftlichen und literaren Cultur emporzuheben sucht.'[24]

Some insight into the life, interests, and sense of priorities of the nobility is obtained when we see the type of education enjoyed by their sons.[25] Whether a nobleman received instruction from private tutors or at one of the *Ritterakademien*, the curriculum was still very much the same. The accent was on languages, particularly French, and often to such an extent that many noblemen could express themselves better in that language than in their mother tongue. Lang writes of Graf Thürheim, for instance: 'Er schrieb und sprach französisch vorzüglich, deutsch richtig . . .', whilst the son of Baron von Bühler, the Württemberg ambassador in Vienna, was taught French but no German at all.[26] There might also be some tuition in English, Italian, and Spanish. Also considered important were history, often taught from contemporary journals, geography, genealogy, and, for future rulers, some law and a little Latin. For the rest, the nobleman's education aimed largely, often exclusively, at equipping him for life at court; Friedrich Karl von Moser writes in his then famous book *Der Herr und der Diener* (1758): 'Die meisten dieser Herrn lernen die Hofstudien, Sprachen, Musik, Reiten, Tanzen, Fechten und Schäkern, sonst nichts.'[27] The famous grand tour of Europe, with as long a stay as possible in Paris, would round off the young aristocrat's education.

Such an education was intended to make the pupil a success in court society. The bookish type of learning was considered 'terribly bourgeois' and absolutely unnecessary if one had money already. All in all the educated nobleman was no more, as J. G. Müller puts it, than 'the most refined peasant on his

estate'[28]—a judgement which hardly seems too harsh when we
hear from Lang that the eighteen-year-old son of the Ansbach
Generalkommissär von Dörnberg had to be sent to the *gemeine
Soldatenschule* ('school for other ranks') on entering the army, so
as to learn the art of reading and writing.[29] The German nobleman, enjoying his inherited privileges but ignoring the duties
which had once justified them, had but one aim in life—to enjoy
it to the full, and for the realization of this aim he could have no
better model than the pleasure-loving French aristocracy of the
age of Louis XV, the age of the 'perfumed, sensual, graceful
rococo'.[30] In every aspect of life he stood under the sway of
Paris, not least in the matter of literary taste.

The chief indoor pastimes of the nobility were the theatre
and opera, card-games, concerts, balls, and redoubts; the chief
pastime of the courtier in his many idle hours was cards. To all
of them reading was hard work rather than a pastime and,
moreover, in the majority of cases French was read far more
fluently than German. For the supreme example of this, of
course, we need go no further than Frederick the Great. Gottsched, describing to a friend his audience with Frederick in
1757, writes with obvious pleasure that he was able to enlighten
the king on the subject of German literature; he continues:

> Als ich sagte, daß die deutschen Dichter nicht Aufmunterung
> genug hätten, weil der Adel und die Höfe zu viel französisch und zu
> wenig deutsch verstünden, alles deutsche recht zu schätzen und
> einzusehen, sagte Er: das ist wahr, denn ich habe von Jugend auf kein
> deutsch Buch gelesen, und je parle comme un cocher, jetzo aber bin
> ich ein alter Kerl von 46 Jahren, und habe keine Zeit mehr dazu.[31]

The same Frederick had not even heard of Gleim's patriotic
Grenadier songs. It is also a sad commentary on the position of
German literature in the courts when Wieland writes of Graf
Stadion's pleasure on reading his *Komische Erzählungen* (1765):
'Er wunderte sich gar zu sehr, daß man das alles in deutscher
Sprache sagen könne—denn bisher kannte er die deutsche
Sprache nur aus Akten, Urkunden und Ministerial-Schriften.'[32]
Even later in the century we find Lang writing of Prince Kraft
Ernst von Hohenaltheim: 'Seine frühere wissenschaftliche Bil-
dung war eine französische, und von eigentlicher klassischer
und deutscher Literatur wußte er nur so viel, was er mit wohl-

berechneter Verschlagenheit sich von seiner Umgebung an-
zueignen verstand.'[33]

During the first half of the century the aristocracy had had
their own branch of fiction in the heroic gallant novels of writers
like Talander, tales of beautiful princesses and heroic knights
moving in the fantastic world of the court masquerades, a
strange mixture of the idealistic, romantic, and sensual sides of
aristocratic social life. This branch of the genre had died out
when, in the second half of the century, novelists turned to the
middle class for their public. The fiction offered at the Leipzig
book fairs at the end of the eighteenth century would have little
appeal to the German nobleman. He was not interested in the
moralizing tales of virtuous family life; to lead a virtuous life
was indeed decidedly 'bad form' in the eyes of the aristocracy.
The humorous novels, which very often depended on the now
proverbial ignorance of the nobility for their humorous situations, would not appeal to him.[34] The emotional outbursts of
the sentimental novelists were to him nothing more than a
deplorable lack of decorum and such books would find no place
in his reading material. The characters of the Storm and Stress
fiction, shunning as they did the ideal of aristocratic life—society
—and welcoming in its place isolation with nature, would hold
no interest for him.

In short, German writers were no longer catering for the
tastes of the nobility. The world of heroic knights and fair
damsels in distress was now confined largely to the branch of
fiction soon to be known as the *Hintertreppenroman*, which provided the reading material for the lower reaches of the reading
public; when a character of noble birth appears in the middle-
class literature he is, as already stated, most often a hated man,
a tyrant, and a threat to the virtue of the good bourgeois
heroine.[35] To find reading material to his taste the nobleman
had to turn to the rococo literature of France; here he found
works suitable for the aristocratic salon with their insistence on
form rather than content, on entertainment rather than instruction, on the piquant rather than on the moralizing. Only the
elegant, form-conscious Wieland amongst German novelists
had found favour in the salons of the nobility. In his *Komische
Erzählungen* (1765), for example, Wieland consciously strove to
please his patron Graf Stadion at Warthausen with these rhymed

tales of frivolous, sensual, and cynical content; the book was well received and he enhanced his reputation still further amongst the German nobility with such works as *Musarion* (1768), *Idris* (1768), *Die Grazien* (1770), *Der verklagte Amor* (1774), and *Oberon* (1780). His novels, too, were attuned to the taste of court circles; the second part of *Don Sylvio von Rosalva* (1764) in particular could appeal only to readers with a liking for the products of the French literary salons and was, as the poet himself said, 'nicht vor jedermann lesbar' ('not suitable for reading aloud before all and sundry'), while *Agathon* (1766–7), of which Wieland had high hopes of its being a financial success, was regarded on its appearance as 'an aristocratic and difficult book'. A minor poet of the period (Lucian) tells us that in such exclusive circles as the court at Warthausen Wieland was so popular 'daß man gar keinen Anspruch auf Witz machen darf, wenn man seine Schriften nicht gelesen hat',[36] but the acclamation of the wider reading public failed to appear, while to the rising generation of poets Wieland was nothing but a *schwächlicher Halbmensch* ('feeble apology for a man'), a *Französling* ('Froggomaniac'), and a *Salontrottel* ('salon lapdog').

There were, of course, some noblemen and some courts that took a lively interest in the welfare of German literature. Biedermann names a few of the aristocratic scholars and writers of the first half of the century, none of them, however, very eminent: von Tschirnhausen, von Seckendorff, von Bühnau-Dahlen, Baron von Boyneburg, Graf von Manteuffel, Freiherr von Münchhausen.[37] Amongst the aristocratic writers of the second half of the century we might mention the Stolbergs, von Thümmel, von Hardenberg, von Knigge, and the Humboldts. Several of the aristocratic salons were noted for their encouragement of German writers, such as those of Graf Stadion at Biberach, Fürstin Gallitzin at Münster, Fürstin Pauline at Lippe, Wilhelm von Bückeburg, Peter von Oldenburg, and those of the courts at Darmstadt, Brunswick, Weimar, and Holstein. It is for this reason that I would regard Marianne Spiegel's detailed analysis of eight libraries of the Schleswig-Holstein aristocracy as by no means representative of the German nobility as a whole; nor does Spiegel claim this, for she herself points out that these noble families were at that time under Danish rule and had never been completely dominated by the culture, norms, and tastes of the French aristocracy. Even so, of the 147 novels found in these eight libraries (for the period 1700–70), 113 are in French, twenty-five in German, and nine in English; lyric poetry, verse epics, and French classical drama are all more strongly represented than the novel in these particular libraries of the Schleswig-Holstein nobility, who clearly belonged to that group of their class who were unusually active and interested in cultural matters in general.[38] Duke Friedrich Christian von Schleswig-Holstein and Graf Schimmelmann, for instance, were both prepared to help Schiller in his need and began their letter as follows: 'zwey Freunde, durch Weltbürgersinn mit einander verbunden, erlassen dieses Schreiben an Sie, edler Mann! Beyde sind Ihnen unbekannt, aber beyde verehren und lieben Sie.'[39] Even one of the old-style die-hards, the Palsgrave Karl Theodor founded an Art Academy, learned societies, and a National Theatre. Scholars have already pointed to the debt owed by German classical writers, Goethe in particular, to the literary-minded courts like Weimar, both for their generous patronage and for the ennobling influence which they exercised on the classical poets' outlook on life.[40]

It was, however, not amongst the aristocracy but in the educated middle class of German society that German classical literature found most of its readers. It had once been the ambition of the patricians and merchants of the large commercial towns like Hamburg to equal the court towns in their own forms of courtly culture, but by following the example of the intellectually more advanced English middle class, the merchant class of Germany was gradually roused to a realization of its own deepest needs, amongst which was a literature of its own. During the first sixty or seventy years of the eighteenth century the German middle class had, so to speak, served its literary apprenticeship; it had been schooled in the field of philosophy by Wolff, introduced to the world of feeling by the Pietist movement, and accustomed to the habit of reading a secular literature by the moral weeklies and the didactic novels of the Age of Enlightenment. By the end of the century the court towns had lost much of their prestige in the world of literature;

Dresden was outshone by Leipzig. Even the few courts which did take an active interest in literary affairs were characterized by a predominantly bourgeois atmosphere.[41]

The German middle class which, a century earlier, had been an insignificant force in the intellectual life of the nation, now felt themselves to be the mainstay of all progress and culture. Typical of the self-confidence and tremendous optimism of this. class is the memorial document (*Gedenkurkunde*) of 1784 found a hundred years ago in a church tower in Gotha:

> Unsere Tage füllen den glücklichsten Zeitraum des 18. Jahr-
> hunderts. Kaiser, Könige, Fürsten steigen von ihrer gefürchteten
> Höhe menschenfreundlich herab, verachten Pracht und Schimmer,
> werden Väter, Freunde und Vertraute ihres Volkes. Die Religion
> zerreißt das Pfaffengewand und tritt in ihrer Göttlichkeit hervor.
> Aufklärung geht mit Riesenschritten. Tausende unserer Brüder
> und Schwestern, die in geheiligter Untätigkeit lebten, werden dem
> Staate geschenkt, Glaubenshaß und Gewissenszwang sinken dahin.
> Menschenliebe und Freiheit im Denken gewinnen die Oberhand.
> Künste und Wissenschaften blühen, und tief dringen unsere Blicke
> in die Werkstatt der Natur. Handwerker nähern sich gleich den
> Künstlern der Vollkommenheit; nützliche Kenntnisse keimen in
> allen Ständen. Hier habt Ihr eine getreue Schilderung unserer
> Zeit.[42]

Literature was, then, at the end of the century, a predominantly bourgeois art, but it was only a small part of the middle class, the better-educated members of this section of the community, that responded most readily to the classical writers of the great age of German literature in their attempt at a fusion of the moral, religious, artistic, and philosophic values of life for the attainment of their ideal of *Humanität*. Writers like Goethe and Schiller found their public in the *Honoratioren* of the large towns, in the university-trained professional men, the ministers of religion, teachers, doctors, and lawyers, in what might be termed the élite of middle-class society. 'High literature' was then even more than now a thing for a small group of scholars; Wilhelm von Humboldt writes: 'Alle unsere guten Schrift-steller und ihre Leser gleichen einer Freimaurerloge; man muß ein Eingeweihter sein.'[43] During his residence in England Moritz was struck by the contrast between the two nations in this respect, for he had found the English national authors 'in all hands, and read by all people' in comparison to their German counterparts whose works were in general read 'only by the learned, or at most by the middle class of people'.[44] Nicolai, too, observes in this connection: 'Der Stand der Schriftsteller beziehet sich in Deutschland beinahe bloß auf sich selber, oder auf den gelehrten Stand.'[45]

For, despite the impression quite often given by literary historians, classical German literature did not enjoy a wide circulation, and the influence it exercised on contemporaries was very much restricted—not infrequently to that on fellow artists or personal friends of the writer. Friedrich Schlegel recognized, and indeed welcomed, this state of affairs: '[Die Leser] jammern immer, die deutschen Autoren schrieben nur für einen so kleinen Kreis, ja oft nur für sich selbst untereinander. Das ist recht gut. Dadurch wird die deutsche Literatur immer mehr Geist und Charakter bekommen.'[46] The reception of the great novel of the Classical Age of German literature, *Wilhelm Meisters Lehrjahre*, illustrates this very clearly. The first and second books of Goethe's novel appeared early in 1795, books III and IV followed in May 1795, V and VI in November 1795, and the last two books in October 1796. Much of its possible effect on the wider reading public would, of course, be lost owing to its gradual and irregular appearance on the market; on the other hand, the fact that it was labelled a *Bildungsroman* by most of the contemporary critics, and the novel's treatment of the theatrical world would increase its appeal amongst the better-off members of German society, for *Bildung* had been the catchword of the century, and the theatre was the latest fashion in most large towns. In the eyes of the wider reading public, however, *Wilhelm Meister* was a difficult book, reserved for the intelligentsia.

Not that Goethe was particularly worried by the limited success of his novel. The fate of *Werther* at the hands of the wider public was never forgotten by him, and to the end of his life that public remained for him *die unbekannte Menge* ('the unknown masses') and the object of his whole-hearted contempt: 'Man sagt, eitles Eigenlob stinket. Das mag sein. Was aber fremder ungerechter Tadel für einen Geruch habe, dafür hat das Publikum keine Nase';[47] he refers elsewhere to the reading public as the 'Parterre-Kloak'.[48] Goethe, and with him most of the

classical writers, was satisfied if his works found 'fit audience
though few'—and few they must have been, for the ideal reader,
in his eyes,

sieht nicht nur die Wahrheit des Nachgeahmten, sondern auch die
Vorzüge des Ausgewählten, das Geistreiche der Zusammenstellung,
das Überirdische der kleinen Kunstwelt; er fühlt, daß er sich zum
Künstler erheben müsse, um das Werk zu genießen, er fühlt, daß
er sich aus seinem zerstreuten Leben sammeln, mit dem Kunstwerk
wohnen, es wiederholt anschauen und sich selbst dadurch eine
höhere Existenz geben müsse.[49]

That there were men who could see in *Werther* nothing more
than the story of an unhappy love-affair came as a bitter disappointment to the young poet who was henceforth to create
for himself his own ideal public, sometimes consisting of one
man, like Herder and later Schiller, or of a small circle of
intimate friends, like his admirers at Weimar, and if this public
was pleased with his work then he was satisfied and confident
that the honour due to him would be granted him by posterity,
his ultimate public: 'Erwachsene gehn mich nicht mehr an, /
Ich muß nun an die Enkel denken.'[50]

Amongst Goethe's critics and 'personal public' at the time of
Wilhelm Meister's appearance, Schiller's voice was the loudest
and the most heeded; Goethe had even asked and received
advice from his fellow poet during the actual composition of the
novel, as shown in the correspondence which passed between
them during these years. Goethe was also pleased with the
reception given to his novel by his two close friends Wilhelm
von Humboldt and Gottfried Körner, whose appreciation was
printed at Goethe's request in Schiller's *Horen* of 1796. The
literary circles of Weimar and Jena showed unqualified admiration for Goethe's novel; Charlotte von Kalb, for instance,
wrote to Goethe: 'Ich sehne mich nach dem dritten Theil Ihres
Wilhelm wie nach der Wärme des Sonnenlichts, wie nach dem
Besuch eines vertrauten Gemüts', and Rahel Levin, one of the
leading personalities in the newly formed Berlin literary circle,
is said to have bribed the 'juniors' of Unger's publishing firm so
that she might be amongst the first to get the instalments of
Goethe's novel.[51] Only Frau von Stein, once Goethe's favourite,
almost only 'public', did not join in the general admiration of
these circles for *Wilhelm Meister*.

The effect which the novel had on the younger generation of Romantic poets is sufficiently well known; the leaders of the new movement proved very adept at finding their romantic ideals expressed in Goethe's work, and through them *Wilhelm Meister* has exercised a great influence on German novelists up to Stifter, Keller, Raabe, and Thomas Mann in the present century. Friedrich Schlegel demonstrates the enthusiasm of the Romantic school for the novel when he writes in his journal *Athenäum*: 'Die französische Revolution, Fichtes Wissenschaftslehre, und Goethes *Meister* sind die größten Tendenzen des Zeitalters.'[52] Amongst the works directly inspired by *Wilhelm Meister* are Tieck's *Franz Sternbalds Wanderungen* (1798), Friedrich Schlegel's *Lucinde* (1799), and not least of all *Heinrich von Ofterdingen* (1802), even though Novalis later turned from a warm admirer into the violent opponent of Goethe's novel. *Wilhelm Meister*, then, was read and appreciated mainly by fellow poets and by members of the exclusive literary circles of the educated middle class and smaller courts;[53] the acclamation of the wider reading public was missing, but Goethe was satisfied: 'Denkt nicht, ich geh' euch dummem Volk zu Leibe, / Ich weiß recht gut, für wen ich schreibe.'[54]

Statements from contemporary booksellers and information on the sale of works prove beyond any doubt that the classics were not a commercial success. The prices of most of the *Klassiker Originalausgaben* were so high as to be almost prohibitive.[55] They were for the most part luxury editions printed on best quality paper and bought to provide 'food for the intellect' for a lifetime and for future generations by a section of the public which was used to paying out such sums for a short journey, for wine supplies, for social functions or for jewellery and the like. Cheaper authorized editions were available in some cases, and there were, of course, the cheaper pirated versions, the reading societies and above all the lending libraries to cut the costs for readers, but in spite of all these facilities, the classics enjoyed a poor circulation. Wilhelm Fleischer, a bookseller of Frankfurt am Main, writes on this subject: 'Man sage mir nichts von dem Absatze dieser Schriften. Im Verhältnisse der ihnen eigentümlichen Popularität, in einem Menschenhaufen von dreißig Millionen, kann der Debit gar nicht in Anschlag kommen.'[56]

Of Goethe's *Collected Works* (1787–90) Göschen printed an ordinary edition of 2,000 and a cheap edition of 3,000, but they sold very slowly. There were only 602 subscribers to the whole series, and after two years only 536 non-subscribed copies of the first four volumes had been sold, together with 200 or 300 copies each of single plays, etc.[57] By far the most successful narrative work by a classical author was Schiller's *Geisterseher* (1789); within four months of its appearance the whole of the first edition had been sold and further editions of as many as 4,000 copies enjoyed a similar success. This was, however, an exception to the general rule.[58]

Ludwig Kehr, another bookseller, learned in a rather costly manner that the taste of the greater reading public was anything but classical; his experience tells us that classical works were read as rarely as they were bought. In 1797 Kehr opened in Kreuznach a very carefully chosen lending library consisting of the works of Gellert, Gleim, Goethe, Hagedorn, Hölty, Kleist, Klopstock, Lessing, Lichtenberg, Matthisson, Rabener, Ramler, Schiller, Tieck, Uz, Wieland, and others; to his great surprise and disappointment he found that no one wanted to borrow his fine books, whilst ghost-stories and romances of chivalry were continually requiring renewals, with several copies of each necessary.[59] Heinrich von Kleist's experience in the Würzburg lending library has already been mentioned.[60] Arnold Mallinckrodt of Dortmund tells us in 1800 that the classical authors, amongst whom he places Klinger and J. G. Müller, were read relatively rarely; their works were swamped by the 'literary mass-produced works'.[61] Finally Karl Preusker, who came to Leipzig as a bookseller's apprentice in 1805, names in his autobiography the authors most in demand at that time; the most classical (as we understand the term today) of the authors on his list is Zschokke, 'whereas the works of Schiller and Goethe were sold in only meagre quantities'.[62]

Even the classical journals were not a commercial success, despite the general vogue for the reading of newspapers, journals, and almanacs. Schiller's *Thalia* could not support itself; his *Horen*, Schlegel's *Athenäum* and Goethe's *Propyläen* all experienced but poor sales. The *Propyläen*, founded in 1798, had in mid 1799 a circulation of only 450 copies and the publisher Cotta had already lost 2,500 Gulden on it. Schiller had promised the reader of his *Horen* 'light entertainment and amusement', and these were indeed the two things demanded of reading material by the wider public, but the strong classic-aesthetic flavouring was entirely against the latter's taste. The favourites with the wider reading public were not publications like those of Schiller, but rather the purely entertaining books and almanacs like W. G. Becker's extraordinarly long-lived *Taschenbuch zum geselligen Vergnügen* (1791–1833), the *Taschenbuch für Damen* (1798–1831), edited at various times by Therese Huber, Lafontaine, Pfeffel, and others, Tromlitz's *Vielliebchen* and Claurens's *Vergißmeinnicht*.

We may say, then, that the public for German classical literature was disproportionately small, and this was not merely because the prices for classical works were extremely high, but also for the simple reason that the majority of readers had no desire to read the works of the great poets—works which demanded of their readers mental alertness, suppleness, concentration, and an appreciation of aesthetic values. The average middle-class reader wanted works which were within his own experience and range of emotion, reflecting his own interests and not conflicting with the demands of his morality. This is not, of course, a phenomenon peculiar only to our period, but for the first time in Germany it reached such huge and obvious proportions. Friedrich Schlegel describes the situation as follows:

Ganz dicht nebeneinander existieren besonders jetzt zwey verschiedene Poesien . . . deren jede ihr eigenes Publikum hat, und unbekümmert um die andere ihren Gang für sich geht. Sie nehmen nicht die geringste Notiz von einander, außer, wenn sie zufällig auf einander treffen, durch gegenseitige Verachtung und Spott; oft nicht ohne heimlichen Neid über die Popularität der einen oder die Vornehmigkeit der andern.[63]

These social and literary divisions of the reading public had always been present, but the intensification of the reading habit had led to a sharper and more obvious distinction between the reading classes, so obvious in fact as to fill contemporaries with a fear for the future of German literature.

In 1780, for example, we hear Göckingk complaining bitterly that the German public showed nowhere near the interest of their English counterpart in 'good literature'; if they did, then he would spend ten years writing a truly great work—'so aber—

ein Hundsfott der für das Publikum nur ein Lied macht'.[64] Göschen writes with equal contempt: 'Unser Publikum nimmt Teil an allem, was für die Neugierde ist.'[65] Lang writes on the same subject: 'Das Publikum ist jetzt ein großer Herr geworden, es will nur Vergnügungen und zahlt nur für Vergnügen; wirklichen Fleiß und Mühe kann es gar nicht ansehen, ohne die Seekrankheit davon zu kriegen.'[66] The most bitter of all, however, is Bürger: he distinguishes between *Publikum* and *Pöblikum* (from *der Pöbel* = the mob, rabble).[67]

The wider reading public drew most of its members from the middle class of German society; what then were the most popular types of narrative literature amongst the middle-class readers at the end of the eighteenth century? First we must distinguish between the more serious-minded reader who demanded more than entertainment from books, and the more common type of reader who regarded reading purely as a pastime. Contemporaries, too, were aware of the existence of these two types of readers; Friedrich Schlegel has already been quoted on this subject and the editors of *Deutsches Museum*, too, regret that they cannot please each class of reader in every issue of their newspaper, and continue: 'Die Eine dieser Klassen will bloß unterhalten, die andere bloß unterrichtet sein.'[68]

Three generations earlier the vast majority of the bourgeoisie had looked for instruction in all their reading material; the Bible, collections of sermons, and the edifying books of religious and moral instruction had been the favourite books of the middle-class reader. To read a work of fiction had once been nothing short of sinful, and it was only when the novel, in the hands of the Rationalistic writers, became a medium for the moral and intellectual enlightenment of the nation, that the middle class had been won over to the novel-reading public. *Insel Felsenburg, Die Schwedische Gräfin*, and *Sophiens Reise* were now to be found next to the Bible in German middle-class homes.

Even at the end of the eighteenth century, however, many readers of bourgeois origin still sought instruction from all their reading material; it is as if they still felt a twinge of their pietistic conscience whenever they picked up a work of fiction from which nothing but entertainment was to be gained. The sort of story that appealed to such readers could not be better described than in the words of the Austrian decree of 1806 which excepted from the general ban on many popular types of fiction those stories which 'im Gewande des Romans ganze Wissenschaften abhandeln, moralische Vorlesungen anbringen, Länder-, Völker-, Natur- und Kunstkenntnisse verbreiten, eine tiefe Kenntnis der menschlichen Natur verraten, das sittliche Leben mit Rührung und Bekehrung des Lesers in einem lebhaften Vortrag darstellen oder mit Witz und Laune die Torheiten und Laster der Menschen züchtigen.'[69] This section of the public wished to read of men and women who had lived their lives in accordance with the demands of bourgeois ethics, stories which justified the reader's pride in his social class with its strict moral code and insistence on the traditional 'bourgeois virtues' of modesty, honesty, industry, temperance, order, and chastity; they wished, in other words, to have models on which they could base their own lives and opinions. Of no other type of reader is Goethe's advice to authors more valid:

Sprichst Du zum Volke, zu Fürsten und Königen, allen
Magst Du Geschichten erzählen, worin als wirklich erscheinet,
Was sie wünschen, und was sie selber zu leben begehrten.[70]

A favourite reading material of this class of the public was the actual biographies of praiseworthy men and those novels which took on biographical form, professing to be true representations of fact. Especially popular were the novels of Jung-Stilling (1740–1817), drawing inspiration as they did from the writer's own experiences and greatly influenced as they were by the Pietist movement.[71] Lang tells us that Stilling was amongst the authors from whose works his uncle, a Lutheran minister, would read aloud to his family during the winter months[72] and the choice is not surprising, for in his *Lebensgeschichte* people read how man could triumph over all adversities so long as he put his trust in the wisdom and goodness of Providence and sought comfort amidst his tribulations in the understanding arms of his friend and father, God; Stilling's life was a worthy model for his readers' own lives, and what better aim could the human being have than that of Stilling: 'Erkenntnis der Wahrheit und Wissenschaften zu erlangen, und Gott und dem Nächsten damit zu dienen.'[73]

It is an expression of the same taste when we find Fritz von
Stolberg (1750–1819), leader of the pious in Germany at this
time and himself a novelist, burning his copy of *Wilhelm Meisters
Lehrjahre* with the exception of Book VI, the *Bekenntnisse einer
schönen Seele*, which he had specially bound as an *Erbauungsbuch*
('devotional work').[74] *Anton Reiser* (1785–90), an autobiogra-
phical novel by Karl Philipp Moritz (1757–93), also enjoyed
popularity amongst this class of the reading public. In it Moritz
tells with convincing truth and unadorned honesty the story of
a young man's initiation into life; the pietistic inheritance of
the author is revealed in his keen psychological insight and un-
equalled powers of self-observation, an art widely practised by
the early Pietists in their desire to record their spiritual progress.
Moritz's novel did not disappear from the libraries of middle-
class homes until the second half of the nineteenth century.

Biographies were looked on as nobler representatives of the
narrative art than novels, mainly because of their foundation
on truth; in the preliminary remarks to these biographical
novels, for example, we are continually coming across such
phrases as, 'Um das Heer schlechter Romane dadurch ver-
drängen zu helfen . . .' ('To help to dislodge the army of bad
novels . . .'). So popular was this branch of writing that we find
a contemporary critic exclaiming in 1799: 'Alles, was nicht
Ritterromane und Hexengeschichten schreiben kann, verliert
sich jetzt in Anekdoten, Biographien und Gallerien.'[75]

The same was the case with books of travel and novels with
some journey as the main theme, after the fashion of Knigge's
Reise nach Braunschweig (1792), another popular branch of
narrative literature amongst readers seeking instruction and
enlightenment. In the Leipzig catalogue of 1740 we find only
six books of travel (*Reisebeschreibungen*) offered, and two of those
were in Latin; in 1770 only five are listed but in the Easter fair
catalogue for 1800 no fewer than fifty-two works of this nature
are offered to the German reader.[76] A contemporary critic
complains in 1784 that no one now ever undertakes a stroll,
a picnic, or a ride without having to tell all Germany what
happened on the way—or worse still, what thoughts occurred to
him on the way;[77] and indeed many of these descriptions really
do overdo the details, faithfully reporting every word exchanged
with each innkeeper and stranger met on the journey. Such

works, together with the biographies, would, it was hoped, help to draw readers away from the soul-destroying chivalrous novels and ghost-stories.[78]

The more serious-minded readers of the middle class were also attracted by novels which portrayed in a realistic manner their own world and problems, and their relationship with, and duties towards, the other classes. Johann Jakob Engel's novel, *Herr Lorenz Stark, ein Charaktergemälde* (1795–6 in *Horen*, 1801 in book form) with its true-to-life picture of middle-class family life and excellent characterization appealed particularly to this section of the public.[79] The same was the case with *Hermann und Ulrike* (1780) by Johann Karl Wezel (1747–1819), whose conception of the ideal novel agrees exactly with that of the practical-minded middle-class citizen: 'Es muß ein Buch sein . . . das ein Beispiel großer, edler, aufstrebender Tätigkeit enthält, wie sie jeder Jüngling nachahmen kann . . . ein Beispiel voll Nerven, Geist, starker, männlicher Empfindung.'[80] Two more novels appealing to this class of the reading public were *Leben des guten Jünglings Engelhof* (1781) by Lorenz von Westenrieder (1748–1829) and *Lebensgeschichte und natürliche Ebenteuer des armen Mannes im Tockenburg* (1789) by Ulrich Bräker (1735–98).

The reader seeking more than entertainment from novels was perhaps most attracted by the moral-pedagogic stories now on the market, like Pestalozzi's (1746–1827) *Lienhard und Gertrud, Vorschläge zur Hebung der häuslichen Erziehung* (1781–5) (*Lienhard and Gertrud, Some Suggestions for the Improvement of Education in the Home*), *Christoph und Else* (1782), *Buch der Mutter* (1803), etc. It was a novel of this type that proved to be the greatest commercial success of the last decade of the century—*Elisa, oder das Weib, wie es seyn sollte* (1795) (*Elisa, or Woman as she ought to be*) by Karoline von Wobeser (1769–1807). This novel went through five more editions during the next sixteen years (1797, 1798, 1799, 1800, 1811), was translated into English in 1799 and 1803, and into French in 1803 and 1812. The almost simultaneous volley of imitations and variations which followed demonstrate not only the popularity of the book, but also the increased intensity of literary life and the existence of a kind of literary mass production: e.g. *Elisa, kein Weib wie es sein soll* (*Elisa, not the Woman she ought to be*); *Louise, ein Weib wie ich es wünsche* (*Louise, a Woman as I would wish her to be*); *Elisa, das Mädchen aus dem Monde* (*Elisa, the Girl from the Moon*); *Maria, oder das Unglück Weib zu sein* (*Maria, or the Misfortune of being a Woman*); *Familie wie es sein soll* (*Family as it ought to be*); *Unterröckchen wie es sein sollte, ein paar Worte unter vier Augen* (*Petticoat as it ought to be, a few Words in Private*), etc. And writers were still exploiting Elisa's success as late as 1800 for, as already mentioned, the Easter catalogue for that year offers eleven imitations (including imitations of imitations): e.g. *Robert, der Mann wie er sein sollte* (*Robert, or Man as he ought to be*), and at once the protest, *Robert, der Mann wie er nicht sein sollte* (*Robert, Man as he ought not to be*).

What is there about *Elisa* that made it a best seller? The scene of the action is contemporary Germany, a setting that readers would know and appreciate, and the story tells of the saving of a marriage, a theme that meant something to all readers. Elisa, through family intrigues, is forced into marriage with a man she does not love—worse still, a man of intemperate habits who is not worthy of her love; but Elisa regards it as her duty to submit to her mother's wishes, enduring all the degradation and humiliation her husband causes her and refusing to abandon him for a man who really loves her; finally she wins over the one-time rake to her virtuous way of life, converts him, and dies in happiness.

The style of the novel is sentimental—often sickly sentimental to the modern reader, with tears flowing on all possible and many impossible occasions. One often gets the impression that partings are engineered by the author just so as to be able to give us another tearful scene of fond embraces—these same partings then also provide occasion to include the many letters which subsequently passed between the separated friends, and novels in letter form had been firm favourites of the German reading public for much of the second half of the eighteenth century. In style and form, in fact, *Elisa* has a great deal in common with the popular sentimental novels of the *Werther* era; Goethe's *Werther*, it would seem, had helped to create a public which remained so constant and so faithful in its taste that it had to reject Goethe's *Wilhelm Meister*.

But the great success of Karoline von Wobeser's novel was not, I would suggest, due primarily to its style, but rather to its

serious content. Here was a woman (the novel appeared anonymously but the Preface made this fact clear) who was not only
justifying but actually extolling the sovereign authority of the
husband in the home, defining and emphasizing a woman's
duties and obligations, and this at a time when educated women
were beginning to show more interest in their rights and privileges and to lay claim to a wider and more active role in life.
The author's chief concern becomes quite clear when we read
in the Preface: 'O, wie wenige Weiber giebt es, welche wahr-
haft aufgeklärt über ihre Pflichten und Bestimmung mit aus-
gebildetem Geiste und edlem Herzen auf der Bahn, auf welcher
sie wandeln, alles das Gute und Nützliche stiften, welches in-
nerhalb ihrem Wirkungskreise liegt!'[81] The interest in *Elisa*, I
would say, was social rather than literary. The main theme
of the story gave its serious-minded readers (obviously mostly
women) a worthy example and ideal to strive after: 'Und Elisa
zeigte allen Weibern, daß des Weibes schönster Ruhm *Tugend*
sei, und daß durch sie das Weib in jeder Sphäre Gutes wirken,
und selbst Generationen beglücken kann';[82] but in addition to
this main theme, the author takes every possible opportunity of
instructing her readers on how to face life's difficult situations,
great and small—she answers the reader's question: 'How am
I to attain happiness?', the question once posed and answered
by the *Erbauungsbücher* ('devotional works'). Karoline von Wobeser manages in the course of her story, for example, to tell
us amongst other things: why women should not attempt to
become too learned; how and why we should honour our
parents; the dangers of violent emotions; the reforms necessary
to improve the lot of the peasant (Elisa takes up, at one stage,
what can only be called social welfare work amongst the poor);
the dangers of coquetry; how to face up to the fact that one's
husband is committing adultery; the advantages of breast-
feeding; how to educate children; what is wrong with the
German schools and private tutors of the 1790s, and so on. One
aspect of the novel in particular aroused critics, reviewers, and
fellow writers, and no doubt attracted even more readers: the
heroine, on her death-bed, dares to express doubts about the
immortality of the soul, the existence of a life hereafter, but
nevertheless dies in peace, secure in the knowledge that she has
put her stay on this earth to good use. And the author, despite

pressure from her publisher and from reviewers, would make no change or modification of this view in later editions.

All of these things combined—the sentimental style, yet serious content, the stress on *Tugend* and on *Vernunft*, the useful information imparted, and the element of topicality, even notoriety, and social criticism in the novel—made *Elisa* a best seller; and anyone who has seen the correspondence columns in the women's weeklies of today will have realized that Elisa's world is not so far removed from that of her modern counterpart as one might perhaps have thought.

Many German writers at the close of the eighteenth century would, of course, give their works titles which were calculated to attract the eye of the pious reader looking for instructive novels; lovers had their letters published so that the young might learn from their mistakes, villains told their life-stories so that others would not follow in their footsteps, and prostitutes published their memoirs as a warning to young girls. Judging from the title alone, for example, there would seem to be no more praiseworthy novel than Heister's *Geständnisse, Leiden und Warnungen. Ein Vermächtniß für die unerfahrene, sich selbst überlassne Jugend* (1785) (*Confessions, Sorrows and Warnings. A Legacy to our Inexperienced and Neglected Youth*). As pointed out by a reviewer of this work, however, the actual content of the novel could have a very pernicious effect on the 'inexperienced youth'; the reviewer ends: 'Wir sehen es als eine unserer ersten Pflichten an, das Publikum vor losen Speisen, die durch solche Aushängeschilder Käufer ankörnen sollen, gewissenhaft zu warnen.'[83] It is obvious from this that such titles had a 'box-office appeal' not to be ignored. Typical examples of the moral-pedagogic novels, or those professing to be such, are the following, offered at the Easter fair of 1800: *Traurige Folgen frühzeitiger Verlobung, eine wahre Geschichte zur Warnung für Eltern, Jüngling und Mädchen* (*The Sad Consequences of Precipitate Betrothal, a True Story, told as a Warning to Parents, Young Men, and Girls*); *Lebensgeschichte der Maria Weinerin — oder Jenseits muß Vergeltung sein. Eine wahre Geschichte zur Belehrung, Trost und Unterhaltung* (*Life-History of Maria Weinerin—or Retribution must come in the Life Hereafter. A True Story to Instruct, Console, and Entertain*).

Not every reader, however, demanded that his reading material be of an edifying nature. By the end of the century novel-reading was to many just as much a pastime as was, say, dancing or card-playing, and the first requirement of a novel was that it should be entertaining. Readers of this type had once been a rarity amongst the middle class but now that the grip of the Church, once the supreme power in matters public and private, had been broken, a secular literature of entertainment found a ready market in all classes of society.

Contemporaries often speak of the changing attitude towards the Church. Perthes, for instance, writes that during his childhood (1772 onwards) enlightenment occupied the place of religion, and freemasonry that of the Church, that men of culture knew the Bible only by hearsay and looked with pity on the peasant and artisan who still read it; even clergymen uttered their tame jokes about Balaam's ass and the walls of Jericho. During the first ten years of his establishment in Hamburg (1796–1806) the only Bibles he sold were to a few bookbinders in neighbouring country towns; he mentions in particular one 'good sort of man' who came into his shop for a Bible and took great pains to assure him it was for a person about to be confirmed, 'fearing evidently lest I should suppose it was for himself'.[84] Herder's wife writes in similar vein: 'Es war damals [c. 1776] bei vielen Mode, von Allem, was kirchliche oder Schul-Einrichtung hieß, äußerst gering zu denken. Der geistliche Stand wurde bei jeder Gelegenheit lächerlich gemacht.'[85] The drop in the production of religious and devotional works for the layman has already been shown.[86]

There can scarcely be a more secular branch of fiction than the comic novel, and this type of narrative literature was amongst the most popular with the novel-reading public during the last decades of the century. One critic writes in 1785: 'Es schreibt jetzo alles komische Romane, wie vor einiger Zeit alles empfindsame, und wird gelesen.'[87] Amongst the most successful comic novels were those of Theodor Gottlieb von Hippel, 1741–1796 (*Lebensläufe nach aufsteigender Linie* (1778–81); *Kreuz- und Querzüge des Ritters A bis Z* (1793), etc.), A. F. F. von Knigge, 1752–96 (*Der Roman meines Lebens* (1781–3); *Die Geschichte Peter Clausens* (1783–5); *Die Reise nach Braunschweig* (1792); *Geschichte des Amtsrats Gutmann* (1794), etc.), J. G. Müller, 1743–1828 (*Siegfried von Lindenberg* (1779); *Komische Romane* (1784–91, in 8 vols.), etc.), and J. K. Wezel, 1747–1819 (*Peter Marks* (1779);

Kakerlak, oder die Geschichte eines Rosenkreutzes (1784), etc.). Knigge
tells us why such works found so many readers when he writes
of his own novels: '. . . sie gehen reißend ab, weil sie lustig zu
lesen sind, nicht viel Kopfbrechens kosten, und nicht über-
mäßig lehrreich sind.'[88]

Perhaps the most popular writer in this field at the turn of
the century was August Friedrich Langbein (1757–1835), who
won the favour of the wider public with his piquant, racy short
stories and comic novels, *Der graue König* (1802), *Der Ritter der
Wahrheit* (1805), *Thomas Kellerwurm* (1806), *Franz und Rosalie*
(1808), etc. So popular were his novels that writers delighted in
sending their wares into the world under his name; critics, too,
agreed that his name alone was sufficient recommendation for
a work: 'Herr Langbein ist längst als Lieblingsschriftsteller des
Publikums bekannt, so daß diese neueste Frucht seiner Laune
(*Franz und Rosalie*) keiner weitern Empfehlung bedarf.'[89] Like the
vast majority of novels written at this time, those of Langbein are
hardly remembered today; they had served their purpose in
entertaining the contemporary public. The Easter fair catalogue
of 1800 lists thirty-one 'satirico-comical' novels: e.g. *Der Mann
mit drei Perücken* (*The Man with three Wigs*); *Die Jungfer Mahm mit
dem Bart* (*Miss Mahm the Bearded Lady*); *Adelhaupt von Stockfisch*;
Der Narr in Folio (*The Fool in Folio*), etc.; and of these, only one is
remembered today—Jean Paul's *Titan*.

Jean Paul Friedrich Richter (1763–1825) was one of the few
writers of his day whose works appealed to all readers of the
German middle class, whether they looked for instruction or for
entertainment in their reading material. One of the explana-
tions for his universal popularity is to be found in the remarkable
combination of popular elements present in his novels. By
combining the turbulence and sentimentality of Storm and
Stress with the stern idealism of Fichte, the moralizing tone of
the older fiction with the subjectivity of the Romantic writers,
the problematic classical novel with the popular sensational
novel, he united, too, the various publics which had separately
followed these trends. His novels were read alike by the admirers
of the didactic enlighteners, of Werther's emotions, of Siegwart's sentimentalism, of Jacobi's cult of feeling, of Herder's
philosophic and Moritz's psychological approach; and no one
was more aware of, or more pleased at, this than Jean Paul

himself for his financial circumstances, especially at the beginning of his career, made it impossible for him to ignore the commercial aspect of writing.

The foundation of Jean Paul's popularity was laid by his novel *Die unsichtbare Loge oder die grüne Nachtleiche ohne den 9. Nußknacker* (1793), the title of which (*The Invisible Lodge, or the Green Nocturnal Corpse without the Ninth Nutcracker*), as the author himself tells us,[90] was chosen purely for commercial reasons, to attract the eye and the imagination of the public and to secure the author's name a place in their memories; further appeal was given to the novel by adding to the title . . . *eine Biographie*.[91] Jean Paul's story may be regarded as a fantastic variation of the type of educational novel brought into vogue by the Enlighteners, but the predominant mood is sentimental. At the same time, there is no lack of exciting incident, and the mysterious element too, so beloved of the wider reading public, is introduced in the shape of Gustav's mentor, 'der Genius'. Part of the story is told in the still popular form of letters. For good measure, the comic prose idyll, *Das Leben des vergnügten Schulmeisterleins Maria Wuz in Auenthal*, was appended to *Die unsichtbare Loge*.

The success of this novel, however, was surpassed by Jean Paul's next book, *Hesperus oder 45 Hundsposttage* (1792–4); again the sub-title . . . *eine Lebensbeschreibung* (*a Biography*) is added. Amongst the many popular elements present in this novel we notice in particular the preoccupation with the theme of love and friendship, the humour and realism, especially in the characterization, and the introduction of exciting and often inexplicable events centring on the mysterious Emanuel-Dahore; both these novels would seem, in fact, to be an attempt to combine the older type of adventure or sensational novel with the new educational novel of development, a combination which appealed very much to the reading public of 1800. But to contemporaries the most popular aspect of Jean Paul's novels was without doubt his sentimentalism; both *Die unsichtbare Loge* and *Hesperus* contain passages which might have come from the pen of Sophie von Laroche, whilst towards the end of *Hesperus* the main 'literary' theme—the conflict of the idealist with the sordid realities of life—tapers away, leaving an ordinary, sentimental romance of the most popular type. After the appearance of *Hesperus* Jean Paul was regarded as the most fashionable sentimental writer of his day, and the rest of his novels were assured of their public. Perhaps the most popular of his later works was the bourgeois-realistic presentation of the *Ehestand, Tod und Hochzeit des Armenadvokaten F. St. Siebenkäs* (1795–6).

To the average novel-reader of his day, Jean Paul was not the problematic, classical author known to German literary history, but the best of the many sentimental novelists now sending their wares to the Leipzig book fair. For the taste for sentimental fiction was still very much alive in the wider reading public, especially amongst the female novel-readers, whose numbers, as already mentioned, had increased immensely during the second half of the century. Any novelist who aimed at good sales and substantial returns ignored this section of the public and its demands at his peril. Interesting in this respect is the following extract from a letter, accompanying a copy of *Die unsichtbare Loge*, sent by Jean Paul to Frau von Streit in 1794: '— um es für Sie zu verschönern, hab' ich's für Sie verkürzt — ich habe die Stellen, die blos Satire enthalten, mit Bleistift verurtheilt, von Ihnen übersprungen zu werden, damit Sie früher zu den sanftern kommen, die wie Adagios blos für das weibliche aufgeweichte Herz gehören.'[92] So well did Jean Paul know his female readers and the importance of catering for their taste.

Not surprisingly the women of Germany were now no longer satisfied with the merely passive role of reading, especially when fiction was drawing so much of its inspiration from the woman's world of the family, love, and friendship, and the feminine mood of sentimentalism. The example of Sophie von Laroche was soon followed and by the end of the century women novelists were no longer the rarity they had once been. Amongst the female authors of the Rationalistic family novels we find, for example, Maria Anna Sagar, Susanne Barbara Knabe, Friedericke Helene Unger, Sophie Tresenreuter, Christianne Sophie Ludwig, Sophie Helmine Wahl, Johanna Isabella von Wallenrodt, Wilhelmine Karoline von Wobeser, and Benedicte Naubert.[93] Typical examples of this type of fiction, a favourite of the female reading public, are to be found in the Leipzig book-fair catalogue of 1800: *Elise von Wahlheim und Bernardo, eine wahre Familiengeschichte mit Originalbriefen* (*Elise von Wahlheim and Bernardo, a True Family History with Genuine Letters*); *Ehestandsgemälde aus der wirklichen Welt* (*Portraits of Married Life from the Real*

World); *Die Familie des Predigers zu Birkenhayn* (*The Family of the Vicar of Birkenhayn*); *Familienszenen* (*Scenes from Family Life*), etc. Three women novelists were particularly successful in their attempt to emulate the success of Sophie von Laroche in the writing of sentimental love-stories. These were Meta Liebeskind (1765–1809) (*Maria, eine Geschichte in Briefen* (1784), etc.), Friederike Lohmann (1749–?) (*Claudine Lahn, oder Bescheidenheit und Schönheit behält den Preis* (1802), etc.), and Eleonore Thon (1757–1807) (*Julie von Hirtenthal, eine Geschichte in Briefen* (1780–1783), etc.). By far the most popular writer of sentimental family novels at the turn of the century, however, was August Heinrich Lafontaine (1758–1831) whose collected works number no less than 160 volumes.[94] From 1800 onwards Lafontaine lived by his pen alone, producing an endless stream of popular novels, which combined the family motifs and moralizing tone of the Rationalistic novel, the adventurous twists of the travel novel, the eroticism of the lower type of fiction and the emotional outbursts of the sentimental novel, and winning for himself a place on the book-shelves of every reading woman and many reading men in Germany; he is said to have been the favourite author of Friedrich Wilhelm III of Prussia.[95] From his more 'literary' colleagues, Tieck and Menzel, Lafontaine earned nothing but mockery and contempt; A. W. Schlegel had indeed praised his early novels as amongst the best Germany could show, but he changed his opinion in later years and joined in his colleagues' derision of Lafontaine, *der Modeerzähler* ('fashionable author').

His numerous readers, however, adored Lafontaine almost to the point of worship. His biographer, J. G. Gruber, tells us that all his novels went through two or three editions in a very short time, were translated into many European languages, were read in the lending libraries until they fell to pieces, and were even bought by fathers for their daughters' dowries; scarcely an almanac, 'pocket-book', or magazine appeared without contributions from Lafontaine, the poems which he included in his novels were set to music—'und er konnte, so gut wie Göthe, das Vergnügen haben, sie auf der Straße bei Leierkästen absingen zu hören'.[96] One incident in connection with Lafontaine's popularity is worth recording in greater detail as it illustrates so concretely and in human terms the whole trend of the eighteenth century, the trend which we have noted in the impersonal statistics of the German book trade; the pastor of Bischdorf, a member of the older generation, tells Gustav Fr. Dinter, a Lutheran theologian and pedagogue:

> Denken Sie, wie es mir mit den Lafontainischen Romanen gegangen ist. Ich bin gewohnt, alle Morgen ein Kapitel aus dem Alten, alle Abende eins aus dem Neuen Testamente in der Grundsprache zu lesen. Ihr Mättig [a village schoolmaster trained by Dinter] ißt abends bei mir und liest nach Tische meiner Frau und meinen zwei Töchtern, während diese nähen und stricken, Lafontaines Romane vor. Ich schmälte im Anfang: Was leset ihr so dummes Zeug? Leset dafür etwas Erbauliches. Aber am Ende interessieren die Geschichten mich selbst. Ich spreche halb zehn Uhr: Höret auf! Ich will mein Kapitel lesen. Morgen muß ich doch hören, wie der Knoten sich entwickelt. Am Ende — hat Lafontaine bei mir die Bibel mehrere Monate lang verdrängt.[97]

A member of the younger generation, a product of the Age of Enlightenment, has introduced the village pastor and his family to the new secular literature of entertainment and even the old clergyman himself, used only to his devotional literature, has been won over.

The admirers of Lafontaine also found reading material to their taste in the novels of August von Kotzebue (1761–1819), which were more or less narrative variations on the same themes as are found in his domestic dramas, Friedrich August Schulze (1770–1849), whose novel *Der Mann auf Freiersfüßen* (1800) is still read today, and H. Clauren (anagrammatical pseudonym of Carl Heun, 1771–1854), the author of some forty volumes of sentimental fiction. The sentimental type of love-story, so popular with the female reading public, is well represented in the book-fair catalogue of 1800: e.g. *Aemil und Julie, die Unzertrennlichen* (*Aemil and Julie, the Inseparable Ones*); *Amalie und Carl, oder die getrennten Liebenden* (*Amalie and Carl, or the Parted Lovers*); *Das Erwachen der Liebe oder der erste Kuß* (*Love's Awakening, or the First Kiss*); *Karl von Kiesmar oder Liebe ohne Genuß, Ehe ohne Eifersucht, Trennung ohne Thränen* (*Karl von Kiesmar, or Love without Lust, Marriage without Jealousy, Parting without Tears*), etc.[98]

Before turning to the lower social classes and their reading material we must first briefly consider two factors which normally lie outside the scope of the orthodox literary historian but which here assume vital importance: firstly, the state of primary education in Germany during the second half of the eighteenth century and secondly, what might be termed 'the economics of book-buying', the relationship between book prices and average earnings. On these two factors and, of course, on the availability of suitable reading material depends the extent to which the peasant and artisan class are to be considered as part of the novel-reading public.

Accurate statistics on the incidence of illiteracy at this time are not available; we can only form a general picture of the situation from the data we have relating to primary education in the various states.[99] One thing, however, is certain—assuming fairly widespread primary education to be a prerequisite for the existence of a wider reading public, we cannot begin to speak of the latter until 1750 at the earliest.

In Württemberg, for example, general compulsory attendance at school was decreed in 1649, and the parents of children who did not attend regularly were to be punished; but a generation later, in 1672, there were still not enough schools to enable the enforcement of the decree, and those schools which did exist were rarely open during the summer months. The chief concern of the authorities in matters of education is indicated by the Württemberg order of 1695, that in those areas still without schools a recapitulation of the catechism, hymn-book, and *Sprüche* had to be given by the clergy every Saturday and Sunday before the sermon. In all primary schools the curriculum was extremely narrow—reading and writing, the barest outline of arithmetic, and a good deal of religion and hymn-singing.

Conditions in the profession of teaching were indicative of the meagre importance attached to things educational. Even university teachers, especially those of the Arts Faculty, teachers in the grammar schools, and private tutors did not command much respect in German society. The respect enjoyed by the village schoolmaster was, naturally, even less. Many teachers regarded their job merely as a stepping-stone to a higher post, the vast majority being theologians waiting for a living in the Church. Almost every schoolmaster had to supplement his income by other means; in the towns some were able to secure a few boarders, some were organists or vergers, some would earn a little by their pens, and all gave private lessons, but in country districts teachers were obliged also to learn some handicraft. Jung-Stilling, for example, was to enter the teaching profession, but as his father, a teacher/tailor, said, 'damit du etwas Gewisses habest, womit du dein Brot erwerben könnest, mußt du mein Handwerk lernen'.[100] In many instances indeed it was more a case of craftsmen supplementing their income by teaching; a Brandenburg decree of 1722 declares that apart from tailors, weavers, smiths, wheelwrights, and carpenters, no other artisans might grace the office of village schoolmaster, and in 1736 we read: 'Ist der Schulmeister ein Handwerker, kann er sich schon nähren; ist er keiner, wird ihm erlaubt, sechs Wochen auf Tagelohn zu gehen.'[101]

In an age that believed so passionately in education one might have expected this situation to be righted by the end of the eighteenth century, and indeed many attempts at reform were made; since the appearance of the first moral weeklies *Erziehung der Jugend* ('education of youth') had been the catchphrase of each new intellectual movement; the question of educational reforms had never been allowed to sink into the background. The age of benevolent despotism and of the absolute sovereign was also not slow in recognizing that the power of the prince rested ultimately on the efficiency and productive capacity of his subjects; by increasing the personal and economic efficiency and welfare of his subjects, the ruler was, in fact, improving his own circumstances, and naturally he could only make contact with his subjects, inform them of their duties as loyal citizens, if they had at least sufficient education to be able to read and obey his decrees and directives. Much of the emphasis on primary education was, in fact, political and economic in origin and not in the first instance philanthropic or even pedagogic. Thus it was that the governments of Frederick the Great, Maria Theresa, and their lesser imitators like Max Joseph in Bavaria had all shown an interest in the improvement of primary schools, providing better training-colleges and better conditions for teachers, and in the practical enforcement of compulsory education. Most of the reforms, however, remained on paper; it was only in the nineteenth century that the work of men like Eberhard von Rochow and Johann Heinrich Pestalozzi began to take effect, bringing about the reform of the whole educational system.

Compulsory education had been ordered in Prussia in 1717, in Saxony in 1772, and in Bavaria only in 1802, but nowhere was it rigidly enforced in practice. In 1786 a census in connection with the Felbiger reforms revealed that of 239,424 children in Bohemia only 142,125 (i.e. 59 per cent) really attended school regularly, and even in an enlightened state like Prussia an inspection made in 1802 showed that Frederick's admirable General-Landschul-Reglement of 1763 had not been followed up by widespread practical measures.

Yet by the end of the century a considerable number of peasants and craftsmen could at least read and write, as indicated most convincingly by the large sales of calendars and similar publications especially written for them. Even early in the century the countryman's *Rossiusche Kalender* of Basel had brought in the, for those days, considerable profit of 200 Thaler annually.[102] One contemporary critic tells us in 1778, when putting the case for the publication of a really good entertaining and edifying newspaper 'for the common man', that even the most poverty-stricken village tavern in Germany now subscribes to some newspaper or other for its customers.[103] There was no greater commercial success during the whole century than Rudolf Zacharias Becker's *Noth- und Hülfsbüchlein oder lehrreiche Freuden- und Trauergeschichte der Einwohner zu Mildheim* (1788) (*Manual of Aid in Times of Need, or the Instructive Story of the Sorrows and Joys of the Inhabitants of Mildheim*), which was written expressly for the peasant and country-dweller. Within one year of its publication 30,000 copies had been sold and four pirated editions had appeared, even though the pirate publishers could not hope to underbid Becker's price of 4 Groschen (about 3p); imitations, like *Noth- und Hülfsbüchlein für Freudenmädchen und ihre Kinder* (*Manual of Aid, . . . for Prostitutes and their Children*), soon appeared on the market. Becker's book had gone through eleven authorized editions by 1791, and if Becker himself is to be believed 1,000,000 copies of the work had been sold by 1811.[104]

In addition to the ability and the desire to read, the capacity to afford to buy books is of obvious relevance in our present context; indeed, for those on the lower economic fringes of the reading public the price of a book is often *the* decisive factor.

Without going into what would here be inordinate detail on the relative purchasing power of money and the cost of living in that age compared with that of our own, a few representative examples, brought into perspective by reference to earnings and prices in general in the eighteenth century, will serve both to illustrate the over-all situation and perhaps also to indicate the nature of the economic considerations in the mind of the individual prospective book-buyer.[105]

From January to December 1785 the *Allgemeine Literatur-Zeitung* reviewed forty-six novels and collections of *Erzählungen*, of which forty-one were in one volume and five in two volumes; the total price for these fifty-one volumes of fiction was 33 Thaler 20 Groschen, thus producing an average price of about 16 Groschen per volume. The highest-priced volume was one at 1 Thaler 16 Groschen (for 592 pages in 8°) and the lowest was at 3 Groschen (for 38 pages in 8°). The average number of pages per volume was 305; one may say, then, that in 1785 1 Groschen could buy about nineteen pages of fiction. But the man who spent 16 Groschen on a novel at this time could also have bought for the same money about 5 lb. of beef or 5 lb. of butter (at its summer price—2 lb. in winter) or about 2 lb. of sugar, remembering that sugar was still very much a luxury article; and if 1 Groschen could buy about nineteen pages of fiction, that same Groschen could also buy more than 1 lb. of black bread or two eggs.

We have further examples of book prices, this time of the most popular types of fiction, in the advertisement mentioned earlier[106] where the book-dealer Sommer announces whole lending libraries for sale. Sommer offers his customers 330 volumes at the 'bargain price' of 77 Thaler—nearly 6 Groschen per volume; as the shop price he quotes 253 Thaler—about 18 Groschen per volume. His further offer of 504 volumes at 137 Thaler works out at nearly 7 Groschen per volume, against a shop price of 407 Thaler—that is 19 Groschen each. It might be thought that the shop price quoted in the advertisement would probably be inflated so as to convince prospective buyers that they were indeed being offered a bargain; but a *Reichsbote* advertisement of 1805[107] shows the prices of lending library favourites ranging from 8 Groschen to 1 Thaler 16 Groschen, and averaging also 18 Groschen. The over-all verdict must be that even the most popular type of novel was by no means cheap. A labourer who spent 8 Groschen on a novel had spent his wages for two whole days, for a master-mason or carpenter it meant one day's wages, while a spinner working on piece-work earned no more than 20 Groschen a week; a skilled factory worker, on the other hand, might expect to earn up to 6 Thaler a week (144 Groschen).[108] At the other end of the social and literary scale, a young jurist who might start at about 140 Thaler per year would be asked 16 Thaler for the Cotta edition of Goethe's works (1806–10) in thirteen volumes; the Vieweg edition of *Hermann und Dorothea* would cost him 2 Thaler 8 Groschen (almost six days' earnings).

We may say, then, that with the possible exception of the skilled industrial worker only very rarely would a member of the lower social classes walk into a bookshop and buy a novel; the severity of economic factors restricted the reading public to this extent, but there were of course other sources of supply, as we have seen—cheaper pirated editions and, above all, the lending libraries where less affluent members of the reading public (and not only they) could borrow novels for a fee well within their means. In Hermannstadt the charge was 6 kr. a week or 20 kr. a month in the 1780s but customers here still had to leave a deposit to the value of the book borrowed; in Gießen in the 1790s the lending library offered its 1,500 volumes to local borrowers at a fee of 1 kr. per day, 4 kr. per week, or 3 fl. 30 kr. per year—a copy of the library's catalogue was also available at a cost of 4 kr. (60 Kreuzer = 1 'Florin' or Gulden; 90 Kreuzer = 1 Thaler; hence 1 Kreuzer = less than 0·2p; 4 Kreuzer = less than 0·7p; the annual fee of 3 fl. 30 kr. = about 35p).[109] There were, too, the travelling book-lenders and book-pedlars who carried their wares to the small towns and villages of all parts of Germany offering books, pamphlets, ballads, journals, etc., for a few Pfennige or Kreuzer.

Country-folk depended to a very large extent for the supply of their reading material on such travelling booksellers, the *Jahrmarktströdler*, and their wares. These men knew the different tastes of their customers and arranged their stocks accordingly. Next to the most devout and edifying works we find books of the most obscene kind, many of them translations of the novels of the popular French writers Crébillon, Rétif de la Bretonne,

Choderlos de Laclos, and Louvet de Couvray. Not that the lower social classes were the only public for this licentious literature; such books have always found readers in every walk of life. All the main works of the above French novelists were to be had either openly or in secret in most of the lending libraries, along with the mass of imitations by German writers like Althing (Christian August Fischer), whose novel, *Hannchens Hin- und Herzüge, nebst der Geschichte dreier Hochzeitsnächte* (1800, repeatedly reprinted) (*Jenny's Journeys To and Fro, together with the Story of Three Wedding Nights*), proved so popular that many similar products were thereafter labelled *in Althings Manier*. Lang tells us, in his *Memoirs*, of noblemen and even one high clergyman who had collected whole libraries of such works.[110] It was not only the lower classes, then, to whom Goethe was referring in his poem *Das Parterre spricht*: 'Lieber will ich schlechter werden, / Als mich ennuyieren.' ('I would suffer corruption, / Rather than endure boredom.')

Also to be found amongst the stocks of the book-pedlars were the old chap-books, which had kept their popularity amongst country-folk for over three hundred years. A contemporary critic tells us in 1668—before the advent of middle-class literature— that apart from prayer-books and household books (*Hausbücher*), the most read books were the chap-books, *Die Finkenritter, Eulenspiegel, Lalenbuch, Markgraf Walther, Herzog Ernst, Der gehörnte Siegfried, Schöne Magelone, Schöne Melusine, Faust, Der ewige Jude, Die Unterweisung der sieben weisen Meister, Herr Tristrant und Wigalois, Der Goldfaden, Der list- und lustige Soldat*, and *Der endlich verzweifelnde Academicus*.[111]

Many of these rudimentary novels had been written, or translated from the French, by members of the German nobility for their fellow aristocrats; they had been passed on to friends in manuscript form. With the invention of printing, however, a stop was put to the monopolizing by the nobility of the pastime of novel-reading, and printed copies were soon to be had in all parts of the country; the novels, and for a time the pastime of novel-reading, went in fact down the social scale. When the success of these originally aristocratic novels amongst the peasantry had become apparent, there soon appeared stories written especially for country-folk, books like *Eulenspiegel* (1515) and *Lalenbuch* (1597, rewritten in 1598 as *Die Schildbürger*), where the peasant was able for once to read of foolish, gullible townsfolk and ingenious, humorous, though roguish, peasants. All of these books were available at the Leipzig and Frankfurt book fairs even in the sixteenth century,[112] and most of them were still available in the eighteenth century, as we know from Goethe's *Dichtung und Wahrheit*.[113]

In three hundred years they had never become outmoded—many of them bore the legend *gedruckt in diesem Jahr* ('printed this year')—nor had they lost any of their popularity. The Frankfurt bookseller Wilhelm Fleischer writes in 1792: 'Der ungebildete Landmann ist bei abentheuerlichen Vorfällen — wie sie die Eulenspiegeliaden erzählen — ganz Ohr: denn sie passen zu seinen rohen Begriffen.'[114] Vulpius speaks of a shepherd whose favourite reading material was the chap-books, especially *Der gehörnte Siegfried, Die schöne Magelone*, and *Die schöne Melusine*.[115] Even the peasants who could not read belonged to the admirers of the chap-books, for these were the books they chose when they were fortunate enough to get someone to read aloud to them. A contemporary, speaking of the countryman, writes: '. . . oft, und vornehmlich im Winter hat er Langeweile, und läßt, wie ich oft gesehen, von seinen Kindern etwas aus dem *Eulenspiegel*, oder den *Schildbürgern* vorlesen'.[116] In Müller's novel, *Siegfried von Lindenberg* (1779), we read of a village schoolmaster who spent one evening weekly reading aloud to a gathering of peasants at the local inn in return for his evening's beer; he was busy at the time reading *Der gehörnte Siegfried*.[117]

Many of the chap-books took their material from legends of Carolingian days, telling stories of knights in armour, their brave deeds and dashing love-affairs. It had once pleased the aristocracy to see in these tales a reflection of their own greatness and glory; as reading material for the lower classes, however, they were simply good adventure stories, packed with stirring and exciting events and free from all problematic, intellectual, and didactic treatises. It was this taste for the adventurous element, most strong in the lower classes who could not themselves hope to travel and enjoy exciting events, that explains also the long-lived popularity of the 'Robinsonades'. Wilhelm Fleischer writes in 1792, over seventy years after the appearance of Defoe's novel: 'Der unstäte Handwerksbursche spürt emsig den Robinsonaden nach';[118] and as late as 1800, as already seen, we find books drawing inspiration from the English novel listed in the Leipzig-fair catalogue; e.g. *Der einsame Inselbewohner, oder Robert Surrais Schicksale in zween Welttheilen* (*The lonely Islander, or Robert Surrai's Fateful Adventures in Two Continents*); *Robinsons wunderbare und merkwürdige Schicksale zu Wasser und zu Lande, mit Bildern für den Bürger und Landmann* (*Robinson's Strange and Remarkable Adventures on Land and at Sea, with Illustrations for Townsfolk and Countrymen*), etc.

Readers with a liking for exciting adventure stories, whatever their social class, found most of their reading material, however, in the host of romances of chivalry, robber, ghost, and horror novels which flooded the German book market and made up the main stocks of every lending library during the last decade of the eighteenth century. August Wilhelm Schlegel writes in the *Jenaische Literatur-Zeitung* in 1797:

> Seit sechs oder sieben Jahren stemmen sich alle Rezensenten des heiligen römischen Reichs, die in diesem Fache arbeiten, gegen die Ritterromane, aber die Menge der ritterlichen Lanzen und Schwerter dringt immer unaufhaltsamer auf sie ein. Vor den Femegerichten, den geheimnisvollen Bündnissen und den Geistern ist vollends gar keine Rettung mehr.[119]

The taste for thrilling tales of brave medieval knights, horrible stories of tyrants and the like had been kept alive in the lower classes not only by the chap-books but also by the so-called historical journals mentioned earlier in this study;[120] several of the more successful *Ritterromane*, the Oriental tales, and heroic gallant novels of the seventeenth century (e.g. *Asiatische Banise, Römische Octavia, Herkules und Valiska*) had also appealed to the same taste and had in fact experienced what is nowadays known as a 'come-back' in the course of the eighteenth century, drawing readers this time, however, from a much wider public and not only from the leisured aristocracy—all in accordance with what Wolfgang Leonhardt has termed 'ein soziologisches Gesetz des Geschmacks: man findet schön, was der sozial Höherstehende vor dreißig Jahren schön fand'.[121] The serious-minded member of the upper bourgeoisie might want to read of his everyday life and problems, but the average reader, certainly the average countryman and the inhabitant of the smaller towns, wanted to forget his problems, his dull everyday life, when he picked up a novel. He delighted in unusual, remarkable, and exciting events set in strange and romantic places in far-off days, rather than in didactic tales of his own life and times; he preferred the supernatural to the sentimental, and the romantic to the realistic.

Yet the popular novels of the last decades of the century, despite their fantastic subject-matter, cannot deny their inheritance from the Enlightenment; they are in effect the sub-literary versions of Wieland's Rationalistic novels of the past. They look at the past from a purely Rationalistic standpoint, exaggerating the part played in life by Reason, they show the concentrated Rationalistic hatred of clericalism, some natural explanation of supernatural happenings is always offered, and they even attempt to assume a moral purpose—the bandit fights for right, ghosts appear as a punishment for wicked deeds, and secret societies exist only for 'the furthering of virtue'.

In the ghost novel *Hinko mit der eisernen Tasche* (1794–7) (*Hinko, the Man with the Iron Pouch*), we have a typical example of this type of fiction. Here we read of bloody fights and violent murders, we move in the company of either very wicked or very holy monks, very noble or very despicable knights, we hear the groans of unhappy maidens and the satanic cursing of hypocritical clergy and raving aristocrats—all set in a world of secret passages, subterranean caves, dense forests, and castle dungeons. There is a total lack of artistic or intellectual ability, the ideas are fantastic, rather than exaggerated; in one instance the blood of a wounded knight runs on to his armour to form the words, 'Pfaffenstolz und Aberglaube färbten mich mit Menschenblut'.[122] Typical of the language of such fiction are the following sentences from *Hinko*: '. . . sein Vatergefühl wurde mit Höllenqual gepeinigt, Zorn zerfleischte sein Eingeweide; er stampfte mit den Füßen, daß der Boden bebte, seine Lippen zitterten und seine Augen rollten wie Feuerkugeln'; '. . . des Abts Wuth war grenzenlos, in convulsivischen Zuckungen dehnte sie sich über die ganze Fleischmasse aus.'[123]

The most popular writers of this type of fiction were Christian August Vulpius (1762–1827), Karl Gottlob Cramer (1758–1817), and Christian Heinrich Spieß (1755–99). Cramer writes, with justification, of his works: 'Meine Romane werden, was auch immer trübsinnige, mürrische Recensenten denken und

sagen mögen, nicht gelesen, sondern verschlungen, nach-
gedruckt und doch viermal aufgelegt';[124] in similar vein he
writes in the Preface to the second part of his *Gefährliche Stunden*
(1800): 'Uns ist daran gelegen, daß die Welt uns lese, darum
kümmern wir uns nicht, es ist uns einerlei, was ihr von uns
schmiert, wenn wir nur den Ton treffen, in welchem Herzen
und Sinne unseres Zeitalters gestimmt sind.'[125] His attitude was
shared by his colleagues. They had no artistic ambitions whatever and were satisfied if their works enjoyed good sales and
brought in good profits.

They had good reason to be satisfied. All of Cramer's novels
went through three or four authorized editions, pirated reprints
were quick to follow their appearance, some of his stories were
dramatized, and several were translated into English. His
popularity is further underlined by the number of writers who
labelled their products 'Vom Verfasser des *Hasper a Spada*' ('By
the author of . . .'), Cramer's most successful novel. Vulpius,
now remembered in literary history only as Goethe's brother-
in-law, was no less popular. His most successful novel, *Rinaldo
Rinaldini, der Räuberhauptmann* (1797), went through eight legal
editions, at least two pirated editions appeared, selections from
the three-volumed work were published separately several
times, and it was translated into English, French, Dutch,
Swedish, Danish, Spanish, Italian, Polish, Russian, and Hun-
garian. Vulpius himself adapted it for the stage in 1800 and,
despite the many imitations which followed the novel's appearance, repeated his success with *Orlando Orlandini* (1802). The
Bibliothek der schönen Wissenschaften (1837–46) of Enslin and
Engelmann, who declared their bibliography would include
'only the superior works of our poetic literature', lists no less
than sixty works by Vulpius. *Rinaldo Rinaldini* is, in fact, still
available to the German novel-reading public in an edition
published by the Karl Rauch Verlag in Düsseldorf in 1959.

The novels of Christian Heinrich Spieß were read in all
classes of Germany society, in higher circles too; the writer's
high position at the court of Count Känigl would no doubt help
him in this respect.[126] Most of his novels went through several
editions, authorized and pirated; they were translated, dramatized, continued, and imitated; works were often assigned to
him by unknown writers who knew the power of his name. His

most popular novels were: *Biographien der Selbstmörder* (1785–9); *Das Petermännchen* (1791); *Der alte Überall und Nirgends* (1792); *Die Löwenritter* (1794); and *Reisen durch die Höhlen des Unglücks* (1796).

Other successful thriller writers, with their most popular works, include Karl Nicolai, 1779–1819 (*Die Banditenhöhle von Carastro*), Ignaz Ferdinand Arnold, 1774–1812 (*Der Brautkuß auf dem Graben; Der berühmte Räuberhauptmann Schinderhannes*), Johann Friedrich Ernst Albrecht, 1752–1816 (*Dolko der Bandit; Lauretta Pisana, Leben einer italienischen Buhlerin*), Karl Grosse, 1761–1847 (*Der Genius*),[127] and Johann Ernst Daniel Bornschein, 1774–1838 (*Der Hundssattler*); even Heinrich Zschokke (1771–1848), before he turned to writing didactic tales (*Goldmacherdorf* (1817)), tried his hand with great success at the popular robber novel— *Die schwarzen Brüder* (1791–5) and *Abällino der große Bandit* (1793), the novel which in the translation by 'Monk' Lewis, *The Bravo of Venice* (1805), gave Zschokke a considerable following in England.

Even women novelists were not averse to writing tales of robbers, knights, ghosts, and witches, although of course any woman who moved or hoped to move in higher circles restricted her writing to the virtuous sentimental family novels. The women who did produce horror novels were usually of more lowly social origin or else they were *déclassées* of the upper class to whom it was a pleasure to follow the tendency of this branch of the genre to tear the mask away from the 'gallant world', and deal with that side of life which was not to be mentioned in good society. Sophie Albrecht (1757–1841), the daughter of an Erfurt professor, for example, was brought up in good bourgeois society; after leaving her husband to become an actress, however, she found herself in great need and shunned by bourgeois friends, and so she turned to writing popular sensational novels of the crudest type—e.g. *Die geheime Geschichte eines Rosenkreutzes* (1792); *Die Geschichte des höflichen Gespenstes* (1797), etc. The same was the case with Frau von Wallenrodt (1740–1819), Friederike Henriette Kühn (1779–1803), and Elisabeth Hollmann (dates not known), author of the novel *Hinko* mentioned above.[128]

Most of the writers of thrillers, however, preferred to remain anonymous; they relied on exciting and impressive titles rather than on reputation to attract readers: *Das Jüdische Großmütter-chen, oder der schreckbare Geist der Frau im schwarzen Gewande* (*The Dear Old Jewish Grandmother, or the Terrifying Ghost of the Woman in the Black Robe*); *Holm von Schlehenhorst, Verteidiger männlicher Rechte, Geschichte aus den Ritterzeiten* (*Holm von Schlehenhorst, Champion of the Rights of Men, a Tale from the Age of Chivalry*); *Der Nachtwächter, oder das Nachtlager der Geister bei Saatz in Böheim, eine fürchterliche Sage aus den Zeiten des grauen Zauberalters* (*The Night-Watchman, or the Ghosts' Encampment near Saatz in Bohemia, a Horrible Saga from the Dark Age of Sorcery*); *Gräfin Nadasdi, Vicekönigin von Ungarn, zwölffache Mörderin aus Eitelkeit. Eine wahre, schaudervolle Geschichte des 17. Jahrhunderts* (*Countess Nadasdi, Vicereine of Hungary, Twelvefold Murderess through Vanity. A True and Terrifying Story from the Seventeenth Century*), etc. This was the type of novel most popular with the greater reading public; such books made up the backbone of every lending library and, as Hauff tells us, 'entweder keinen Rücken mehr hatten, oder vom Lesen so fett geworden waren, daß sie mich ordentlich anglänzten'.[129]

Literary historians, when dealing with this period, have tended in the past to neglect the fictional works popular with the wider reading public, saying that they entertained contemporary readers and leaving it at that. The robber and ghost novels, the tales of horror, and the popular romances of chivalry certainly did entertain contemporaries but they were also not without influence on the development of German letters.

In fulfilling the popular demands of the day, by yielding to popular taste and placing their stories in far-off days amidst romantic settings, these novels kept alive the interest in historical and pseudo-historical material. When the heroic gallant novels and romances of chivalry of the seventeenth century had been superseded by the Rationalistic novel the attention of writers had turned from the past to the present; the sentimental novelists had also disregarded history and legend as a source of material. The taste for stories with a historical setting, however, was already too strong in the wider reading public to be forgotten so easily. They liked to read of splendid and horrible deeds in past ages and for that reason this section of the public had clung so determinedly to the chap-books, had welcomed the popular historical journals of the early eighteenth century, and had ultimately availed themselves of the *gesunkenes Kulturgut* of the aristocratic fiction of the previous age. There was still a serious literary undertaking which proves beyond doubt the interest of many readers in the older romances of chivalry; this was Reichard's *Bibliothek der Romane* (1778–94), in which were published not full novels but excerpts from the best *Ritterromane*, offering not complete stories but only the bare motifs which went to make up these stories. How hungry must then the public have been for the old historical tales when a collection of naked, undeveloped motifs was so successful as to last sixteen years and grow to twenty-one volumes.

Writers whose sole ambition it was to provide the greater public with the reading material it wanted could not afford to ignore this taste, and so it was that the popular authors turned once more to history, the chap-books, and the *Ritterromane* for their material. Vulpius, despite his insistence on the originality of his novels, received much of his inspiration and material from Reichard's collection; and the rest of his colleagues, Spieß, Cramer, Albrecht, Arnold, Nicolai, etc., made the same liberal use of the old motifs from the romances of chivalry, in settings often reminiscent of the historical novels of a century earlier.

It is, therefore, not strictly accurate to say that Goethe's *Götz* and Schiller's *Räuber*, *Geisterseher*, and *Verbrecher aus verlorener Ehre* called forth the mass of popular chivalrous, robber, ghost, and horror novels, as has been asserted; the taste for such material had been present in the lower classes since the appearance of the chap-books, had been nurtured by the popular historical journals and some of the older representatives of the genre and, now that writing for the wider reading public had become financially rewarding, was finally fully satisfied by the novels of writers like Vulpius. The whole world and the motifs of this branch of fiction were in fact part of the German literary tradition long before *Götz* appeared. It was, however, the example of Goethe and Schiller that gave cautious and hesitating authors courage to come forward with these popular motifs —motifs which had long been scorned by the more literary novelists and abused by critics—and to seek their material in the inexhaustible store-room of history and legend.

Ancient history had provided Wieland with the settings for

many of his novels but the ideas propounded and the way of thought expressed in them were those of his own day; they were in fact 'unhistorical historical novels'. The same was the case with the works of his imitators, Ignaz Aurelius Feßler, 1756–1839 (*Marc Aurel* (1790–2); *Aristides und Themistokles* (1792), etc.), and August Gottlieb Meißner, 1753–1807 (*Alcibiades* (1785–8); *Bianca Capello* (1785), etc.). More successful were the *Sagen der Vorzeit* (1787–98) by Veit Weber (1762–1837).[130] But it was not until the novels of Benedicte Naubert (1756–1819) appeared that the truly historical approach was made in German fiction. She was the first to attempt the representation of past ages and the characterization of personalities as recorded in historical sources. Her novels were intended not for higher intellectual circles but for the average middle-class reader, and the success which they enjoyed is obvious from the number of authorized and pirated editions of each work, and by the amount of speculation as to the identity of their anonymous author; since many of her novels bear the words 'Vom Verfasser des *Walther von Montbarry*', '. . . der *Thekla von Thurn*', '. . . des *Hermann von Unna*' we may take it that these were her most popular novels.[131]

Through the work of Benedicte Naubert a public was prepared for the historical novels of the Romantic writers, and for the translations of Scott's novels. The foundation had been laid for the future development of this branch of the genre in the hands of Hauff, Häring, Fontane, C. F. Meyer, and Ricarda Huch. The German historical novel, then, had been born in the upper classes in the seventeenth century, slid down the social scale during the eighteenth century to become the *Unterhaltungsroman*, the favourite of the masses, and was then finally reinstated by Benedicte Naubert and the Romantics and made acceptable once more to educated middle- and upper-class readers of fiction.

In addition to the part it played in the establishment of the German historical novel, the popular fiction of these years, by virtue of its very large public, contributed a great deal to the final subversion of the purely rationalistic view of life set forth in the Age of Enlightenment and, in its material and motifs if not in form and style, anticipated much that we now characterize as *Mondscheinromantik* and 'der magische Einblick in die Nachtseiten der Natur'.[132] Furthermore, the reading material of the lower social classes and the wider reading public, the chap-books, romances of chivalry, and the sensational novels, exercised direct influence on the rising generation of poets, the Romantics. We have their own evidence that they were well acquainted with this reading material. Brentano and Tieck were ardent students of the old chap-books and together they brought about the reissue of many of them; Tieck was also very much impressed by his reading of Grosse's *Genius*. Dorothea Schlegel revived *Merlin* and *Loher und Maller*, while Kleist was early acquainted with the old *Ritterromane*. Heine enthused about *Rinaldo Rinaldini*; Immerman, Grillparzer, and Uhland all confess to an early partiality to the popular fiction of Cramer, Spieß, and Vulpius, and Kerner writes: 'In die damalige unschöne Literatur arbeitete ich mich durch die reichlich mit Kramerschen, Spießischen und Lafontainischen u. s. w. Schriften versehene Leihbibliothek des Herrn Antiquars Nast ein.'[133]

The writers of the first decades of the new century had grown up in the world of lending libraries, and the reading material of their youth was not without lasting effect on them and on their works. Tieck's first novels *Abdallah* (1792) and *William Lovell* (1795–6) betray a strong interest in the horrific, terrifying happening so beloved of the popular novelists, whilst his later stories *Der blonde Eckbert, Der getreue Eckhart,* and *Der Liebespokal* all treat the magic powers of the supernatural forces of nature, as countless popular ghost novels had done years before. The adventure novels of Friedrich de la Motte Fouqué may be superior to those of Spieß in technique, language, and style but the motifs and material used by these writers are almost identical; his lion-hearted heroes from the courts of Provence and Moorish Spain might have stepped straight from the old romances of chivalry—the mere titles of his works show their affinity to the popular fiction of the day: *Historie vom edlen Ritter Galmy (The History of Galmy the Noble Knight)* (based on Wickram's *Ritter Galmy uss Schottland*); *Fahrten Thiodulf des Isländers (The Journeys of Thiodulf the Icelander)*; *Der Zauberring (The Magic Ring)*, etc. There were ghosts and supernatural powers in plenty in Arnim's *Kronenwächter,* whilst in the stories of E. T. A. Hoffmann and the early works of Hauff the 'literary tale of terror' surely reached its height.

The popular reading material of the last decades of the eighteenth century had played its part in German letters by giving the younger generation of writers a stimulant for their imagination, a new source of powerful and popular material, and a most assiduous novel-reading public.

APPENDIX I
(AFTER JENTZSCH)

BOOK PRODUCTION AT THE EASTER FAIRS
OF 1740, 1770, AND 1800

Narration	1740					1770					1800				
	Number of publications German	Latin	Percentage of Latin in group	Percentage of total production	Percentage of main group (I etc.)	Number of publications German	Latin	Percentage of Latin in group	Percentage of total production	Percentage of main group (I etc.)	Number of publications German	Latin	Percentage of Latin in group	Percentage of total production	Percentage of main group (I etc.)
TOTAL PRODUCTION	545 and 1 Ital.	209	27·68			981	163	14·25			2,442 and 19 French	102 and 6 Ital.	3·97		
I. THEOLOGY	246	45	15·46	38·54		244	36	12·86	24·47		339	9	2·59	13·55	
(a) For the expert	95	45	31·65	18·41	47·77	110	36	24·14	12·67	52·89	147	9	5·16	6·03	44·54
(b) For the layman	143			19·08	49·48	123			10·84	44·28	148			5·80	42·82
(c) Religious instruction	8			1·06	2·75	11			0·96	3·93	44			1·71	12·64
II. LAW	39	58	59·79	12·85		36	25	40·98	5·33		121	8	6·2	5·02	
III. MEDICINE	31	19	38	6·62		68	23	25·27	7·95		200	9	4·306	8·135	
IV. GENERAL WORKS FOR THE SCHOLAR	23	17	42·5	5·298		39	13	25	4·46		32	5	15·625	1·44	
V. HISTORY AND GEOGRAPHY	65	20	23·53	11·38		101	9	8·18	9·615		267	5	1·84	10·59	
(a) History	53	16	23·19	9·13	81·18	76	8	9·52	7·34	76·36	142	4	2·74	5·68	53·68
(b) Geography	12	2		1·86	16·47	19	1		1·75	18·18	115	1		4·51	42·65
(i) Books of travel	4	2			7·06 of V	5				4·54 of V	52				19·12 of V
VI. POLITICAL SCIENCE	10			1·34		32			2·80		93			3·62	
VII. PHILOSOPHY	24	20	45·45	5·83		27	7	20·59	2·97		87	7	7·45	3·66	
VIII. PEDAGOGY (incl. school books)	4			0·535		20			1·75		105			4·09	

IX. Classical Philology	8	10	55·55	2·45	17	18	51·43	3·06	46	32	41·03	3·04
X. Non-classical Philology	1	4	80	0·662	10	6	37·5	1·4	27	1	3·57	1·09
XI. Imaginative Literature and Fine Arts	40 and 1 Ital.	3	6·82	5·83	181	7	3·72	16·43	523 and 19 French, 6 Ital.	3	0·54	21·45
(1) General, theoretical, etc.	5				12	2		2·36	9			1·52
(2) Various branches:												
(a) Fine Arts	5 and 1 Ital.	1		0·93	12	1			29	1		
(b) Music				15·91	8			0·7	63 and 19 French, 6 Ital.			3·43
(c) Literature:												
(i) Collected works, etc.	8	2	22·71	1·32	27	1	2·45		11	1		1·32
(ii) Poetry	2		4·545	0·26	34	3	3·23		34			2·49
(iii) Drama	20		43·45	2·65	42		3·67		64			
(iv) Narrative literature					46		4·02		300			11·68
XII. Popular-moral Works, etc.	23	8		3·31	39		3·41		102			3·97
XIII. Popular Periodicals	2	2		0·27	34	1	3·06		49			1·907
(a) Moral weeklies	2	2			19							
XIV. Practical House-books, Games, etc.	7			0·93	16		1·4		53			2·06
XV. Mathematics and Natural Sciences	14	11		3·31	54	17	23·61	6·206	161	22	12·02	7·12
XVI. Agriculture, Industry, Engineering, War, and Commerce	8			1·06	59	1		5·24	220	1		8·06

APPENDIX II

PRODUCTION OF NOVELS 1740–1810

(Based on Heinsius, *Alphabetisches Verzeichnis* . . . (Leipzig, 1813). Included in the count: all novels published in German, whether original works or translations; both new and repeated editions in as far as the latter are listed; collections of short stories. Multi-volumed novels counted as *one* item, dated by appearance of first volume. Not included: novels and short stories in languages other than German.)

(*a*)

Year	No. of Novels	Year	No. of Novels	Year	No. of Novels	Year	No. of Novels
1740	10	1758	9	1776	63	1794	171
1741	11	1759	10	1777	45	1795	181
1742	9	1760	8	1778	55	1796	178
1743	7	1761	6	1779	46	1797	182
1744	16	1762	15	1780	75	1798	185
1745	17	1763	15	1781	94	1799	200
1746	18	1764	21	1782	104	1800	270
1747	21	1765	18	1783	90	1801	252
1748	22	1766	18	1784	86	1802	336
1749	26	1767	15	1785	95	1803	300
1750	25	1768	34	1786	81	1804	271
1751	21	1769	50	1787	104	1805	254
1752	27	1770	43	1788	131	1806	150
1753	34	1771	39	1789	112	1807	133
1754	23	1772	38	1790	141	1808	128
1755	30	1773	27	1791	166	1809	113
1756	20	1774	36	1792	179	1810	157
1757	10	1775	51	1793	163		

Note the drop in production (i) during the Seven Years War, 1756–63 and (ii) after the Battle of Jena, 1806.

(*b*)

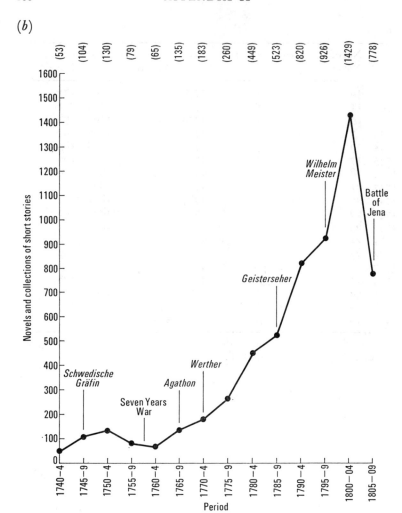

NOTES

PREFACE

1. 'We literary historians are attuned either totally to aesthetic-formal considerations or else to matters concerning the history of the mind or that of literary development, forgetting too easily that the most widespread effects in the history of literature often spring from impulses that appear perhaps strange to us, from factors that are more remote from us and not primarily of an aesthetic or philosophical nature.' H. Schöffler, *Protestantismus und Literatur* (Leipzig, 1922), p. 74.

2. It is, however, most gratifying to note a growing interest in this subject; see especially the works by Beaujean, Becker, Burger, Greiner, Killy, Nutz, Schulte-Sasse, Spiegel, and Thalmann listed in Bibliography.

3. 'Our literature does not begin until 1740.' *Litteratur und Völkerkunde* (1784), v. 275.

CHAPTER I

1. 'They are gardens in which, on the stems of history, the fruits of political science and ethics blossom forth and ripen amongst the flower-beds of delightful verse, in truth they are veritable academies for the high-born, court schools which ennoble the mind, the intellect, and the manner, and tutor the tongue in pleasing courtly conversation.' Quoted by H. Hettner, *Geschichte der deutschen Literatur im 18. Jahrhundert*, 2nd revised edn. (Brunswick, 1872), Bk. 1, p. 155.

2. See H. Schöffler, *Protestantismus und Literatur* (Leipzig, 1922), and W. Gebhardt, *Religionssoziologische Probleme im Roman der Aufklärung*, Gießen Diss. (Gießen, 1931).

3. See H. Beck, *Die religiöse Volksliteratur der evangelischen Kirche Deutschlands in einem Abriß ihrer Geschichte* (Gotha, 1891).

4. Gebhardt, op. cit., pp. 29–30.

5. A. F. F. von Knigge, *Die Reise nach Braunschweig* (1792) (*Deut. Nat. Lit.*, vol. cxxxvi), p. 263.

6. F. Nicolai, *Sebaldus Nothanker* (1773–6). (*Deutsche Literatur, Reihe Aufklärung*, vol. xv), pp. 30 ff.

7. 'But refuse profane and old wives' fables, and exercise thyself rather unto godliness.' 1 Tim. 4: 7.

8. '... as it was an all-too-romantic work on such a sacred subject.' Quoted by Gebhardt, op. cit., p. 25.

9. *Dichtung und Wahrheit*, Pt. I, Bk. 2. (*Goethes Werke* (Weimar, 1887–1912), vol. xxvi, p. 123.)

10. '. . . gladly suffer that all novels, the best one included, be thrown on to a heap and set alight.' Quoted by Gebhardt, op. cit., p. 109, note 19.

11. J. K. A. Musäus, *Der deutsche Grandison* (1781), i. 110.

12. *Miscellaneous Prose Works of Sir Walter Scott* (Edinburgh, 1827), iii. 121–2.

13. See, for example, the Preface to Schnabel's *Insel Felsenburg* (1731–43); and later in the century we read in a review of *Lorenz Arndt von Blankenburg, keine Liebesgeschichte, von dem Verfasser der Emilie Sommer*: 'Die Versicherung, daß es *keine* Liebesgeschichte sei, ist in dem Verstande zu nehmen, wie so oft die Romanschreiber beteuern, daß sie uns keinen Roman, sondern eine wahre Geschichte geben.' ('The assurance that it is *not* a love-story is meant in the sense applied so often by protesting novelists, namely: that they are offering us not a novel, but a true story.' *Allgemeine Literatur-Zeitung* (1785), No. 2.)

14. See Chap. 5, pp. 152–3.

15. 'What harm and what damage has been brought about by pernicious works like *der Amadis* . . .' Candorin, *Zimber-Swan* (1666), p. 150; cf. Goedeke, *Grundriß*, iii, § 192, p. 245.

16. '. . . bad and disreputable books and novels.' Quoted by J. Goldfriedrich, *Geschichte des deutschen Buchhandels* (Leipzig, 1908–9), ii. 323.

17. '. . . good novels may, of course, be given to young girls; but alas! Where are the good ones? I have . . . seen not one . . .' J. T. Hermes, *Sophiens Reise von Memel nach Sachsen* (Worms, 1776), iv. 132. Cf. here also A. F. F. von Knigge, *Der Roman meines Lebens* (Frankfurt, 1781), i. 277.

18. 'Above all else, be on your guard against the host of childish stories, comedies, and novels which do not make you any wiser or more virtuous but which do overcharge the powers of the imagination . . .' C. F. Bahrdt, *Handbuch der Moral für den Bürgerstand* (Tübingen, 1789), p. 181.

19. J. H. von Wessenberg, *Über den sittlichen Einfluß der Romane* (Constance, 1826), p. 176.

20. Similarly *Seellehre* and *Seelenforscher* (psychologist).

21. 'This we regret most of all, that such venomous things are not only bought and read most frequently but are also more likely to find a publisher than what is intended to serve God's honour and further the cause of goodness.' Quoted by J. Schmidt, *Geschichte des geistigen Lebens in Deutschland von Leibnitz bis auf Lessings Tod* (Leipzig, 1862–4), i. 322.

22. *Sequel to the Life of James Lackington*; quoted by Q. D. Leavis, *Fiction and the Reading Public* (London, 1932), p. 298.

23. For an evaluation of Wolff's work in this sphere see E. A. Blackall, *The Emergence of German as a Literary Language* (Cambridge, 1959), pp. 26 ff.

24.   'Scarce had old Latin ceased to rule
                  When radiant Truth came into Season;
                  With German as the teacher's tool
                  The very Rabble turned to Reason.'
                                    (Translated by Duncan M. Mennie)

Quoted by G. Steinhausen, *Der Aufschwung der deutschen Kultur vom 18. Jahrhundert bis zum Weltkrieg* (Leipzig and Vienna, 1920), p. 6.

25. John Stuart Mill, *Autobiography* (New York, 1924), p. 74.

26. See Schmidt, i. 161, for a list of typical titles of devotional works, all by August Pfeiffer (1640–?).

27. See *Die Soziologie der literarischen Geschmacksbildung* (Munich, 1923), chap. VII, section 3. A rough English equivalent of Schücking's expression would be: 'the new characteristic type upholding trends in taste.'

28. 'Novels are all kinds of love-stories and tales of the gods and heroes of high rank—or even of other persons, filled with all manner of secret and surprising amorous intrigues.'

29. 'A man worthy of the name will show one how to practise courtesy, accomplish brave deeds, conduct oneself with modesty towards respectable ladies, observe the correct form in dealings with persons of rank, and how to demonstrate one's intelligence in all conversation.'

30. *Robinson Crusoe* (1719), p. 2.

31. See especially H. Ullrich, *Robinson und die Robinsonaden* (Weimar, 1898); A. Kippenberg, *Robinsonaden in Deutschland* (Hanover, 1892); Goedeke, *Grundriß*, iii, § 192, p. 263.

32. J. H. Hartung, *Universalkatalog* (Königsberg, 1746), pp. 247 ff.

33. F. Nicolai, *Sebaldus Nothanker*, ed. cit., p. 30. Schnabel's much more traditional *Der im Irrgarten der Liebe herumtaumelnde Cavalier . . .* (1738) was equally popular in these circles according to Nicolai. It would seem that Schnabel's name alone was sufficient guarantee for the true Christian nature and integrity of a work of fiction.

34. Further editions of *Insel Felsenburg* appeared in 1736–51, 1744–6, 1763, 1772, 1780–9, and 1827. It was also reprinted by numerous pirates. Modern reprint, edited by Fritz Brüggemann, in *Deutsche Literatur, Reihe Aufklärung*, vol. iv, and in Reclam's *Universal-Bibliothek*, Nos. 8419–28.

35. John Wain in a review in the *Observer*, 13 Dec. 1959.

36. '. . . that many bookshops should no longer be called bookshops but journal shops, and moreover that book-dealers should be dispatching and forwarding journal information-sheets rather than book information-sheets . . .' M. P. H., *Curieuse Nachricht von denen Heute zu Tage grand mode gewordenen Journal-, Quartal-, und Annual-Schriften* (Freyburg, 1715); quoted by Goldfriedrich, ii. 58.

37. Figures from Goldfriedrich, ii. 58.

38. Figures on moral weeklies taken from Goldfriedrich, ii. 60–1, and iii. 320, and from Steinhausen, op. cit., pp. 9 ff.

39. 'For several years now, dear fellow countrymen, you have been used to reading a few moral periodicals each week . . .'
'From the French frontier to Moscow is a distance of about 300 German miles; so great is the area where the *Patriot* is held in high esteem.' Quoted by Steinhausen, op. cit., p. 10.

40. 'Nowadays the name "Poet", as an imperial title, denotes a kind of learned nobility but is otherwise held in great contempt.' Quoted by Schmidt, i. 61.

41. W. Rehm, *Geschichte des deutschen Romans* (Berlin, 1927), p. 70.

42. 'The art of writing is looked upon favourably only if a man has some other source of income enabling him to support himself and win respect. . . . To be sure, no father would wish on his son the insecure life led by Opitz.' Quoted by Schmidt, i. 61.

43. 'The production of poetical works was regarded as something sacred, and it was considered almost simony to accept or negotiate a fee.' *Dichtung und Wahrheit*, Pt. III, Bk. 12. (*Goethes Werke* (Weimar, 1887–1912), vol. xxviii, p. 113.)

44. 'The author, whether he has been paid for his work or not, certainly does not lose by it and can be well satisfied when he sees that his book is read with eager eyes.' J. A. Bernhard, *Kurzgefaßte curieuse Historie derer Gelehrten* (1718), p. 144.

45. Steinhausen, op. cit., p. 16.

46. It was for long looked on with displeasure if the son of a 'good house' became a professional writer; authors of noble birth continued even in the nineteenth century to use bourgeois pseudonyms (e.g. Anastasius Grün = Graf von Auersperg; Nikolaus Lenau = Niembsch, Edler von Strehlenau; Halm = Freiherr von Münch-Bellinghausen); consider here, too, the difficulties which both Annette von Droste-Hülshoff and Heinrich von Kleist experienced with their families.

47. Preface to his *Täglicher Schauplatz der Zeit* (1695).

48. Schmidt, i. 344.

49. For a detailed study of the changing relationship between writer and public during these years see H. Riefstahl, *Dichter und Publikum in der ersten Hälfte des 18. Jahrhunderts, dargestellt an der Geschichte der Vorrede*, Frankfurt a. M. Diss. (Limburg, 1934).

50. 'Plenty of others have written about, and cried out against, the princes and the gentry; people just as undistinguished as I myself will find that this is the book for them.' Preface to Weise's *Erznarren* (1672).

51. 'So the fact remains that reading, writing, and conversing are of use to people of all ranks; the mighty of this world find a clear mirror in these works, the statesmen find a magnetic compass showing which course to steer and where to drop anchor, the middle class and townsfolk see that a virtuous way of life is more profitable and more honourable than the way of vice, and . . . even the peasant is gladdened when stories are read to him. . . . Reading, writing, and talking about something sensible is of benefit to all classes and, in time, the middle class may thereby elevate themselves to become almost the peers of the higher ranks, provided that fortune favours them and the gall of envy plays no part. Even the lowliest of men can derive comfort and encouragement from these stories.' Preface to Schnabel's *Lustige Gesellschaft* (1745).

CHAPTER 2

1. 'His wares are produced by, and intended for, no one but scholars; if, at times, someone from the other professions does buy a German book, or one printed in his mother tongue in a foreign country, then it is but a casual purchase and so rare in occurrence that it is not really worth bothering about.' Adrian Beier, *Kurtzer Bericht von der Nützlichen und Fürtrefflichen Buch-Handlung* (Jena, 1690), pp. 5 ff., 44.

2. For important accounts of the Leipzig fair and the German book trade in general see the works by Goldfriedrich, Heinsius, Jentzsch, Kayser, Krünitz, and Schwetschke listed in Bibliography.

As Schwetschke has pointed out, it is as well to remember when consulting the Leipzig catalogues: (1) that not every book that appeared in Germany is listed (cf. above, pp. 61–2); this is especially the case with works on Catholic theology; (2) some books are listed in two and sometimes more places in one catalogue; and (3) a few works listed were never in fact published. Figures derived from these catalogues, then, are not *absolutely* accurate, but they do give us the over-all picture and illustrate the *relative* changes within the book market. The two catalogues compiled by Heinsius and Kayser are invaluable for checking the information in the Leipzig lists.

A vast bibliography of printing and allied techniques, book trade, publishing, bookselling, etc., with much German material, is to be found in *Katalog* (Leipzig, 1885), published by the Börsenverein der deutschen Buchhändler. German material, both of private and institutional libraries, is contained in: G. Pollard and A. Ehrman, *The Distribution of Books by Catalogue from the Invention of Printing to A.D. 1800, based on Material in the Broxbourne Library* (Cambridge, Roxburghe Club, 1965). For the history of bookselling, book trade, etc., at all periods and in all countries see: Chicago, Newberry Library, J. M. Wing Foundation, *Dictionary Catalogue of the History of Printing*, 6 vols. [with] 1st suppl. 3 vols. (Boston, 1961, 1970).

3. Figures here and following from J. Goldfriedrich, *Geschichte des deutschen Buchhandels* (Leipzig, 1908–9), ii. 17, 23–4, 69, 80, 390.

4. Goldfriedrich, ii. 390.

5. Figures from W. Gebhardt, *Religionssoziologische Probleme im Roman der Aufklärung*, Gießen Diss. (Gießen, 1931), pp. 30–2, and R. Jentzsch, *Der deutsch-lateinische Büchermarkt . . .*, Leipzig Diss. (Leipzig, 1912), Appendix 1.

6. Jentzsch, op. cit., p. 323.

7. Goldfriedrich, ii. 70 ff. and Jentzsch, op. cit., pp. 57 ff.

8. See Chap. 3, p. 86.

9. See W. H. Bruford, *Germany in the Eighteenth Century* (Cambridge, 1935), pp. 182 ff.

10. For an excellent picture of Leipzig during the time of the book fair see Goldfriedrich, ii. 260 ff.

11. J. S. Pütter, *Der Büchernachdruck nach ächten Grundsätzen des Rechts geprüft* (Göttingen, 1774).

12. 'This whole organization of the German book trade is as convenient for the public as it could possibly be and such as no other country in Europe can boast of.' Pütter, op. cit., p. 143.

13. An 'Imperial resolution' published by Joseph II in 1788 contains the sentence: 'Um aber Bücher zu verkaufen, braucht es keine mehrere Kenntnis, als wie um Käs zu verkaufen.' ('The selling of books, however, requires no more knowledge than that needed to sell cheese.' Quoted by Heinemann in his edition of *Goethes Werke* (Leipzig and Vienna, 1900), iii. 285, note 6.) Cf. here Goethe's *Xenien*, No. 286:

Einem Käsehandel verglich er eure Geschäfte?
Wahrlich der Kaiser, man sieht's, war auf dem Leipziger Markt.

('Compared your business to the cheese trade, did he?
Clearly the Emperor has been to the Leipzig Fair.')

14. Figures from Goldfriedrich, ii. 180.

15. See Chap. 3, pp. 66–7.

16. 'To have faith in Gellert, in virtue, and in religion—these are almost one and the same thing to our reading public.' Goethe in his review of *Briefe über den Werth einiger Dichter* . . . by Mauvillon and Unzer, in the *Frankfurter Gelehrte Anzeigen* (1771); quoted by J. Schmidt, *Geschichte des geistigen Lebens in Deutschland von Leibnitz bis auf Lessings Tod* (Leipzig, 1862–4), ii. 487.

17. See Eva D. Becker, *Der deutsche Roman um 1780* (Stuttgart, 1964), pp. 6–7.

18. 'There was altogether such a general openness among these people that one could speak to no individual or write to no one without at once regarding one's words as directed to several. One spied out one's own heart and that of the others and, with the indifference of the several governments towards such a communication . . . this practice of ethical and literary exchanges soon became more and more widespread. Such correspondence, especially with important persons, was carefully collected and extracts were then read aloud when friends gathered together.' *Dichtung und Wahrheit*, Pt. III, Bk. 13. (*Goethes Werke* (Weimar, 1887–1912), vol. xxviii, p. 178.)

19. See Fritz Brüggemann's Introduction to his edition of Hermes's novel in *Deutsche Literatur, Reihe Aufklärung*, vol. xiii (Leipzig, 1941). See also Chap. 3, pp. 70 ff.

20. These figures are from Jentzsch; important sources for confirming and/or supplementing the information given in the Leipzig catalogues are the catalogues compiled by Heinsius (covering the period 1700–1810) and Kayser (for the period 1750–1832).

21. 'Whether it would not be in order, for the convenience of compositors, to have certain names cast as one type.' G. C. Lichtenberg, *Die Bibliogenie oder die Entstehung der Bücherwelt* (Weimar, 1942), p. 20.

22. On the subject of estimates of the total production of fictional works in Germany during this period see Chap. 3, pp. 63–5.

23. Jentzsch, op. cit., p. 146, note 1.

24. See Chap. 5, pp. 137–40.

25. Ian Watt, *The Rise of the Novel* (Peregrine Books, 1963), p. 302.

26. '... that novels like these would be of no use even [as wrapping-paper] to a shopkeeper since, before they could reach him, they have already passed through so many hands that they are completely tattered; they serve to prove that good taste just cannot begin to become more general in this age of good taste and that the public as a whole chooses to put up with such plain rye bread rather than be served a better prepared dish.' *Allgemeine Deutsche Bibliothek* (1785–1806), vol. xiv, Pt. I, p. 278.

27. 'But rarely do clever minds devote their time to writing novels. These products of man's wit have been debased by the many pen-pushers almost as much as has occasional verse.' Ibid., vol. xv, Pt. I, p. 247.

28. See Chap. 5, pp. 160–1.

29. See especially the bibliography in J. Schulte-Sasse, *Die Kritik an der Trivialliteratur seit der Aufklärung* (Munich, 1971), pp. 149–52.

30. M. Beaujean, *Der Trivialroman in der zweiten Hälfte des 18. Jahrhunderts*, 2nd enlarged edn. (Bonn, 1969), pp. 187 ff.

31. H. F. Foltin, 'Zur Erforschung der Unterhaltungs- und Trivialliteratur, insbesondere im Bereich des Romans' in *Studien zur Trivialliteratur* (ed. H. O. Burger) (Frankfurt a. M., 1968), pp. 242–70.

32. 'They effect nothing but evacuations of the lachrymal bag and a sensually gratifying vascular relief; but the intellect goes away unreplenished and the more noble force in man receives no sustenance whatever from them.' Quoted by Schulte-Sasse, op. cit., p. 74.

33. But see here the extremely well documented theoretical basis for supporting such a proposition, provided by Schulte-Sasse, op. cit.

CHAPTER 3

1. 'The general public does little reading .... It is hardly credible how little is read by people in this country. Anyone connected, either closely or remotely, with court circles reads a lot so as to avoid the nausea of idleness .... Amongst the others you will rarely find anyone who has time to read.' Quoted by Walther Gebhardt, *Religionssoziologische Probleme im Roman der Aufklärung*, Gießen Diss. (Gießen, 1931), p. 28. It may be, as Gebhardt suggests, that Sulzer is here thinking only of a secular literature of entertainment and either does not know of the widely read devotional literature or considers it unworthy of special mention, taking that part of the reading public in fact for granted. In any case, Sulzer's observation retains its interest and relevance in our present context.

2. 'As long as books remain only in the hands of professors, students, and contributors to journals I do not think it is worth the trouble to write for the present generation.' Quoted by J. Schmidt, *Geschichte des geistigen Lebens in Deutschland von Leibnitz bis auf Lessings Tod* (Leipzig, 1862–4), ii. 186.

3. 'Never has there been more written and more read.' *Teutscher Merkur* (1779), 1st Quarter, p. 216.

4. 'This incessant reading has become an almost indispensable and general requisite of life.' Kant, *Über die Buchmacherey* (Königsberg, 1798), p. 65.

5. 'Our literature does not begin until 1740.' *Litteratur und Völkerkunde* (1784), v. 275.

6. 'People are reading even in places where, twenty years ago, no one ever thought about books; not only the scholar, no, the townsman and craftsman too exercises his mind with subjects for contemplation.' *Neues Archiv für Gelehrte, Buchhändler und Antiquare* (Erlangen, 1795), p. 295.

7. '. . . the need to read which is becoming more and more generally felt, even in those classes of society where the state is wont to contribute so little in the field of education'. Schiller in his *Merkwürdigen Rechtsfällen als ein Beitrag zur Geschichte der Menschheit*; quoted by J. Schulte-Sasse, *Die Kritik an der Trivialliteratur seit der Aufklärung* (Munich, 1971), p. 73.

8. 'It would not be easy today to find a woman of some education who does not do some reading; readers are now to be found in all classes of society, in towns and in the country, and even musketeers in the cities have books brought to them from the lending library to the main guardhouse.' *Deutsches Museum* (1780), p. 176; cf. here also *Allgemeiner Litterarischer Anzeiger* (1797), p. 1241.

9. J. Goldfriedrich, *Geschichte des deutschen Buchhandels* (Leipzig, 1908–9), iii. 256.

10. J. Möser, *Patriotische Phantasien* (*Deutsche Bibliothek in Berlin*), pp. 57 ff.

11. 'When these poor girls of ours were supposed to be milking the cows, they would be found poring over a book they did not understand.' *Deutsches Museum* (1776), Feb., p. 152.

12. *Schlesische Provinzialblätter* (1806), Nov.; quoted by Goldfriedrich, iii. 256.

13. '. . . that the art of printing had indeed led to a wider dissemination of learning but also to a contraction of its content. Reading a lot is harmful to the ability to think.' G. C. Lichtenberg, *Die Bibliogenie oder die Entstehung der Bücherwelt* (Weimar, 1942), p. 35.

14. See Chap. 4, pp. 111–13.

15. Quoted by Raymond Williams, *The Long Revolution* (Pelican Book, 1965), p. 183.

16. 'In the second half of the previous century reading took the place of other, no longer fashionable pastimes . . . The new demand produced a new business, seeking to earn one's living and to add to one's wealth by supplying the goods: the book trade.' Fichte, *Über das Wesen des Gelehrten* (1805); quoted by Goldfriedrich, iii. 147. See also above, pp. 85 ff.

17. 'Every year between 6,000 and 7,000 new books are printed; moreover, more than 20,000 people are writing for a living. No nation has ever

experienced anything like this.' *Berner Zeitung* (1799), p. 287; quoted by Goldfriedrich, iii. 148.

18. 'The art of the 3,000 German book-producers, who were able to manufacture 4,709 books in three years, is beyond my comprehension.' *Deutsches Museum* (1776), May, p. 440; a footnote gives the source for the statistics as *Gatterers Historisches Journal*, Pt. I, p. 266. The *Allgemeiner Litterarischer Anzeiger* (1797, p. 690) saw the reasons for this increase as threefold: (1) the increase in the so-called *gelehrter Stand* ('men of learning'), (2) *Deutschlands Lage*, i.e. its division into numerous individual semi-independent states, each with its own form of government, its own customs, and interests; each district wished to be served by its own literature and yet everyone everywhere showed an interest in everything in general, and (3) the interplay of *Vielschreiberei* and *Vielleserei* ('ceaseless pen-pushing' and 'incessant reading').

19. 'If England's forte is race-horses, then ours is race-authors.' Lichtenberg, op. cit., p. 52.

20. Cf. Goldfriedrich, iii. 147. The population figure of about 20,000,000 is that estimated by Professor Bruford for the end of the eighteenth century in the territories forming the pre-war German Empire. W. H. Bruford, *Germany in the Eighteenth Century* (Cambridge, 1935), p. 158.

21. Figures from Marjorie Plant, *The English Book Trade* (London, 1939), p. 445. Cf. here also Ian Watt, *The Rise of the Novel* (Peregrine Books, 1963), pp. 36 ff.

22. *Memoirs of the Forty-Five First Years of the Life of James Lackington*, . . . *Written by Himself* (1791), 13th edn., with Index (n.d.), p. 257.

23. K. Chr. Reiche, *An die sämmtlichen Autoren* . . . *von Seiten der Buchhandlung der Gelehrten* (Leipzig, 1783); see Goldfriedrich, iii. 273.

24. W. Fleischer, *Über bildende Künste* (Frankfurt, 1792); see Goldfriedrich, iii. 274.

25. 'The present age cannot stomach solid and profound works. It ignores them. Only translations from English and French, only novels, only facetious fiddle-faddle, these are the lap-dogs, these are the darlings of our day and age.' *Johann Jakob Reiskens Von ihm selbst aufgesetzte Lebensbeschreibung* (Leipzig, 1783), p. 99.

26. '. . . as long as the *purveyors of novels in Leipzig* are able to acquire entire estates through publishing *Werthers Leiden*, *Siegwarts Klostergeschichte* and similar foul rubbish, whereas books of the highest moral integrity often serve no purpose other than as wrapping-paper for cheese and butter dealers.' *Damen-Journal* (Leipzig, 1784), December-Heft.

27. 'A novel? Let's call it this, it could be that it will get a few more readers because of this.' Lessing, *Hamburgische Dramaturgie* (1767-8), St. 69.

28. Marion Beaujean, *Der Trivialroman in der zweiten Hälfte des 18. Jahrhunderts*, 2nd enlarged edn. (Bonn, 1969), and J. Schulte-Sasse, op. cit.

29. See Chap. 2, pp. 32-3.

30. Marianne Spiegel, *Der Roman und sein Publikum im frühen 18. Jahrhundert,* *1700–67* (Bonn, 1967).

31. J. G. Heinzmann, *Appel an meine Nation über Aufklärung und Aufklärer . . .* (Bern, 1795); cf. Goldfriedrich, iii. 274. Heinzmann's estimate is, as we have seen, confirmed by the Leipzig Easter-fair catalogue for 1800.

32. Cf. Introduction to 1st edition of *Pamela* (1740).

33. 'Furthermore, I would include in this category [of moral verse] the good prose poems, especially *Clarissa* and *Grandison*. But what's this? Novels being advocated from the chair of philosophy? Yes, if they are the works of a man like Richardson then I consider it my duty to recommend them. . . . In years gone by, as I read Part Seven of *Clarissa* and Part Five of *Grandison*, my heart, in a manner of sweet melancholy, wept away some of the most wondrous hours it has experienced; for that, Richardson, I am grateful to you even now.'

34. 'For the whole of Germany it is without question Gellert's fables that have given a new direction to the entire nation in matters of taste. They have stolen their way gradually into homes where otherwise nothing is ever read. Ask the good daughter of your nearest country parson about Gellert's fables. She will know them! The works of other poets? Not a word! In this way what is good has been proclaimed through examples and not through rules, and what is evil has been made an object of contempt.' Thomas Abbt, *Vom Verdienst* (1765); quoted by J. Schmidt, ii. 295.

35. A correspondent of the *Deutsches Museum* writes from Holland about his surprise and pleasure on seeing a review in a Dutch journal of *Eerwaarden Heer Sebaldus Nothanker*; the correspondent adds: 'Sehr begierig ist diese Übersetzung gelesen, gekauft und angepriesen worden.' ('This translation has been read, bought, and praised with great enthusiasm.' *Deutsches Museum* (1776), Aug., p. 700.)

36. '. . . it is not necessary to afford pleasure . . . one must sermonize, lull them to sleep'. Wieland in a letter of 6 Apr. 1759; quoted by J. Schmidt, ii. 165.

37. For a discussion of the important part played by the Protestant clergy and former students of theology in the development of German literature during these years readers are referred to Herbert Schöffler, *Protestantismus und Literatur* (Leipzig, 1922), pp. 227 ff.

38. 'The time is approaching when we as preachers shall scarcely be able to reach the people; and then the essence of truth and beauty must needs be presented in a pleasing garb, and you, should you continue as you are, can then become a German Richardson.' Quoted by Georg Hoffmann, *Johann Timotheus Hermes* (Breslau, 1911), p. 15.

39. 'Why that's wonderful! At last they're again printing something that's written in the manner of Grandison.' Hermes, *Geschichte der Miss Fanny Wilkes, so gut als aus dem Englischen übersetzt,* 2nd edn. (1770), i. 5.

40. Cf. H. Kunze, *Lieblingsbücher von Dazumal. Eine Blütenlese* (Munich, 1938), pp. 60–1.

41. Brüggemann's Introduction to his edition of Hermes's novel in *Deutsche Literatur, Reihe Aufklärung*, vol. xiii (Leipzig, 1941).

42. 'In short, among all our novelists . . . this author is supreme in his knowledge of the world and his treatment of German customs.' *Teutscher Merkur* (1773), ii. 76 ff. Most of the contemporary reviewers greet *Sophiens Reise* as the first original German novel, e.g. *Magazin der deutschen Critik* (1772), vol. i, Pt. 2, pp. 245 ff. Previously German writers had hesitated to lay the scenes of their novels in Germany, and in many stories English characters travelling or residing in Germany supply the seemingly indispensable un-German element.

43. '. . . just ask the book-dealers; just search the dressing-tables! I know the importance of the early hours of the morning. The woman who wishes to be edified will of course spend them reading a serious book. And every other woman will be reading a novel at that time. Are we writers . . . really to abandon these novel-readers to their perilous fate?' Hermes, *Sophiens Reise von Memel nach Sachsen* (Worms, 1776), iii. 141.

44. 'Anyone who can cherish all three without ornamentation, or anyone . . . who would simply add fuel to the flame, can sell his copy; for it was not for him that I wrote it.' Ibid. v. 218.

45. Ibid. iv. 310.

46. See Chap. 2, pp. 32–4.

47. 'Whereas in the past there were only few ladies, even amongst those of rank, who were acquainted with any printed matter apart from their prayer-book and the family almanac and who sought entertainment in their leisure hours through reading *Hercules und Herculiscus*, *Römische Oktavia*, and then on to *Asiatische Banise* and Neukirch's *Telemach* and other generally popular books of their own day, reading has now become a general necessity even in the middle classes and amongst people barely above those who have never learned to read at all; and for every woman who, fifty years ago, read a book written in her own day there are now (at a conservative estimate) one hundred who read everything that they can lay their hands on and that holds promise of some entertainment without overtaxing the intellect—and this is particularly true of the small towns and in country areas where the diversion of city life is wanting.' Wieland, *Der neue teutsche Merkur* (1791), Feb., p. 201.

48. Cf. here J. Schmidt, i. 649 ff. I find Leo Balet's objections against this interpretation (in *Die Verbürgerlichung der deutschen Kunst, Literatur und Musik im 18. Jahrhundert* (Leiden, 1936), pp. 323 ff.) untenable. He states that no valid reason has ever been put forward to explain why the religious element in Pietism should, from about mid eighteenth century onwards, have receded and granted pre-eminence to the subjective emotional element; surely one of the main themes of the whole century is that very secularization (in philosophy, music, art, and literature) which brought about this change of emphasis and which indeed, in other contexts, receives due acknowledgement from Balet. His second and only other objection is that Pietism was 'a purely German

movement' whereas Sentimentalism was a European phenomenon; Germany was, of course, by no means the only country to experience this wave of pietistic thought—in contemporary England we find the Quakers, in France the movement led by Port Royal and Pascal, and in the Netherlands a similar group under the leadership of the Frenchman Labadie. English Sentimentalism, too, first took the form of religious meditation upon death and judgement. For a discussion of the role of Feeling in English religious life and in English devotional literature see Schöffler, op. cit., pp. 138 ff.

49. 'Herr Handsom was the most beautiful, the most talented, most courteous, and moreover the most pious man in all Scotland . . . And he wept so gently that one scarcely noticed it . . .' Hermes, *Geschichte der Miss Fanny Wilkes*, 2nd edn. (1770), i. 32.

50. 'I shall not dwell on the gentle, manly tone of his voice which seems to be utterly and perfectly made for the expression of the sentiments within his noble soul; the fire in his beautiful eyes, subdued by a touch of melancholy, the inimitably pleasing blend of grandeur and grace in all his movements, and the thing that distinguishes him from all other men, of whom I . . . have seen a large number—that is the virtuous look in his eyes . . .' Sophie von Laroche, *Die Geschichte des Fräuleins von Sternheim* (*Literaturdenkmale des 18. und 19. Jahrhunderts*, vol. cxxxviii (Berlin, 1907)), p. 61.

51. 'Almost without exception the girls of today are, alas, of a melancholy and sentimental disposition.' Quoted by G. Steinhausen, *Der Aufschwung der deutschen Kultur* . . . (Leipzig and Vienna, 1920), p. 34.

52. J. Schmidt, ii. 25.

53. 'My heart is by nature sensitive, disposed to the most passionate, most tender, and most constant friendship, ever open to receive each impression of compassion and tenderness but at the same time so sorely inclined to melancholy that I must frequently seek refuge and relief in tears.' Quoted by Steinhausen, op. cit., p. 30.

54. See Steinhausen, op. cit., pp. 33 ff. and J. Schmidt, ii. 389.

55. 'Just like the influence exercised on the present generation by the two extremes of *Werther* and *Siegwart* along with all the intervening voices in the middle register heard in the chord of sentimentalism; the way in which they have increased the elasticity of the soul, strained every nerve, bewitched all the senses, melted every heart, ruptured the lachrymal dams of continence, released a wave of lamentations . . . in just such a way were the hearts and minds of the preceding generation affected by these foreign drugs [Richardson's novels].' J. K. A. Musäus, *Der deutsche Grandison* (1781), i. 96.

56. 'What *I* do not like, is that our author sets such great store by weeping. Indeed, not only does he himself weep on every possible occasion, tears of sorrow and tears of joy, but he also causes all who come near him to burst into tears too: God, angels, human beings, the devil, and so on.' Quoted by J. Schmidt, ii. 23.

57. See Christine Touaillon, *Der deutsche Frauenroman im 18. Jahrhundert* (Vienna and Leipzig, 1919), p. 129, and V. Stockley, *German Literature as known in England 1750–1830* (London, 1929), p. 106.

58. J. Schmidt, ii. 468.

59. See Ridderhof's introduction to the novel in *Literaturdenkmale des 18. und 19. Jahrhunderts*, vol. cxxxviii (Berlin, 1907).

60. The English translation of 1776, for example, announced itself as *The History of Lady Sophia Sternheim, attempted from the German of Mr. Wieland*; the translator was Joseph Collyer. A further translation, by Edward Harwood, appeared the same year.

61. See here especially J. W. Appell, *Werther und seine Zeit*, revised edn. (Leipzig, 1865), and H. H. Borcherdt, *Der Roman der Goethezeit* (Stuttgart, 1949).

62. See Chap. 1, pp. 22 ff.

63. 'Countless daily newspapers and monthly journals are dispatched every day in our post-bags and are now found lying on dressing-tables and desks, in club-rooms, inns, and village pubs.' Quoted by Steinhausen, op. cit., p. 89.

64. *Vorspiel auf dem Theater*, l. 116 and l. 46.

65. 'Even amongst professors, and by no means rarely, you will find men who in ten years have taken no food for the intellect apart from the miserable pickings from a few journals.' Lichtenberg, op. cit., p. 37.

66. K. H. von Lang, *Aus der bösen alten Zeit*, 2 vols. (Stuttgart, 1910), i. 174; cf. also ibid. i. 137.

67. 'Was not the *Wandsbeckermerkur* bought by the ordinary man in this country, and it was read with great relish in all public houses.' *Deutsches Museum* (1778), Feb., pp. 148 ff.

68. Cf. here and below, Münster University *Sommersemester Referat 1948* (Professor Hagemann), Institut für Publizistik.

69. '. . . which can confidently be described as the most distinguished in Germany.' *Deutsches Museum* (1778), Aug., p. 97.

70. Figures from Goldfriedrich, iii. 314 ff., and Marianne Kohl, *Die National-zeitung der Deutschen, 1784–1830* (Stuttgart, 1936). We must also remember in this connection that with the reading societies, coffee-houses, and inns which took newspapers, one newspaper sold often meant as many as twenty readers. Raymond Williams (op. cit., p. 207) tells us that the leading morning newspapers in England at this time had circulations varying between 2,000 and 3,000; the first regular evening paper, the *Star* (founded 1788), gained a circulation of 2,000, the figure for the *Courier* (founded 1789) was 7,000.

71. Cf. here particularly the article by J. W. Eaton, 'The Beginnings of German Literary Criticism', in *Modern Language Notes*, vol. liii, pp. 351 ff.

72. 'At long last my *Asiatische Banise* . . . dares to present itself on the stage of the book-sickened world.' Preface to *Asiatische Banise* (1688).

73. 'As the know-alls of this world are wont to pour the most virulent abuse on every action of their often innocent neighbour, how much more real are the fears of the man who through his pen introduces himself on a stage before the whole world.' Preface to *Täglicher Schauplatz der Zeit* (1695).

74. 'We have to answer to you and your good sense, dear reader . . . for these present pages! I turn to you as to a judge, to whom I am accountable and to whose verdict I . . . most willingly submit.' Preface to Hagedorn's *Poetische Nebenstunden* (1729).

75. 'In as far as I myself play any part in the article, I shall loyally and scrupulously abide by the verdict of the public and thus regard myself as nothing more than the organ of public opinion.' Quoted by L. L. Schücking, *Die Soziologie der literarischen Geschmacksbildung* (Munich, 1923), p. 99. Available in the series *DALP-Taschenbücher*, vol. 354, 3rd and revised edn. (Munich and Bern, 1961).

76. 'They are applauding! What have I said that's rubbish?' Ibid., pp. 59, 99.

77. 'When a book and a head collide and there is a hollow sound, the fault lies always with the book.' Lichtenberg, op. cit., p. 25; cf. here also Goethe's poem *Der Rezensent*.

78. 'Bad writers (their number is legion) should be the last to cry out against the *Allgemeine Deutsche Bibliothek*. After all, they achieve through it a sort of immortality that their own works could never bring them.' *Allgemeine Literatur-Zeitung* (1785), No. 76.

79. 'I see reviews as a kind of children's disease which attacks all new-born books to a greater or lesser extent . . . people have often tried to protect them with amulets like a preface or dedication, or have even attempted to innoculate them by writing the review themselves; but the cure does not always work.' Lichtenberg, op. cit., p. 48.

80. Quoted by W. H. Bruford, *Germany in the Eighteenth Century* (Cambridge, 1935), p. 272. For a detailed account of the rise of the profession of letters in Germany, readers are referred to Professor Bruford's chapter on this subject, ibid., pp. 271 ff.

81. Cf. here and below, Nicolai, *Sebaldus Nothanker* (*Deutsche Literatur, Reihe Aufklärung*, vol. xv), pp. 58 ff., and also F. Koch, *Deutsche Kultur des Idealismus* (Potsdam, 1935), pp. 268 ff.

82. Quoted by Ian Watt, *The Rise of the Novel* (Peregrine Books, 1963), pp. 56–7.

83. Goldfriedrich, iii. 305 and note 179.

84. '. . . for these books fall into the hands of all too many people, and the critics pounce on them straightaway and are only rarely discouraged from fault-finding by the appearance of a famous name.' Nicolai, loc. cit.

85. 'There is no doubt whatever that we have in Germany more writers than could cater for the welfare of all four continents.' Lichtenberg, op. cit., p. 35.

86. 'Everyone is writing—the youngster, the greybeard, the matron. / May the gods create a race for whom the race of writers can write.' Goethe, *Xenien* (*Nachlaß*), No. 146.

87. Cf. here Goldfriedrich, iii. 249 ff., from which most of the following figures are taken.

88. '. . . that the army of writers in Germany was about 5,500 strong.' See *Allgemeine Literatur-Zeitung* (1785), No. 85.

89. Quoted by Otto von Leixner, *Geschichte der deutschen Litteratur*, 6th edn. (Leipzig, 1903), p. 723.

90. James Lackington, op. cit., p. 260.

91. Weiz, *Das gelehrte Sachsen* (1780); quoted by Goldfriedrich, iii. 249.

92. See Chap. 1, pp. 25–7.

93. For a detailed account of the various attempts at self-publication and subscription publication see Goldfriedrich, iii, chap. 3.

94. Cf. here and below, Goldfriedrich, iii. 118 ff. I give the examples of authors' fees in Thaler and add in parentheses a rough equivalent in English money, based on Professor Bruford's estimate of 1 Thaler = 3*s*. = 15p. The main points in the present context—the discrepancy between publishers' and writers' profits and the marked improvement in authors' fees as the century proceeded—will emerge from this. Obviously the question of modern equivalents in purchasing power is a very complex one and one which cannot be gone into here. For some idea of the purchasing power of money and an indication of the cost of living in eighteenth-century Germany, see Bruford, op. cit., Appendix 1.

95. For further examples of authors' honoraria see Bruford, op. cit., p. 278, and F. Koch, op. cit., pp. 268 ff.

96. '. . . of sitting down in seclusion, pottering about with pen and ink, and perhaps, at most as a side-line, doing something of direct use to the state.' *Deutsches Museum* (1783), p. 489.

97. The ultimate stage in this development would now seem to have been reached; Robert Graves is reputed to have said that he wrote novels so that he could afford to write poetry.

CHAPTER 4

1. See H. H. Houben, *Verbotene Literatur* (Berlin, 1924), p. 541.

2. '. . . conducive to the common welfare and particularly beneficial to the lower social classes.' Quoted by J. Goldfriedrich, *Geschichte des deutschen Buchhandels* (Leipzig, 1908–9), iii. 89.

3. *Memoirs of Frederick Perthes* (translated from the German) 3rd edn., 2 vols. (London and Edinburgh, 1857), i. 295 ff.

4. 'The unmistakable loving-kindness of the author and his desire, shining through every word he writes, to bring as much happiness as possible to all men, give me cause to hope that he himself, far from objecting to my action, will indeed regard it as consonant to his own design.' *Allgemeine Literatur-Zeitung* (1785), No. 67.

5. 'No privilege can ever again afford protection against Trattner the book-dealer recently created a baron by His Imperial Majesty. With the support

184   NOTES CHAPTER 4

of court funds he is now flooding the whole of Germany [with his wares] and even dares to presume to lay down the law in our own country . . . .' Quoted by Goldfriedrich, iii. 19.

6. Cf. here Perthes, op. cit., i. 17, and Goldfriedrich, iii. 51 ff.

7. *Deutscher Zuschauer* (1788), vol. ix, Bk. 25, p. 116.

8. '. . . in all truth, in an issue where this prize is at stake, a gold guinea cuts a sorry figure.' Quoted by Goldfriedrich, iii. 90.

9. 'Just imagine the good that will result in Germany when the best writers are represented in future not only in the libraries of the wealthy, the majority of whom do not read them but keep them simply as show-pieces, but also in the houses of ordinary citizens, among the possessions of every man!' *Briefwechsel über den Nachdruck von Shakespeares Theater* (1778), p. 5; quoted by Goldfriedrich, iii. 91.

10. See Chap. 5, pp. 149–51.

11. Goldfriedrich, iii. 93 ff.

12. 'We all know that he [the door-to-door pedlar] was all too successful in this respect. And so within a few years pirated editions had penetrated into even the most remote corners of all the provinces to which no bookseller, even with the best of intentions and sparing no pains, could ever have gained access. The bargain prices and the choice from among the best books attracted the connoisseur, and many who would never in all their lives have dreamed of buying a book now gradually acquired a small collection.' *Neues Archiv für Gelehrte, Buchhändler, und Antiquare* (Erlangen, 1795), p. 102; quoted by Goldfriedrich, iii. 100.

13. 'Whatever is easiest to write, whatever will enjoy the quickest sales, whatever involves the smallest loss—these are the things that authors must write and dealers must publish as long as the plague of piracy persists.' Quoted by Goldfriedrich, iii. 92.

14. See Goldfriedrich, iii. 82.

15. 'A miserable flop is found in the warehouse of a pirate publisher just as rarely as an empty nut amongst those filched by squirrels.' Quoted by H. Kunze, *Lieblingsbücher von Dazumal. Eine Blütenlese* (Munich, 1938), p. 20. On the apparently insurmountable difficulty of taking the number of editions as a criterion of popularity in the eighteenth century see Kunze, op. cit., pp. 8 ff.

16. Cf. here and following Goldfriedrich, iii. 343 ff., H. H. Houben, *Verbotene Literatur* (Berlin, 1924), and *Hier Zensur, wer dort?* (Leipzig, 1918).

17. Houben, *Verbotene Literatur*, p. 571.

18. '. . . the whole genre which one refers to contemptuously as "the novel"'. Houben, *Hier Zensur . . .*, p. 117.

19. '. . . since I perceive that the liberty of the Press is degenerating into the licence of the Press, and that book censorship has ceased altogether.' Quoted by Goldfriedrich, iii. 413. During the whole period from 1716 to 1763, for example, only twenty-six books had been forbidden by the Prussian censorship (Houben, *Hier Zensur . . .*, p. 17).

20. 'From the time I first became a citizen of these two states until the present day . . . I have not heard a word about restriction of the freedom of the Press, nor about forbidden or confiscated books.' *Über Aufruhr und aufrührerische Schriften* (Brunswick, 1793), p. 112; quoted by Goldfriedrich, iii. 426.

21. . . . so that 'vicious people could not find out the vicious books from it, nor clever people the clever books'. Quoted by Goldfriedrich, iii. 345.

22. Houben, *Verbotene Literatur*, p. 97.

23. *Dichtung und Wahrheit*, Pt. I, Bk. 4. (*Goethes Werke* (Weimar, 1887–1912), vol. xxvi, p. 237.)

24. 'Set to and write something for my firm that will be confiscated.' Quoted by Goldfriedrich, iii. 431.

25. 'If we ignore Bibles, hymn-books, almanacs, and political newspapers, then there is no question but that scholars, incomparably more than any other section of society in the land, are in fact the true mainstay of the whole book trade and the most frequent book-buyers without whose custom any book-dealer would be in a most precarious position.' *Weitere Ausführung, die Buchhandlungen und Druckereyen in den Königl. Preuß. Staaten betreffend* (1781), p. 33; quoted by Goldfriedrich, iii. 270.

26. 'My best customers are schoolboys, itinerant journeymen, peasants, and sweet old women.' F. Nicolai, *Sebaldus Nothanker* (*Deutsche Literatur, Reihe Aufklärung*, vol. xv), p. 70.

27. '. . . unless the librarian is prevented by some matter of consequence and gives prior notification of this *per scedulam*.' Cf. here Goldfriedrich, ii. 14 ff.

28. Cf. here Goldfriedrich, iii. 265 ff.

29. 'Anyone wishing to look more closely at a book must direct his request to the librarian who will then show him the book and, if warranted, even permit him to read some of it.' Quoted by Goldfriedrich, iii. 266.

30. Cf. here F. Paulsen, *Geschichte des gelehrten Unterrichts*, 2nd edn. 2 vols. (Leipzig, 1896–7), ii. 12, 138 ff.

31. Quoted by Goldfriedrich, iii. 268.

32. 'Dusty, desolate, and unfrequented rooms in which the librarian, by virtue of his office, must stay for a few hours each week to spend the whole of this time in solitude. The deep silence is unbroken save for the occasional doleful gnawing of some bookworm.' Quoted by Kunze, op. cit., p. 15.

33. 'Furthermore, His Excellency Lieutenant-General von Platen was kind enough to permit the reading public of the town to make use of this valuable establishment in return for a small monthly subscription. . . . In recent years, however, the number of people reading in the town has increased considerably and the officers, for whose benefit this library had in fact been established, would not always be able to get the books they wanted if the circle of readers were to become too large; consequently the inhabitants of the town have, for a number of years, not been allowed access to the regiment's books and a good number of them have now joined together for the

acquisition of books and journals whereby the advancement of good taste and a love of contemporary literature will be greatly furthered.' *Allgemeine Literatur-Zeitung* (1785), No. 23.

34. Cf. here and following, Goldfriedrich, iii. 250 ff.

35. Cf. here also U. Bräker, *Der arme Mann im Tockenburg* (*Bräkers Werke in einem Band*) (Berlin and Weimar, 1964), pp. 229–31.

36. *Allgemeine Literatur-Zeitung* (1785), No. 47.

37. Quoted in *The Times Literary Supplement*, 3 Feb. 1966.

38. Cf., here and following, Goldfriedrich, iii. 257 ff.

39. J. Brauchli, *Der englische Schauerroman um 1800*, Zürich Diss. (Weida, 1928), p. 136, and *The Times Literary Supplement*, 3 Feb. 1966.

40. '. . . that the worthy public, here and in the neighbouring country districts, and including also those members of the lowest social classes, would cease offering up their honest work and labour, and their higher duties, as a sacrifice to their mania for reading and their addiction to present-day, for the most part utterly useless, time-consuming, character-mutilating reading matter.' Quoted by Goldfriedrich, iii. 259.

41. Ibid.

42. 'In this place useful books are those which are almost always available. You can recognize them by the newness of their covers, sometimes they have passed through many hands, yet are still uncut; love-stories and romances of chivalry, on the other hand, look very much the worse for wear.' *Hieroglyphen* (Berlin, 1780), i. 32; quoted by Goldfriedrich, iii. 260.

43. 'Listen to what I found there and I shall need to say no more about the tone of Würzburg.

"I should like to have a few good books."
The collection is at your disposal, sir.
"Perhaps something by Wieland."
I hardly think so.
"Or by Schiller, Goethe."
You would not be likely to find them here.
"Why is that? Are all these books out? Do people read so much here?"
Not exactly.
"What sort of people do the most reading here then?"
Lawyers, merchants, and married women.
"And the unmarried women?"
They are not permitted to apply for books.
"And students?"
We have orders not to give them any.
"But if so little is read, could you tell me then where in heaven's name the works of Wieland, Goethe, and Schiller have got to?"
Begging your pardon, sir, but these books are not read here at all.
"I see. You have not got them in the library?"
We are not allowed to.
"Then what sort of books have you got here along all these walls?"

Romances of chivalry, those and nothing else. To the right those with ghosts, to the left without ghosts, according to taste. "Aha, I see!"'
Heinrich von Kleist, *Briefe 1793–1804* (*Heinrich von Kleist dtv-Gesamtausgabe,* vol. vi) (Munich, 1964), p. 97.

44. See *Schlesische Provinzialblätter* (1806), Nov., No. 11, and Goldfriedrich, iii. 260.

45. 'In all reputable lending libraries you will find the following highly entertaining works: *Celestine's Garters* (3rd edn.); *Corona. The Necromancer; The Ghost of my Girl, her Appearance and my Wedding Feast; The Chambers of Horror, a Ghost Story (Repository of Ghost Stories,* vol. i); *Kunigunde, or The Robbers' Cave in the Forest of Firs; Lisara, the Amazon from Habyssinia, a Romantic Portrait; Legends from the World of Ghosts and Magic* (new edn.); *The Suicide, a Tale of Terror and Wonder; Escapades in Sorcery, a Comic Tale; The Old Man of the Woods, or The Underground Dwelling; The Strange Adventures of an Englishman in America; Diverting Anecdotes and Side-splitting Cross-cuts* by G. C. Cramer.' *Reichsbote* (Leipzig, 1805), St. 1, 20 June; quoted by Goldfriedrich, iii. 261.

46. Cf. here Perthes, op. cit. i. 60 ff.

47. '. . . that the scholar who does not want to be left behind has time for little else but reading.' *Neues Archiv . . .* (Erlangen, 1795), p. 103; quoted by Goldfriedrich, iii. 104.

48. W. H. Bruford, *Germany in the Eighteenth Century* (Cambridge, 1935), p. 290.

CHAPTER 5

1. Cf. G. Steinhausen, *Der Aufschwung der deutschen Kultur vom 18. Jahrhundert bis zum Weltkrieg* (Leipzig and Vienna, 1920), p. 91.

2. 'And where, pray, is the fatherland to be found in this Germany of ours, at present suffering the afflictions of war and devastation? Germans are fighting against Germans. The contingent of our prince is serving with the one army, yet in our small province they are seeking to raise recruits for the other. Which side are we supposed to join? Whom are we supposed to attack? Whom are we supposed to defend? For whom are we supposed to die?' Nicolai, *Sebaldus Nothanker* (*Deutsche Literatur, Reihe Aufklärung,* vol. xv), p. 34. Cf. here also W. Wenck, *Deutschland vor hundert Jahren* (Leipzig, 1887), vol. 1, chap. 4, and W. H. Bruford, *Germany in the Eighteenth Century* (Cambridge, 1935), pp. 291 ff.

3. 'We have no capital city which could perhaps function as a general academy for the nation's great artists and, as it were, an arbiter in matters of taste.' *Teutscher Merkur* (1773), p. x.

4. Bruford, op. cit., p. 45.

5. 'Is there anywhere in Germany where taste remains constant over a distance of 10 miles and does this taste ever remain unchanged for 10

consecutive years?' A. F. F. von Knigge, *Die Reise nach Braunschweig* (*Deut. Nat. Lit.*, vol. cxxxvi), p. 277.

6. 'There is little that can be done about the Catholics here; most of them remain stupid and uncouth.' Cf. here and following, Steinhausen, op. cit., pp. 80 ff.

7. See Chap. 4, pp. 99–101.

8. J. Goldfriedrich, *Geschichte des deutschen Buchhandels* (Leipzig, 1908–9), iii. 383.

9. 'These priests from the good old days were, as a rule, quite content to leave well alone in matters concerning scholarship, they were men of the people in the Capuchin tradition, peasants who had completed a course of religious studies and whose homespun conception of the priesthood was admirably suited to the homespun nature of their penitents. It was these remarkable men who did most to ensure that the people of Bavaria moved from the seventeenth into the nineteenth century without noticing anything of the eighteenth.' Quoted by Steinhausen, op. cit., p. 82.

10. Nicolai, op. cit., p. 68.

11. '. . . where truth and good taste are still struggling against superstition, prejudices, and barbarism, and where out of stupidity or malice such writings [as the new journal] are suppressed by censors and inspectors, since more enlightenment might result from their perusal.' *Bibliothek der schönen Wissenschaften und freyen Künste* (1757), vol. i, pt. 1, p. viii.

12. *Deutsches Museum* (1777), Foreword.

13. 'In that area a poet is held to be a time-corrupting good-for-nothing.' Quoted by F. Sengle, *C. M. Wieland* (Stuttgart, 1949), p. 51.

14.   O, I'm a lass from Yorkshire
              With cheeks as brown's can be,
              And London girls' accomplishments
              Are not, I swear, for me.

              The books they're always reading!
              Their Richardsons and Grays!
              How dainty their deportment,
              How honey-sweet their ways!

              This flirting, reading, writing
              Mars lasses horribly.
              The man for me that's chosen
              He'll read one day for me.
                         (Translated by Duncan M. Mennie)

Ibid., pp. 247–8; cf. here also K. A. Kortum, *Jobsiade* (1784–99) (*Deut. Nat. Lit.*, vol. cxl), pt. 2, chap. 2, ll. 147–8.

15. Hilde Neumann, *Der Bücherbesitz der Tübinger Bürger von 1750–1850*, Diss. (Tübingen, 1955). Quoted by Marion Beaujean, *Der Trivialroman in der zweiten Hälfte des 18. Jahrhunderts*, 2nd enlarged edn. (Bonn, 1969), p. 19.

16. 'What's this, we thought! A big thick book about belles-lettres produced in a region whose inhabitants and neighbours hardly know whether Germany does or does not possess writers like Klopstock and Uz.' See Sengle, op. cit., p. 235.

17. '. . . man of letters, which term in Courland by no means signifies a man of learning but rather some wretched middling species between nobleman and peasant.' T. G. von Hippel, *Lebensläufe nach aufsteigender Linie* (1778–81), pt. 1, p. 21.

18. 'Reutlingen, October 1798. We are pleased to announce that all kinds of pirate editions from here, Tübingen . . . and Vienna are available in our shop on the easiest of terms and at bargain prices with half-yearly settlement of accounts. Our stock is such that we are in a position to offer immediate delivery, in a cheap yet tasteful edition, of any outstanding work which has appeared in the literary world of Saxony, thus combating the scandal of the enormous book prices in Saxony and fulfilling the wishes of many thousands of people.' Quoted by Goldfriedrich, iii. 104.

19. See Perthes, *Memoirs* (transl.), 3rd edn., 2 vols. (Edinburgh and London, 1857), i. 17, 293 ff. and ii. 290 ff.

20. Marion Beaujean (op. cit., p. iv) objects to such 'classification by social group' on the grounds that 'in this period [choice of] reading material becomes, significantly enough, dependent on level of education (*Bildungsniveau*) and intellectual-spiritual attitudes (*geistig-seelische Haltung*), which means that the frontiers of taste cut right through the social classes and for that reason social classification becomes unimportant.' I find this reasoning hard to follow and would maintain that precisely those factors mentioned by Beaujean, level and type of education and intellectual-spiritual attitudes, varied so much from class to class that social origins played in fact a decisive part in the question of literary taste though, as we shall see, *some* authors and *some* types of fiction did, of course, find readers in all sections of German society.

21. 'If one were to set out to describe the present-day nobility, then it would perhaps be seen as mere derision; it would have to be a portrait of the ridiculous, and the truth would be all too near the mark in most cases: let us rather keep silence, hide our shame, take counsel and mend our ways.' J. M. von Loen, *Freye Gedanken von der Besserung des Staats* (1740); quoted by Steinhausen, op. cit., p. 64.

22. 'Ignorance is very nearly a sign of noble birth.' J. M. von Loen, *Freye Gedanken vom Hof*, 3rd edn. (1768), p. 21.

23. 'Not even books, a subject most dear to me, were given a moment's thought. The people around me knew nothing about the arts and sciences; they were German courtiers and at that time this class consisted of people of not the slightest culture.' *Wilhelm Meisters Lehrjahre*, Bk. VI. (*Goethes Werke* (Weimar, 1887–1912), vol. xxii, p. 269.)

24. 'Good-natured mental limitation, striving to attain the heights of a learned and literary culture.' 'Schemata zur Fortsetzung von "Dichtung

und Wahrheit"' in *Goethe-Jahrbuch*, xxviii (1907), 9. See here also Bruford, op. cit., p. 64, and *Culture and Society in Classical Weimar* (Cambridge, 1962), p. 56.

25. For a full account of this subject see Bruford, op. cit., pp. 67 ff.

26. 'His written and spoken French was excellent, his German was correct.' K. H. von Lang, *Aus der bösen alten Zeit*, 2 vols. (Stuttgart, 1910), i. 123, and ii. 82.

27. 'Most of these gentlemen learn courtly pursuits, languages, music, riding, dancing, fencing, and flirting, and nothing else.' Quoted by J. Schmidt, *Geschichte des geistigen Lebens* . . . (Leipzig, 1862–4), ii. 261.

28. J. G. Müller, *Siegfried von Lindenberg* (1779).

29. K. H. von Lang, op. cit., ii. 194.

30. Cf. here especially A. Kleinberg, *Die europäische Kultur der Neuzeit* (Leipzig and Berlin, 1931), p. 28.

31. 'When I said that German writers did not receive sufficient encouragement, as the aristocracy and the courts spoke too much French and understood too little German to be able to grasp and appreciate fully anything written in German, He said: that is true, for I haven't read no German book since my youth and je parle comme un cocher, but now I am an old fellow of forty-six and have no time for such things.' Quoted by J. Schmidt, ii. 138.

32. 'He was greatly amazed to find that all this could be expressed in German—for till now his only knowledge of the German language was from files, official documents, and ministerial papers.' Wieland in a letter of 8 Oct. 1764; quoted by Sengle, op. cit., p. 175.

33. 'His first training as a scholar was concerned only with things French, and his acquaintance with classical and with German literature proper was confined to what he had, with a nicely calculated shrewdness, managed to appropriate from the people around him.' K. H. von Lang, op. cit. i. 51.

34. Cf. here especially J. G. Müller's *Siegfried von Lindenberg* (1779).

35. As, for example, in *Schwedische Gräfin* (1747–8), *Wilhelmine* (1764), *Fräulein von Sternheim* (1771), *Emilia Galotti* (1772), and many others.

36. . . . so popular 'that one could lay no claim whatever to being a man of wit unless one had read his works'. Cf. here F. Sengle, *C. M. Wieland* (Stuttgart, 1949).

37. See K. Biedermann, *Deutschland im 18. Jahrhundert* (Leipzig, 1854–80), ii. 133.

38. See Marianne Spiegel, *Der Roman und sein Publikum im frühen 18. Jahrhundert, 1700–67* (Bonn, 1967), pp. 96 ff.

39. 'Two friends, joined together as citizens of the world, direct this letter to you, noble Schiller! Both are unknown to you but both hold you in great esteem and affection.' Quoted by Steinhausen, op. cit., p. 65.

40. See here especially Bruford, op. cit., pp. 71 ff., 321 ff., and *Culture and Society in Classical Weimar* (Cambridge, 1962).

41. Ibid.

42. 'Our present time is witnessing the happiest period of the eighteenth century. Emperors, kings, and princes, full of benevolence, descend from their awesome heights, hold pomp and splendour in contempt, and become the fathers, friends, and trusted companions of their people. Religion tears asunder the priestly garb and emerges in her true godliness. Enlightenment forges ahead with gigantic strides. Thousands of our brothers and sisters, who once led lives of hallowed inactivity, are consigned to the state. Religious antagonism and restraint of conscience are on the wane. Love of mankind and freedom of thought are getting the upper hand. The arts and sciences are flourishing, and our gaze is penetrating deeply into nature's workshop. Craftsmen, together with artists, are approaching perfection. The seeds of useful knowledge are putting forth shoots in all classes of society. This is a true description of our age.' Quoted by Steinhausen, op. cit., p. 79.

43. 'All our good writers and their readers are like a Masonic Lodge; one must first be initiated.' Quoted by H. Kunze, *Lieblingsbücher von Dazumal* . . . (Munich, 1938), p. 14.

44. See G. M. Trevelyan, *English Social History*, 3rd edn. (London, 1947), pp. 412–14.

45. 'In Germany our men of letters have reference almost exclusively to themselves alone or to the scholars in our society.' See Nicolai, op. cit., pp. 71–2.

46. '[Readers] are for ever complaining that German authors write for such a small circle, often in fact for themselves as a group. I find this a good thing. German literature gains more and more in spirit and character because of it.' Quoted by J. Schulte-Sasse, *Die Kritik an der Trivialliteratur seit der Aufklärung* (Munich, 1971), pp. 117–18, note 17.

47. 'It is said that self-praise stinks. That may be so. But the smell of unjust criticism from outsiders seems to escape the collective nose of the reading public.' Goethe, *Maximen und Reflexionen*.

48. 'parterre-sewer'. Goethe, *Invektiven*.

49. '[The ideal reader] sees not only the truth of what is portrayed but also the merits of the selected material, the ingenious quality of the structure, the divine nature of the world of art in miniature; he senses that he must raise himself to the level of the artist so as to appreciate the work, he senses that he must concentrate his efforts, ignore the distractions of the world about him, he must live with the work, contemplate it again and again and so create for himself a higher existence.' Quoted by Schulte-Sasse, op. cit., p. 93.

50. 'Adults no longer concern me, / I must now think of the grandchildren.' On the subject of Goethe and the reading public see Köster's lecture 'Goethe und sein Publikum' in *Goethe-Jahrbuch*, xxix (1908), Anhang.

51. 'I yearn for Part III of your *Wilhelm* as I yearn for the warmth of the sun, for the visit of a friend and kindred spirit.' See Heinemann's

Introduction to *Wilhelm Meisters Lehrjahre* in *Goethes Werke* (Leipzig and Vienna, 1900), ix. 13 ff.

52. 'The French Revolution, Fichte's philosophy, and Goethe's *Wilhelm Meister* mark the most significant trends of our epoch.' Ibid., p. 15.

53. The not uneducated Perthes, for example, had first to be admitted to the exclusive circle of scholars (Spekter, Reinhold, Runge, Halsenbeck, and others) in Hamburg before becoming acquainted with the works of Goethe and Schiller. In certain circles it was more or less 'a social necessity' to know the works of such men. Cf. here Perthes, op. cit. i. 50.

54. 'Don't imagine I intend to set about you, stupid rabble, / I know full well for whom I am writing.' Goethe, *Invektiven*.

55. See Goldfriedrich, iii. 270 ff. For further discussion of book prices see above pp. 149–51.

56. 'Don't talk to me about the sale of these works. The popularity they enjoy and the market for them, seen in relation to a mass of 30,000,000 people, are really not worth mentioning.' W. Fleischer, *Über bildende Künste* (Frankfurt, 1792), p. 122; quoted by Goldfriedrich, iii. 272.

57. Figures from Bruford, op. cit., p. 280.

58. The works of Jean Paul enjoyed a wide circulation; to contemporaries, however, he was not the classical author we now know, but one of the many *Modeschriftsteller* ('fashionable writers'). See above, pp. 142 ff. For comparison it may be noted that in England 6,500 copies of *Joseph Andrews* were sold in thirteen months, of *Roderick Random* 5,000 in a year, and of *Sir Charles Grandison* 6,500 in a few months. (R. Williams, *The Long Revolution* (Pelican, 1971), p. 183.)

59. L. Chr. Kehr, *Selbstbiographie* (Kreuznach, 1834); see Goldfriedrich, iii. 272, and Kunze, op. cit., p. 33.

60. See Chap. 4, pp. 108–9.

61. A. Mallinckrodt, *Über Deutschlands Litteratur und Buchhandel* (Dortmund, 1800); see Goldfriedrich, iii. 272.

62. Quoted by Goldfriedrich, iii. 273.

63. 'In our present age in particular two types of literature are to be found, the one bordering closely on the other, each having its own public and each going its own way quite unconcerned about the other. They take not the slightest notice of each other unless their paths should happen to cross, in which case is manifest a mutual contempt and derision—frequently alongside a secret envy of the popularity of the one or the exclusiveness of the other.' Quoted by Schulte-Sasse, op. cit., p. 115.

64. '. . . but the way things are—[who wants to be] a foul miscreant yelping out some tune just to entertain the public?' Göckingk to Bürger, 30 Mar. 1780; quoted by Goldfriedrich, iii. 273.

65. 'Our public will occupy itself with anything that humours its curiosity.' Ibid.

66. 'The public has now become lord and master, it seeks nothing but entertainment and will pay only for being entertained; honest diligence and effort it cannot contemplate without an attack of seasickness.' K. H. von Lang, op. cit. ii. 227.

67. Goldfriedrich, iii. 273. Schulte-Sasse (op. cit., p. 37) points out that Mendelssohn, Lessing, and Herder still follow earlier usage in applying *Publikum* and *Pöbel* as opposing concepts; only later in the century is the once 'neutral' *Publikum* invested with the pejorative sense of *Pöbel*, gradually superseding it as a literary term of contempt (as in the extracts cited from Göckingk, Göschen, and Lang). One of the first to use the word *Publikum* as a derogatory term is Klopstock in his essay 'Von dem Publiko' (1759).

68. 'One of these classes wishes only to be entertained, the other wishes only to be instructed.' H. Chr. Boie and Chr. W. Dohm in Foreword to the second year of *Deutsches Museum* (1777).

69. ... stories which 'in the guise of a novel treat of whole fields of learning, introduce lectures on ethics, add to our knowledge of other countries, nations, the world of nature and art, betray a profound knowledge of human nature, and present either a vivid portrayal of man's social and moral life, moving and perhaps even converting the reader, or else a witty and humorous condemnation of man's follies and vices.' Quoted by H. H. Houben, *Hier Zensur, wer dort?* (Leipzig, 1918), p. 117.

70. 'When you speak to the people, to princes, and to kings, / You can tell them all stories which give the appearance of reality / To all that they themselves wish and desire to experience in life.' Goethe, *Erste Epistel*, ll. 45–7.

71. Joh. Hein. Jung-Stilling (1740–1817): *Heinrich Stillings Jugend* (1777), ... *Jünglingsjahre* (1778), ... *Wanderschaft* (1778), ... *häusliches Leben* (1789), ... *Lehrjahre* (1804), ... *Alter* (1817); also *Geschichte des Herrn von Morgenthau* (1779), *Das Heimweh* (1794), *Das Leben der heiligen Thekla* (1814), etc.

72. Lang, op. cit., i. 35. Lang's list also includes the works of Lavater, and Claudius, further *Siegwart*, *Sebaldus Nothanker*, and 'several other novels by Wetzel, Sattler, etc.'.

73. '... to attain to a knowledge of the truth and man's learning, and to use this in the service of God and one's neighbour.' Jung-Stilling, *Lebensgeschichte* (Leipzig, 1908), p. 140.

74. Goethe's brother-in-law Schlosser, too, could not hide his disgust 'daß Goethe dieser reinen Seele einen Platz angewiesen hat ... in dieser Herberge für vagabundierendes Lumpengesindel' ('that Goethe has given this "pure soul" a place in such a den of worthless rogues and vagabonds'). Both Herder and Jacobi objected to 'this whole business of Mariane and Philine' and were bitterly disappointed when Goethe did not, in the later books, treat them with the contempt they deserved. See Heinemann's Introduction to the novel in *Goethes Werke* (Leipzig and Vienna, 1900), ix. 14.

75. 'Everyone who is unable to write romances of chivalry and tales of witches is now frantically occupied with turning out anecdotes, biographies, and "galleries".' *Neue Allgemeine Deutsche Bibliothek*, xlviii (1799), 405.

76. See Appendix I.

77. *Berliner Monatsschrift* (1784), pp. 319 ff.

78. Cf. here particularly *Neue Allgemeine Deutsche Bibliothek*, xlviii (1799), 175.

79. Interesting from the sociological point of view is the fact that the German bourgeoisie as portrayed in Engel's novel is no longer (as in the Rationalist novel) fighting for recognition, by the other social classes, of its way of life and moral code, but living quietly in its own sphere and turning to the problems peculiar to its own class. *Lorenz Stark* can in this respect be regarded as the forerunner of Hebbel's *Maria Magdalena*. Cf. here H. H. Borcherdt, *Der Roman der Goethezeit* (Stuttgart, 1949), p. 242.

80. 'It must be a book . . . that contains an example of splendid, noble, purposeful activity such as can serve as a model for every young man . . . an example full of courage and vigour, intellect, and keen, manly sensibility.' Wezel in the Foreword to his translation of *Robinson Crusoe* (1779).

81. 'How few women there are, alas, who are truly informed about their duties and their allotted task of employing a cultivated mind and a noble heart along the path which they tread, thereby propagating all that is good and beneficial within their sphere of activity.' K. von Wobeser, *Elisa, oder das Weib wie es seyn sollte*, 3rd edn. (Leipzig, 1798), p. vii.

82. 'And Elisa showed all women that their crowning glory lay in *virtue* and that through this quality all women could do good in every sphere of life, bringing happiness even to generation after generation.' Ibid., p. 351.

83. 'We regard it as one of our first duties to warn the public most earnestly about the unsavoury dishes to which customers are lured by such display signs.' *Allgemeine Literatur-Zeitung* (1785), No. 43.

84. Perthes, op. cit. ii. 243.

85. 'It was widely fashionable at that time [*c.* 1776] to have a low opinion of everything connected with the Church and with education. The clergy were held up to ridicule at every possible opportunity.' Quoted by J. Schmidt, ii. 689.

86. See Chap. 2, pp. 32–4, and Appendix I.

87. 'Everybody is writing comic novels nowadays, just as everyone was writing sentimental ones a few years ago—and all get read.' *Allgemeine Literatur-Zeitung* (1785), No. 2.

88. '. . . they enjoy good sales because they are funny to read, make no great demands of the brain, and are not excessively instructive.' Knigge, *Die Reise nach Braunschweig* (*Deut. Nat. Lit.*, vol. cxxxvi), p. 269.

89. 'Herr Langbein has long been acknowledged to be a favourite author of the reading public, and so this most recent product of his humour (*Franz und Rosalie*) requires no further recommendation.' *Intelligenz-Blatt zum Morgenblatt für gebildete Stände* (1808), No. 16. It is also interesting in this connection to see the sort of 'company' in which Langbein found himself in an anthology of stories published in 1810 and listed in Heinsius's *Verzeichnis*:

Erholungen, eine Sammlung neuer Erzählungen . . . von Göthe, Kotzebue, Lafontaine, Jean Paul Richter, Rochlitz, Langbein und anderen.

90. Cf. here H. H. Borcherdt, op. cit., p. 178.

91. A glance at any of the book-catalogues of this time shows to what extent writers relied on 'promising' titles to attract readers; only the writers with higher literary ambitions remained aloof from this method of boosting sales. Interesting in this respect is the following extract from a German journal of our own time: 'Seitdem die Städtische Bücherei Ingolstadt *Michael Kohlhaas* als *Rächer der Enterbten* und Goethes *Wahlverwandtschaften* als *Ehe im Schatten* anbietet, soll die Nachfrage nach Klassikern erheblich gestiegen sein.' ('Since Ingolstadt Municipal Library put *Michael Kohlhaas* on offer as *Avenger of the Disinherited* and Goethe's *Wahlverwandtschaften* as *Marriage under a Cloud*, the demand for classical authors is said to have risen considerably.') *Neue Illustrierte* (Cologne, 20 Sept. 1950), 5 Jahrg., No. 38, p. 40.

92. '—to afford you more pleasure, I have shortened it for you—the passages that contain only satire I have marked with pencil, condemning them to be ignored by you so that you may the sooner come to the more gentle sections which, like *adagios*, are designed solely for the tear-laden, feminine heart.' Berend (ed.), *Die Briefe Jean Pauls* (Munich, 1922), ii. 13. Jean Paul often uses the terms *Adagio* and *Allegro* to refer respectively to the sentimental and satirical styles of writing. (I am indebted to Dr. J. W. Smeed of the University of Durham for this reference.)

93. Cf. here Christine Touaillon, *Der deutsche Frauenroman im 18. Jahrhundert* (Vienna and Leipzig, 1919).

94. *Der Naturmensch* (1791), *Der Sonderling* (1792), *Saint Julien* (1798), *So geht es in der Welt* (1803), *Fedor und Marie* (1805), etc.

95. Lang tells us, for example, how Hardenberg arranged for the Queen of Prussia to read out Lang's own *Baireuther Geschichte* to her husband 'to cultivate in the King, with his many hours of leisure, a taste for the more serious type of book, as all he ever wanted were the novels of Lafontaine'. See Lang, op. cit. ii. 42.

96. '. . . and he, no less than Goethe, was able to enjoy the pleasure of hearing them sung in the streets accompanied by hurdy-gurdies.' J. G. Gruber, *August Lafontaines Leben und Wirken* (1833), p. 289.

97. 'Just imagine what has happened to me because of Lafontaine and his novels. It is my custom every morning to read, in the original, a chapter from the Old Testament and every evening a chapter from the New Testament. Your fellow, Mättig [a village schoolmaster trained by Dinter], always has his evening meal with us and afterwards he reads Lafontaine's novels aloud to my wife and my two daughters, while they are sewing and knitting. At first I used to chide them with: Why do you read such rubbish? You should be reading something instructive instead. But in the end I am interested in the stories myself. At half-past nine I call out: Stop! I want to read my chapter. I shall have to hear tomorrow how the plot develops. The end result for me—for several months Lafontaine took the place of the

Bible.' The incident is from *Dinters Leben* (Neustadt a. d. Orla, 1829) and quoted by H. Schöffler, *Protestantismus und Literatur* (Leipzig, 1922), p. 195.

98. For a satirical account of feminine tastes in fiction at this time see the essay 'Versuch über den Roman, nicht von Blankenburg, sondern von einer Mamsell. Schreiben an die Herren Romanschreiber' in *Morgenblatt für gebildete Stände* (1808), No. 164.

99. Cf. here F. Paulsen, *Geschichte des gelehrten Unterrichts*, 2nd edn., 2 vols. (Leipzig, 1896–7), Bruford, op. cit., pp. 122 ff., 248 ff., Goldfriedrich, ii. 391 ff., and Steinhausen, op. cit., pp. 70 ff.

100. '... so that you have some dependable means of earning a living you must learn my trade.' Jung-Stilling, *Lebensgeschichte* (Leipzig, 1908), p. 58.

101. 'If the schoolmaster is a craftsman his livelihood is assured; if he is not, he is permitted to seek casual labouring work for six weeks.' Quoted by Goldfriedrich, ii. 393.

102. Goldfriedrich, ii. 394.

103. *Deutsches Museum* (1778), Feb., p. 148.

104. As Bruford points out (op. cit., p. 280) this works out at an average of over 40,000 copies a year maintained over twenty-three years. For comparison it may be noted that the highest figure recorded for a single work in eighteenth-century England was 105,000 but this was for a somewhat sensational religious pamphlet by Bishop Sherlock, published in 1750—and many copies were distributed free of charge (see Ian Watt, *The Rise of the Novel* (Peregrine Books, 1963), pp. 37–8).

Despite the obviously wide appeal of the subject-matter and the extremely low price of the book, Becker's figures must be open to doubt; he would, of course, have no reliable information on the sale of unauthorized editions and probably overestimated the pirate publishers' share of the takings. Nevertheless, even allowing for exaggeration, the success of this book clearly demonstrates the existence of a considerable number of readers amongst the less-well-off social classes.

105. Cf. here especially Bruford, op. cit., Appendix I, and Bruford, *Culture and Society in Classical Weimar* (Cambridge, 1962), Appendix I. For a discussion of book prices in England in the eighteenth century see I. Watt, op. cit., pp. 42 ff.

106. See Chap. 4, p. 108.

107. See Chap. 4, p. 110.

108. In eighteenth-century England the situation was even worse; the average price of popular Gothic tales was 14*s.* per novel, or 5*s.* 2*d.* per volume (they were usually lengthy works of, on average, three volumes). Against this we find that the average labourer earned about 10*s.* a week and £1 a week was considered a decent wage for skilled journeymen or small shopkeepers. Cf. here J. Brauchli, *Der englische Schauerroman um 1800*, Zürich Diss. (Weida, 1928), pp. 136 ff. and I. Watt, op. cit., p. 42.

109. Cf. here Goldfriedrich, iii. 257 ff.

110. Lang, op. cit. ii. 150.

111. Becher, *Politischer Diskurs* (Frankfurt, 1668), pp. 64 ff.

112. Cf. here H. Rausse, *Geschichte des deutschen Romans bis 1800* (Kempten and Munich, 1914), p. 31.

113. Goethe, *Dichtung und Wahrheit*, Bk. I. (*Goethes Werke* (Weimar, 1887–1912), vol. xxvi, p. 51.) See also Beaujean, op. cit., pp. 20–1).

114. 'The uneducated countryman is all ears when exciting incidents are being related—as in stories like *Eulenspiegel*—for they suit his rough and ready notions.' W. Fleischer, *Über bildende Künste* (Frankfurt, 1792); quoted by Goldfriedrich, iii. 285.

115. C. A. Vulpius, *Pantheon berühmter und merkwürdiger Frauen* (Leipzig, 1816), pt. V, p. 161.

116. '. . . he is often bored, especially in winter, and, as I have often seen, he will then get one of his children to read aloud to him from *Eulenspiegel* or *Schildbürger*.' *Deutsches Museum* (1778), Feb., p. 148.

117. J. G. Müller, *Siegfried von Lindenberg* (Munich, 1918), pt. I, chap. 4. It may be of interest here to note that the chap-books enjoyed a similar popularity in contemporary Holland; we are told by an eighteenth-century observer that when members of the lower social classes in Holland read at all, then they usually turned to *Orson en Valentyn*, *De schoone Helena*, *De vier Heemskinderen*, *Fortunatus*, etc.; see G. W. Huygens, *De Nederlandse Auteur en zijn Publiek* (Amsterdam, 1946), pp. 42–3.

118. 'The restless journeyman is always keenly on the look-out for "Robinsonades".' Quoted by Goldfriedrich, iii. 285.

119. 'For six or seven years now all the critics of the Holy Roman Empire who are working in this field have been resisting the romances of chivalry, but the host of gallant lances and swords is relentlessly closing in upon them. There is now absolutely no hope of rescue from the Vehmic Courts, the ghosts, and the secret societies.' Quoted by Borcherdt, op. cit., p. 248.

120. See Chap. 1, p. 22.

121. '. . . a sociological law governing matters of taste: one likes what one's social superior liked thirty years ago'. R. W. Leonhardt, *Xmal Deutschland* (Munich, 1961), p. 187. On the subject of the heroic-gallant novel in the eighteenth century see Touaillon, op. cit., pp. 367 ff. For details of eighteenth-century reprints of some of these novels see E. A. Blackall, *The Emergence of German as a Literary Language* (Cambridge, 1959), p. 196.

122. 'Priestly pride and superstition caused these stains of human blood.' *Hinko mit der eisernen Tasche* (Wolfenbüttel, 1794–7), i. 33.

123. '. . . his paternal feelings were racked by the pains of hell, rage ripped his belly asunder; he stamped his feet, making the ground quake, his lips trembled, and his eyes rolled like balls of fire'; '. . . the abbot's fury was boundless, in paroxysmal convulsions it spread out over the entire mass of his flesh.' Ibid. i. 8, 50.

124. 'Whatever gloomy, cantankerous critics may say and think, my novels

are not read but devoured, pirated, and still they go through four editions.' In Foreword to *Erasmus Schleicher* (1789); quoted by Kunze, op. cit., p. 118.

125. 'Our main concern is that the world should read us, and for that reason the stuff you scribble about us does not worry us at all, we could not care less, as long as we do succeed in keeping in tune with the hearts and minds of our own day and age.' Preface to Part II of *Gefährliche Stunden* (1800).

126. He was Känigl's companion and steward (*Wirtschaftsdirektor*). Spieß started his career as a dramatist; several of his plays were produced by Goethe at Weimar, whilst his *Ritterschauspiel, Klara von Hohenheim* (1790), was seen by Körner in Vienna as late as 1811. An edition of his collected works, in eleven volumes, appeared in 1840—forty-one years after his death. See Kunze, op. cit., p. 107.

127. It is interesting to note a modern reprint of the English translation of Grosse's *Genius* under the title of *Horrid Mysteries*, published by Holden in 1927. Cf. here V. Stockley, *German Literature as known in England 1750–1830* (London, 1929), p. 217.

128. Cf. here Touaillon, op. cit., pp. 444 ff.

129. '. . . either had no back left on them or had become so greasy from reading that they really beamed at me.' W. Hauff, *Memoiren des Satans* (1826–7); quoted by Kunze, op. cit., p. 108.

130. Scott knew Weber's *Sagen der Vorzeit*. From one of them he borrowed the plot of his *House of Aspen*. See Stockley, op. cit., p. 216.

131. *Walther von Montbarry* (1786), *Hermann von Unna* (1788), *Geschichte der Gräfin Thekla von Thurn* (1788). Schiller is known to have been acquainted with her novels, the material of which provided some stimulus to his own work in the historical drama. (Letter from Körner to Schiller, dated 2 Nov. 1788, referred to by Beaujean, op. cit., p. 112.)

132. Marianne Thalmann (*Die Romantik des Trivialen* (Munich, 1970)) has demonstrated this most forcefully, with particular reference to the work of Grosse and Tieck.

133. 'Through the lending library, which was run by Herr Nast, the dealer in second-hand books, and which was very well stocked with the works of Cramer, Spieß, Lafontaine, and the like, I became well versed in the not-so-polite literature of those days.' Quoted by Kunze, op. cit., p. 32.

BIBLIOGRAPHY

I. LITERARY HISTORY

(a) General

BECK, H., *Die religiöse Volksliteratur der evangelischen Kirche Deutschlands in einem Abriß ihrer Geschichte* (Gotha, 1891).

BIESE, A., *Geschichte der deutschen Literatur*, 3 vols., 24th edn. (Munich, 1930).

BLACKALL, E. A., *The Emergence of German as a Literary Language* (Cambridge, 1959).

BRÜGGEMANN, F., *Vorboten der bürgerlichen Kultur* (*Deutsche Literatur, Reihe Aufklärung*, vol. iv) (Leipzig, 1931).

GERVINUS, G. G., *Geschichte der deutschen Dichtung*, 5 vols., 4th edn. (Leipzig, 1853).

GOEDEKE, K., *Grundriß zur Geschichte der deutschen Dichtung*, vols. iii and iv.

HAUSER, A., *Sozialgeschichte der Kunst und Literatur*, 2 vols. (Munich, 1953).

HETTNER, H., *Geschichte der deutschen Literatur im achtzehnten Jahrhundert*, 2nd revised edn. (Brunswick, 1872).

KLEINBERG, A., *Die deutsche Dichtung in ihren sozialen, zeit- und geistesgeschichtlichen Bedingungen* (Berlin, 1927).

KÖSTER, A., *Die deutsche Literatur der Aufklärungszeit* (Heidelberg, 1925).

LEIXNER, O. VON, *Geschichte der deutschen Litteratur*, 6th edn. (Leipzig, 1903).

MERKER, P., and STAMMLER, W. (eds.), *Reallexikon der deutschen Literaturgeschichte*, 4 vols. (Berlin, 1925–31).

MORGAN, B. Q., and HOHLFELD, A. R., *German Literature in British Magazines* (Wisconsin, 1949).

RIEFSTAHL, H., *Dichter und Publikum in der ersten Hälfte des achtzehnten Jahrhunderts, dargestellt an der Geschichte der Vorrede*, Frankfurt a. M. Diss. (Limburg, 1934).

ROBERTSON, J. G., *A History of German Literature*, new and revised edn. (Edinburgh and London, 1944).

SCHERER, W., *Geschichte der deutschen Literatur*, revised by O. Walzel, 4th edn. (Berlin, 1928).

SCHÖFFLER, H., *Protestantismus und Literatur* (Leipzig, 1922).

SCHÜCKING, L. L., *Die Soziologie der literarischen Geschmacksbildung* (*Philosophische Reihe*, vol. lxxi) (Munich, 1923); available in the series *DALP-Taschenbücher*, vol. 354, 3rd and revised edn. (Munich and Bern, 1961).

STEPHEN, L., *English Literature and Society in the Eighteenth Century* (University Paperbacks, 1963).

STOCKLEY, V., *German Literature as known in England 1750–1830* (London, 1929).

STRAUSS, W., *Vorfragen einer Soziologie der literarischen Wirkung*, Cologne Diss. (Cologne, 1934).

WALZEL, O., *Deutsche Dichtung von Gottsched bis zur Gegenwart* (Potsdam, 1927–9).

WITTE, W., 'The Sociological Approach to Literature' in *Modern Language Review*, xxxvi (1941), 86–94.

(b) History of the Novel and the Reading Public

APPELL, J. W., *Die Ritter-, Räuber- und Schauerromantik* (Leipzig, 1859); R.P. Leipzig, 1967 and Munich–Pullach, 1968.

—— *Werther und seine Zeit*, revised edn. (Leipzig, 1865).

BEAUJEAN, M., *Der Trivialroman in der zweiten Hälfte des 18. Jahrhunderts* (*Abhandlungen zur Kunst-, Musik- und Literaturwissenschaft*, vol. xxii), 2nd enlarged edn. (Bonn, 1969).

BECKER, E. D., *Der deutsche Roman um 1780* (*Germanistische Abhandlungen*, vol. v) (Stuttgart, 1964).

BOBERTAG, F., *Geschichte des Romans . . . bis zum Anfange des 18. Jahrhunderts*, 2 vols. (Berlin, 1881–4).

—— (ed.), *Erzählende Prosa der klassischen Periode* (*Deutsche National-Literatur*, vol. cxxxvi) (Stuttgart, 1886).

BORCHERDT, H. H., *Geschichte des Romans und der Novelle in Deutschland* (Leipzig, 1926).

—— *Der Roman der Goethezeit* (Urach and Stuttgart, 1949).

BRAUCHLI, J., *Der englische Schauerroman um 1800*, Zürich Diss. (Weida, 1928).

BRAUN, J. W., *Goethe im Urteil seiner Zeitgenossen*, 3 vols. (Berlin, 1883–5).

BRÜGGEMANN, F., *Gellerts Schwedische Gräfin* (Aachen, 1925).

BURGER, H. O. (ed.), *Studien zur Trivialliteratur* (*Studien zur Philosophie und Literatur des 19. Jahrhunderts*, vol. i) (Frankfurt a. M., 1968).

EBELING, F. W., *Geschichte der komischen Literatur in Deutschland während der zweiten Hälfte des 18. Jahrhunderts*, 3 vols. (Leipzig, 1869).

EICHENDORFF, J. VON, *Der deutsche Roman des 18. Jahrhunderts in seinem Verhältnis zum Christentum* (Leipzig, 1851).

GARTE, H., *Kunstform Schauerroman*, Leipzig. Diss. (Leipzig, 1935).

GEBHARDT, W., *Religionssoziologische Probleme im Roman der Aufklärung*, Gießen Diss. (Gießen, 1931).

GERHARD, M., *Der deutsche Entwicklungsroman bis Goethes Wilhelm Meister* (Halle, 1926).

GREINER, M., *Die Entstehung der modernen Unterhaltungsliteratur. Studien zum Trivialroman des 18. Jahrhunderts* (*Rowohlt Taschenbuch*, r.d.e., No. 207, 1964).

HEINE, C., *Der Roman in Deutschland von 1774 bis 1778* (Halle, 1892).

HIRSCH, A., *Bürgertum und Barock im deutschen Roman*, 2nd edn., prepared by H. Singer (Cologne, 1957).

HOFFMANN, G., *Johann Timotheus Hermes: Lebens-, Zeit- und Kulturbild* (Breslau, 1911).

HUYGENS, G. W., *De Nederlandse Auteur en zijn Publiek* (Amsterdam, 1946).

KAYSER, W., *Entstehung und Krise des modernen Romans* (Stuttgart, 1955).

KILLY, W., *Deutscher Kitsch. Ein Versuch mit Beispielen* (Göttingen, 1961).

KIPPENBERG, A., *Robinsonaden in Deutschland* (Hanover, 1892).

KÖSTER, A., 'Goethe und sein Publikum' in *Goethe-Jahrbuch*, xxix (1908), Anhang.

KÜHN, J., *Der junge Goethe im Spiegel der Dichtung seiner Zeit* (Heidelberg, 1912).

KUNZE, H., *Lieblingsbücher von Dazumal. Eine Blütenlese* (Munich, 1938).

LEAVIS, Q. D., *Fiction and the Reading Public* (London, 1932).

MÜLLER-FRAUREUTH, C., *Die Ritter- und Räuberromane* (Halle, 1894).

NOLLAU, A., *Das literarische Publikum des jungen Goethe von 1770 bis zu seiner Übersiedlung nach Weimar* (Weimar, 1935).

NUTZ, W., *Der Trivialroman. Seine Formen und seine Hersteller. Ein Beitrag zur Literatursoziologie* (Cologne, 1962).

RAUSSE, H., *Geschichte des deutschen Romans bis 1800* (Kempten and Munich, 1914).

REHM, W., *Geschichte des deutschen Romans*, vol. i (*Vom Mittelalter bis zum Realismus*) (Berlin, 1927).

REHORN, K., *Der deutsche Roman. Geschichtliche Rückblicke und kritische Streiflichter* (Cologne and Leipzig, 1890).

RITTER, H., *Die pädagogischen Strömungen im letzten Drittel des 18. Jahrhunderts in den gleichzeitigen deutschen pädagogischen Romanen* (Halle, 1939).

ROSE, W. (ed.), *Essays on Goethe* (London, 1949).

SCHMIDT, E., *Richardson, Rousseau und Goethe* (Jena, 1875).

SCHULTE-SASSE, J., *Die Kritik an der Trivialliteratur seit der Aufklärung. Studien zur Geschichte des modernen Kitschbegriffs* (*Bochumer Arbeiten zur Sprach- und Literaturwissenschaft*) (Munich, 1971).

SENGLE, F., *C. M. Wieland* (Stuttgart, 1949).

SINGER, H., *Der galante Roman* (Stuttgart, 1961).

SOMMERFELD, M., 'Romantheorie und Romantypus der deutschen Aufklärung' in *Deutsche Vierteljahrsschrift*, iv (1926), pp. 459–90.

SPIEGEL, M., *Der Roman und sein Publikum im frühen 18. Jahrhundert 1700–1767 (Abhandlungen zur Kunst-, Musik- und Literaturwissenschaft*, xli) (Bonn, 1967).

SPIERO, H., *Geschichte des deutschen Romans* (Berlin, 1950).

THALMANN, M., *Der Trivialroman des 18. Jahrhunderts und der romantische Roman* (Berlin, 1923).

—— *Die Romantik des Trivialen. Von Grosses 'Genius' bis Tiecks 'William Lovell' (List Taschenbücher*, No. 1442) (Munich, 1970).

TOMPKINS, J. M. S., *The Popular Novel in England 1770–1800* (London, 1932).

TOUAILLON, C., *Der deutsche Frauenroman im 18. Jahrhundert* (Vienna and Leipzig, 1919).

ULLRICH, H., *Robinson und die Robinsonaden: Bibliographie* (Weimar, 1898).

WATT, I., *The Rise of the Novel* (Peregrine Books, 1963).

WOLFF, O. L. B., *Allgemeine Geschichte des Romans*, 2nd edn. (Jena, 1850).

An excellent and most comprehensive Bibliography, of both source material and secondary literature, is:

BECKER, E. D., and DEHN, M., *Literarisches Leben. Eine Bibliographie. Auswahlverzeichnis von Literatur zum deutschsprachigen literarischen Leben von der Mitte des 18. Jahrhunderts bis zur Gegenwart (Schriften zur Buchmarktforschung*, xiii) (Hamburg, 1968).

II. EIGHTEENTH-CENTURY CRITICISMS

(a) *Literary*

BERNHARD, J. A., *Kurzgefaßte curieuse Historie derer Gelehrten* (Frankfurt a. M., 1718).

BLANKENBURG, C. F. VON, *Versuch über den Roman* (Leipzig, 1774). Facsimile reprint: Metzler Verlag, Stuttgart, 1965.

BODMER, J. J., *Critische Abhandlung* (1740).

BREITINGER, J. J., *Critische Dichtkunst* (1739).

GOETHE, J. W. VON, *Dichtung und Wahrheit* (1811–33).

GOTTSCHED, J. C., *Kritische Dichtkunst* (1730).

KNIGGE, A. F. F. VON, *Über Schriftsteller und Schriftstellerei* (Hanover, 1793).

MEUSEL, J. G., *Lexicon der vom Jahre 1750 bis 1800 verstorbenen teutschen Schriftsteller* (Leipzig, 1802–16).

REHBERG, A. W., 'Goethe und sein Jahrhundert' in *Minerva*, iv (Aug. 1835).

SCHLEGEL, F., *Brief über den Roman* (1800).

WESSENBERG, J. H. VON, *Über den sittlichen Einfluß der Romane* (Constance, 1826).

(b) A Selection of Newspapers, Journals, etc.

Allgemeine Deutsche Bibliothek (Berlin, 1765–1806).

Allgemeine Literatur-Zeitung (Jena, 1785–1833).

Auserlesene Bibliothek der neuesten deutschen Literatur (Lemgo, 1772–8).

Berlinische Monatsschrift (1783–96).

Der Mensch. Eine moralische Wochenschrift (1751–4).

Der Teutsche Merkur (1773–89), then as Neuer Teutscher Merkur (1790–1810).

Deutsches Museum (1776–88), then as Neues Deutsches Museum (1789–91).

Erfurtische Gelehrte Zeitung (1781–96).

Morgenblatt für gebildete Stände (Tübingen, 1808).

Neue Bibliothek der schönen Wissenschaften und freien Künste (1765–1806).

III. THE BOOK TRADE AND THE PROFESSION OF LETTERS

(a) Catalogues

Leipziger Meßkataloge 1740, 1770, and 1800.

HEINSIUS, W., Alphabetisches Verzeichnis der von 1700 bis zu Ende 1810 erschienenen Romane und Schauspiele . . . (Leipzig, 1813); reprint Zentralantiquariat der D.D.R., Leipzig, 1972.

KAYSER, C. G., Vollständiges Verzeichnis der von 1750 bis Ende des Jahres 1832 in Deutschland und in den angrenzenden Ländern gedruckten Romane und Schauspiele (Leipzig, 1836); reprint Zentralantiquariat der D.D.R., Leipzig, 1972.

SCHWETSCHKE, G., Codex Nundinarius Germaniae literatae bisecularis. Meß-Jahrbücher des deutschen Buchhandels von dem Erscheinen des ersten Meß-Katalogus im Jahre 1564 bis zu der Gründung des ersten Buchhändler-Vereins im Jahre 1765. Mit . . . Fortsetzung 1766 bis einschließlich 1846 (Halle, 1850–77); reprint, two parts in one vol., Folio (Nieuwkoop, 1963).

(b) Eighteenth-century Writers

FLEISCHER, W., Über bildende Künste (Frankfurt a. M., 1792).

KRÜNITZ, J. G., Oeconomische Encyclopädie, oder, Allgemeines System der Land-, Haus-, und Staats-Wirtschaft, 242 vols. (Berlin, 1773–1858). Vol. 7 (1776), under 'Buchhandlung', gives a contemporary account of the German book trade and book-fair practices.

LICHTENBERG, G. C., Die Bibliogenie oder die Entstehung der Bücherwelt (Weimar, 1942).

MALLINCKRODT, A., Über Deutschlands Litteratur und Buchhandel (Dortmund, 1800).

PERTHES, C. T., Friedrich Perthes Leben nach dessen schriftlichen und mündlichen Mittheilungen, 3 vols. (Gotha, 1848–55); new revised edn. Stuttgart, 1951.

PERTHES, F., Memoirs of Frederick Perthes, 2 vols., 3rd edn. (Edinburgh and London, 1857).

PERTHES, F. (*cont.*), *Der deutsche Buchhandel als Bedingung des Daseins einer deutschen Literatur* (*Reclam U-B*, No. 9000) (Stuttgart, 1967).

PÜTTER, J. S., *Der Büchernachdruck nach ächten Grundsätzen des Rechts geprüft* (Göttingen, 1774).

REIMARUS, J. A. H., *Der Bücherverlag in Betrachtung der Schriftsteller, der Buchhändler und des Publikums erwogen* (Hamburg, 1773).

(c) *Later Writers*

BUCHNER, K., *Beiträge zur Geschichte des deutschen Buchhandels*, 2 vols. (Gießen, 1873–4).

COLLINS, A. S., *Authorship in the Days of Johnson* (London, 1927).

—— *The Profession of Letters* (London, 1928).

GOLDFRIEDRICH, J., *Geschichte des deutschen Buchhandels*, vols. ii and iii (Leipzig, 1908–9).

HOUBEN, H. H., *Hier Zensur — Wer dort?* (Leipzig, 1918).

—— *Verbotene Literatur von der klassischen Zeit bis zur Gegenwart* (Berlin, 1924).

JENTZSCH, R., *Der deutsch-lateinische Büchermarkt nach den Leipziger Ostermeß-Katalogen von 1740, 1770 und 1800 in seiner Gliederung und Wandlung*, Leipzig Diss. (Leipzig, 1912).

UNWIN, S., *The Truth about Publishing* (London, 1926).

IV. SOCIAL AND CULTURAL

BAHRDT, C. F., *Handbuch der Moral für den Bürgerstand* (Tübingen, 1789).

BALET, L., *Die Verbürgerlichung der deutschen Kunst, Literatur und Musik im 18. Jahrhundert* (Leiden, 1936).

BIEDERMANN, K., *Deutschland im 18. Jahrhundert* (Leipzig, 1854–80).

BRÄKER, U., *Der arme Mann im Tockenburg* (1789); R.P., ed. by Hans-Günther Thalheim in *Bräkers Werke in einem Band* (Berlin and Weimar, 1964).

BRUFORD, W. H., 'Goethe's *Wilhelm Meister* as a Picture and a Criticism of Society' in *Publications of the English Goethe Society*, n.s. ix (1933), 22–45.

—— *Germany in the Eighteenth Century* (Cambridge, 1935).

—— *Theatre, Drama and Audience in Goethe's Germany* (London, 1950).

—— *Culture and Society in Classical Weimar, 1775–1806* (Cambridge, 1962).

BRÜGGEMANN, F., 'Der Kampf um die bürgerliche Welt- und Lebensanschauung in der deutschen Literatur des 18. Jahrhunderts' in *Deutsche Vierteljahrsschrift*, iii (1925), 94–127.

—— *Die bürgerliche Gemeinschaftskultur der vierziger Jahre* (*Deutsche Literatur, Reihe Aufklärung*, vols. v and vi) (Leipzig, 1933).

ERMATINGER, E., *Deutsche Kultur im Zeitalter der Aufklärung* (Potsdam, 1935).

GOOCH, G. P., *Germany and the French Revolution* (London, 1920).

HALLER, J., *Die Epochen der deutschen Geschichte*, new, enlarged edn. (Stuttgart, 1940).

JUNG-STILLING, H., *Lebensgeschichte* (Leipzig, 1908).

KLEINBERG, A., *Die europäische Kultur der Neuzeit* (Leipzig and Berlin, 1931).

KOCH, F., *Deutsche Kultur des Idealismus* (Potsdam, 1935).

LANG, K. H. VON, *Aus der bösen alten Zeit*, 2 vols. (Stuttgart, 1910).

MAHRHOLZ, W. (ed.), *Der deutsche Pietismus* (Berlin, 1921).

MORITZ, K. P., *Anton Reiser* (Munich, 1912).

MORLEY, E. J. (ed.), *Crabb Robinson in Germany 1800–1805* (Oxford, 1929).

MÖSER, J., *Patriotische Phantasien* (1774–86); selection in *Deutsche Bibliothek in Berlin* (No date).

PAULSEN, F., *Geschichte des gelehrten Unterrichts*, 2 vols., 2nd edn. (Leipzig, 1896–7).

RITSCHL, A., *Geschichte des Pietismus*, 3 vols. (Bonn, 1880–6).

SCHMIDT, J., *Geschichte des geistigen Lebens in Deutschland von Leibnitz bis auf Lessings Tod*, 2 vols. (Leipzig, 1862–4).

STEINHAUSEN, G., *Der Aufschwung der deutschen Kultur vom 18. Jahrhundert bis zum Weltkrieg* (Leipzig and Vienna, 1920).

—— *Geschichte der deutschen Kultur*, 3rd edn. (Leipzig, 1929).

WILLIAMS, R., *Culture and Society 1780–1950* (London, 1958); published in Penguin Books, 1961.

—— *The Long Revolution* (London, 1961); published in Pelican Books, 1965.

INDEX